Poses for Artists Series, Volume 9 by Justin R. Martin
www.PoseMuse.com for details and links

PoseMuse
PO Box 2105
Edwards, CO 81632 USA
www.PoseMuse.com
justin@posemuse.com

Ordering Information:
Available on Amazon.com in paperback or Kindle formats, and Gumroad.com in pdf format via PoseMuse.com. All ebook formats available on SmashWords.com. Special discounts are available on quantity purchases by businesses, corporations, associations, and others. For details, contact PoseMuse above.

Publisher's Cataloging-in-Publication Data:
Martin, Justin R.
Poses for Artists Volume 9: An essential reference for figure drawing and the human form. Inspiring Art and Artists
Series/ Justin R. Martin
1. Nonfiction - Art - Techniques - Drawing
2. Nonfiction - Art - Reference
3. Nonfiction - Art - Illustration

First Edition, First Printing 2023
ISBN: 978-1-7377937-3-1
Imprint: POSEmuse
14 13 12 11 10 9 8 7 6 5 4 3 2 1

The poses included in the Pose for Artists Book Series were first available online to encourage all artists to create. The purpose of sharing the poses is to help artists get over 'artist's block' that occurs at the very beginning of a new drawing. Staring at that blank page can be daunting. These poses are here to jump-start the whole process.

If you draw, you know the fear of wasting energy starting at a blank page. Use these poses to side-step the problem, and get drawing.

These books are not step-by-step drawing tutorials. There are PLENTY of those available. Here is a "middle step" not a "step by step" to get you moving forward quickly on your new art.

Thank you for supporting our project by purchasing this book. Keep drawing. Share your work often so others may be inspired, by YOU.

All the best,
Justin R. Martin
April 2023

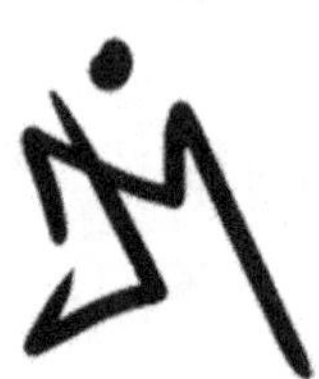

TABLE OF CONTENTS

UNSHADED FEET

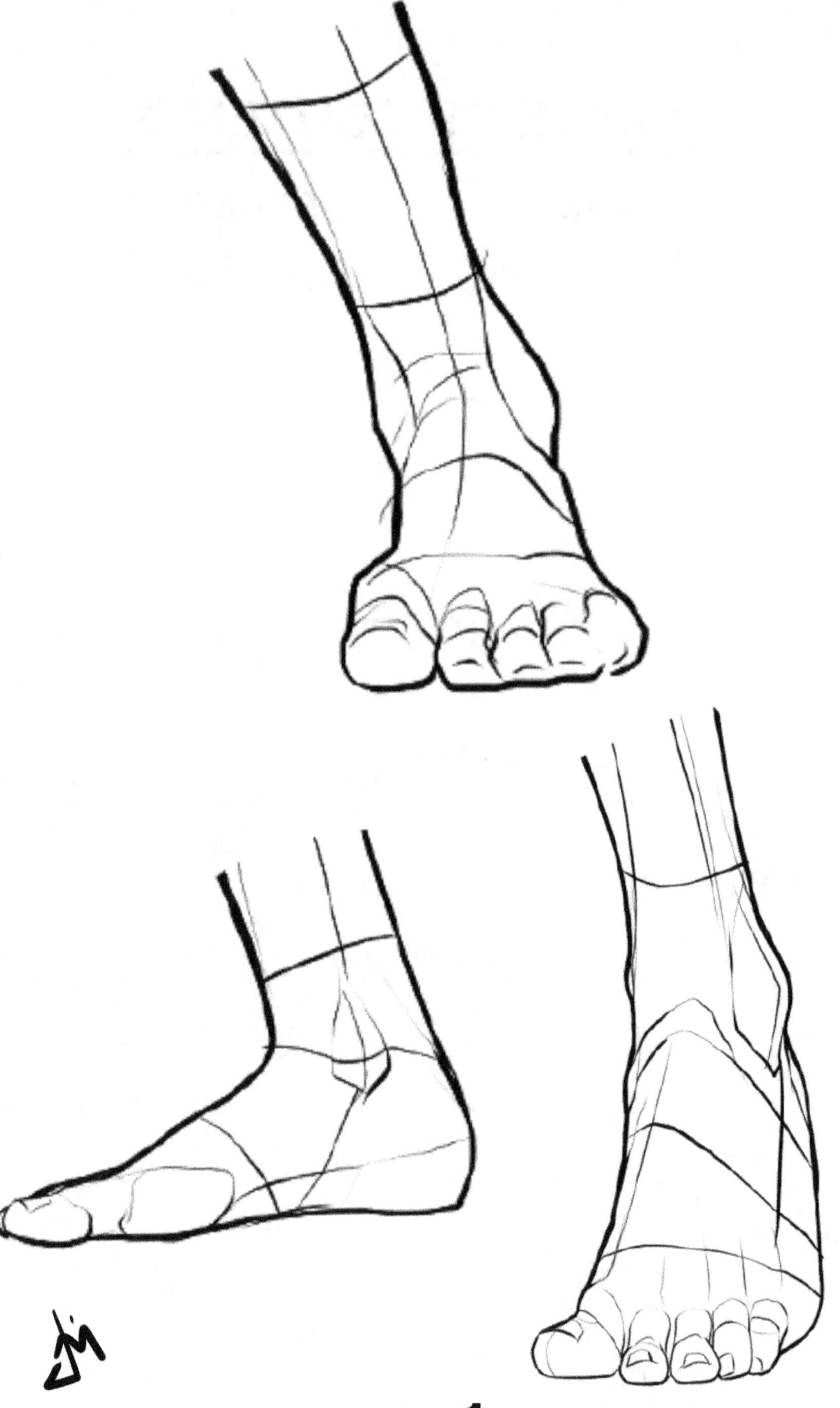

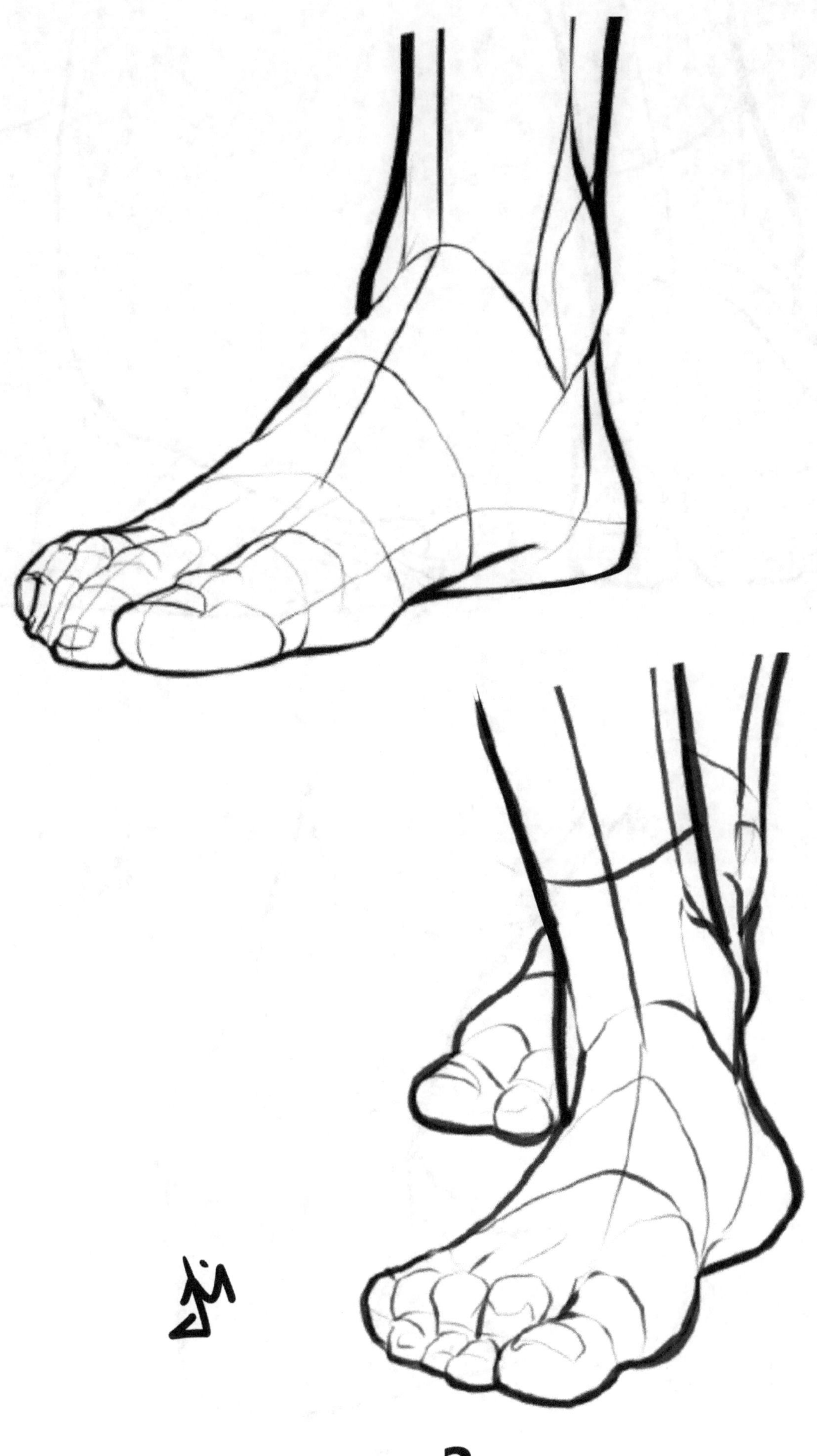

2

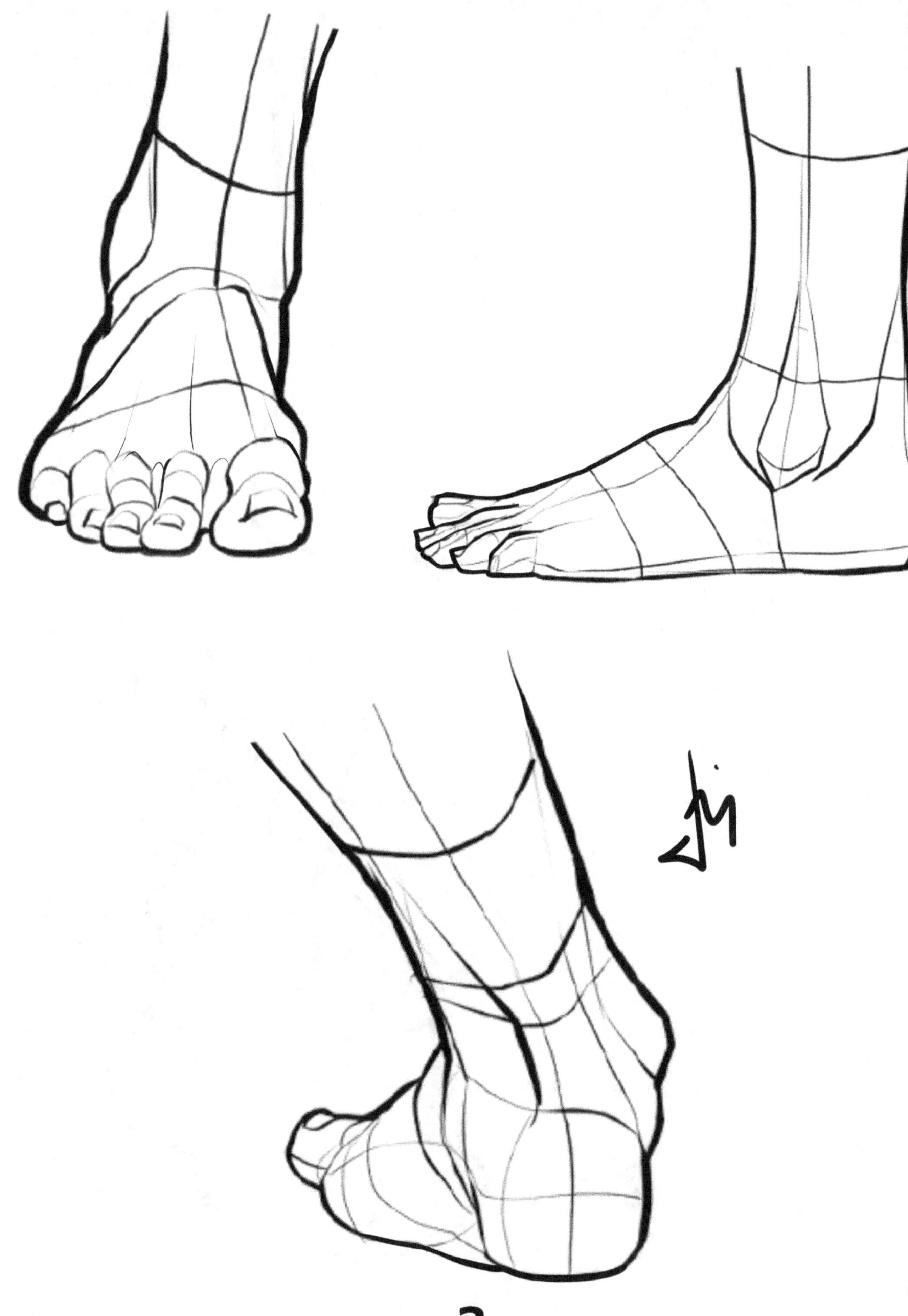

3

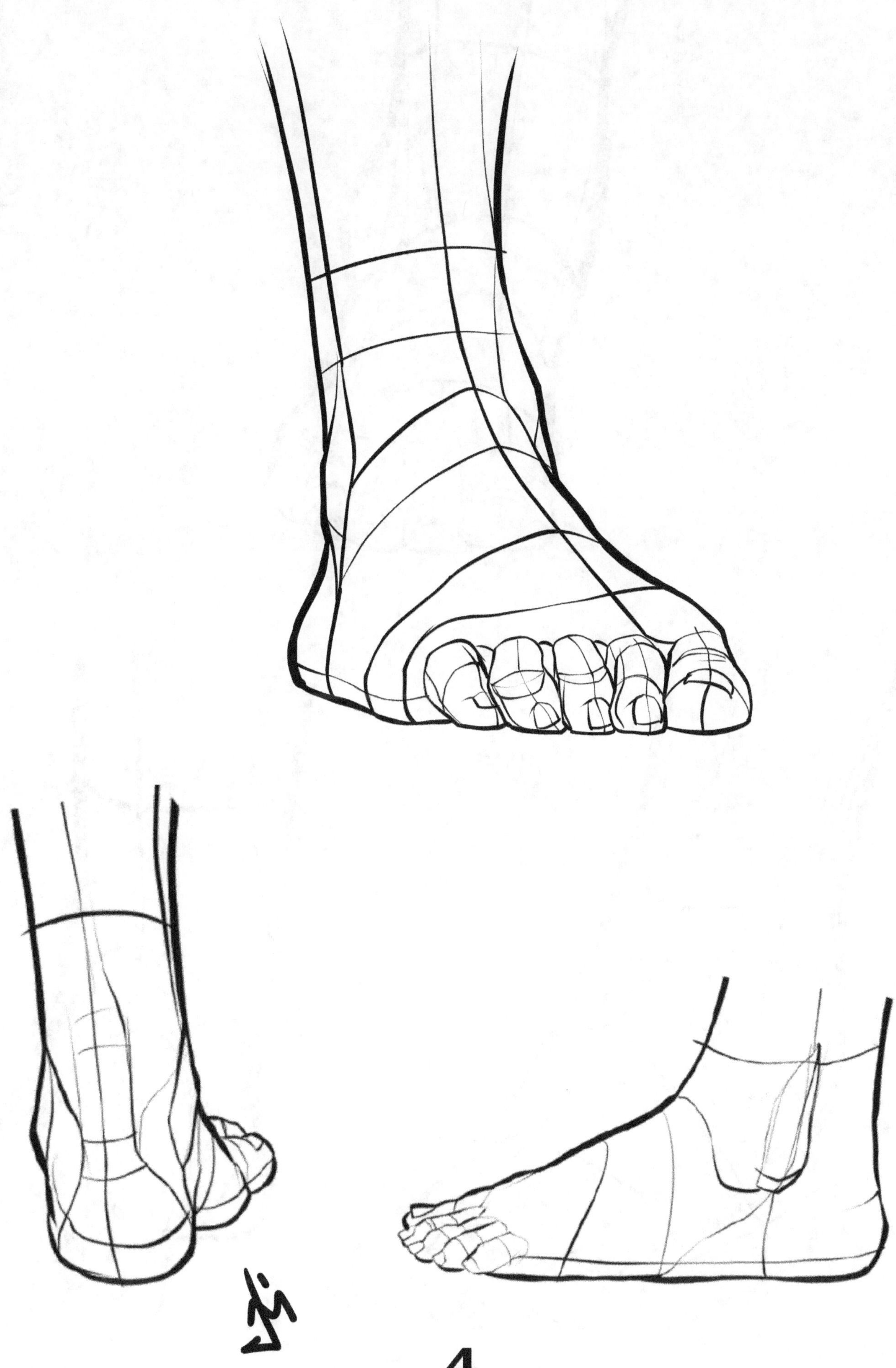

4

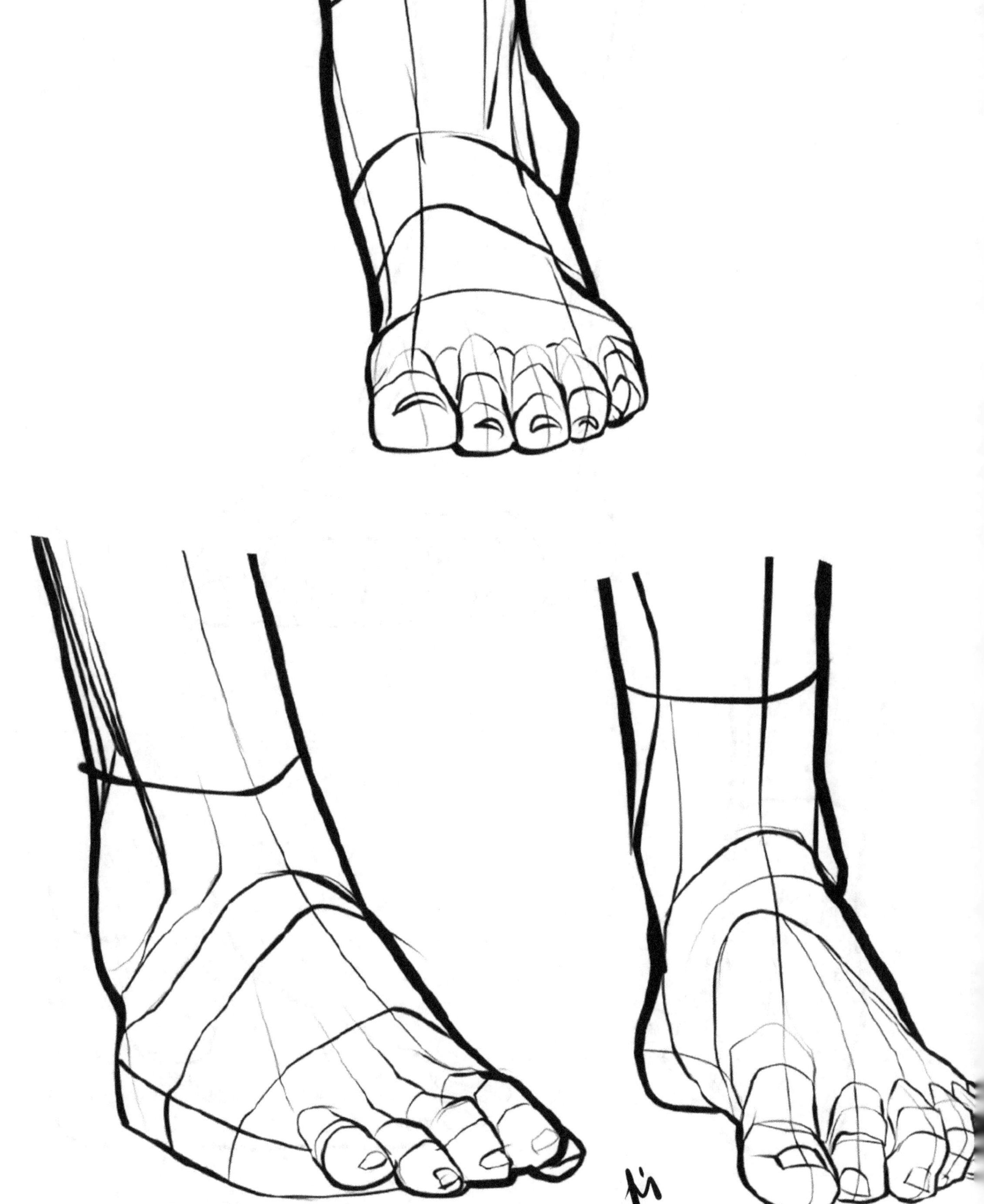

5

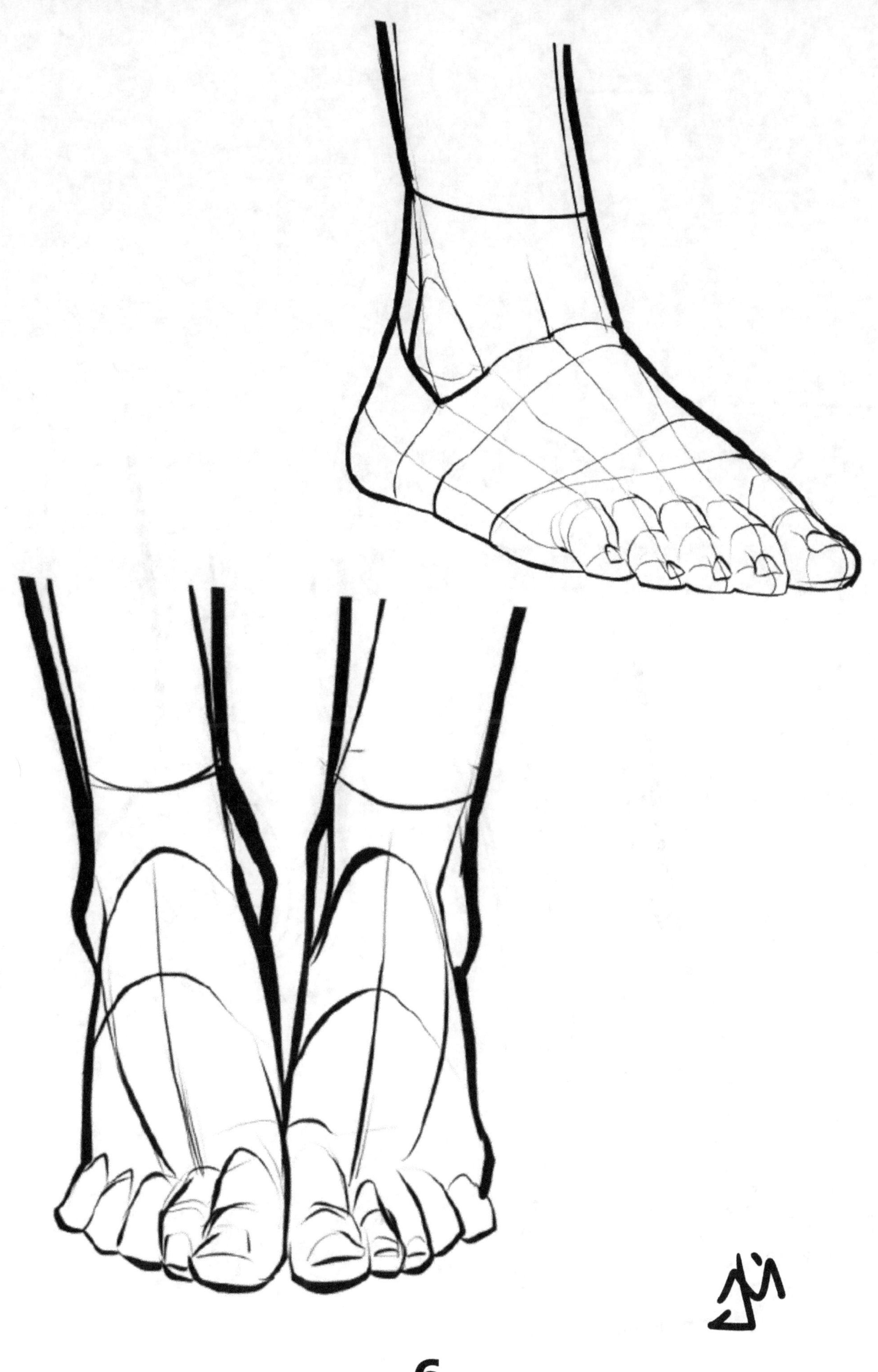

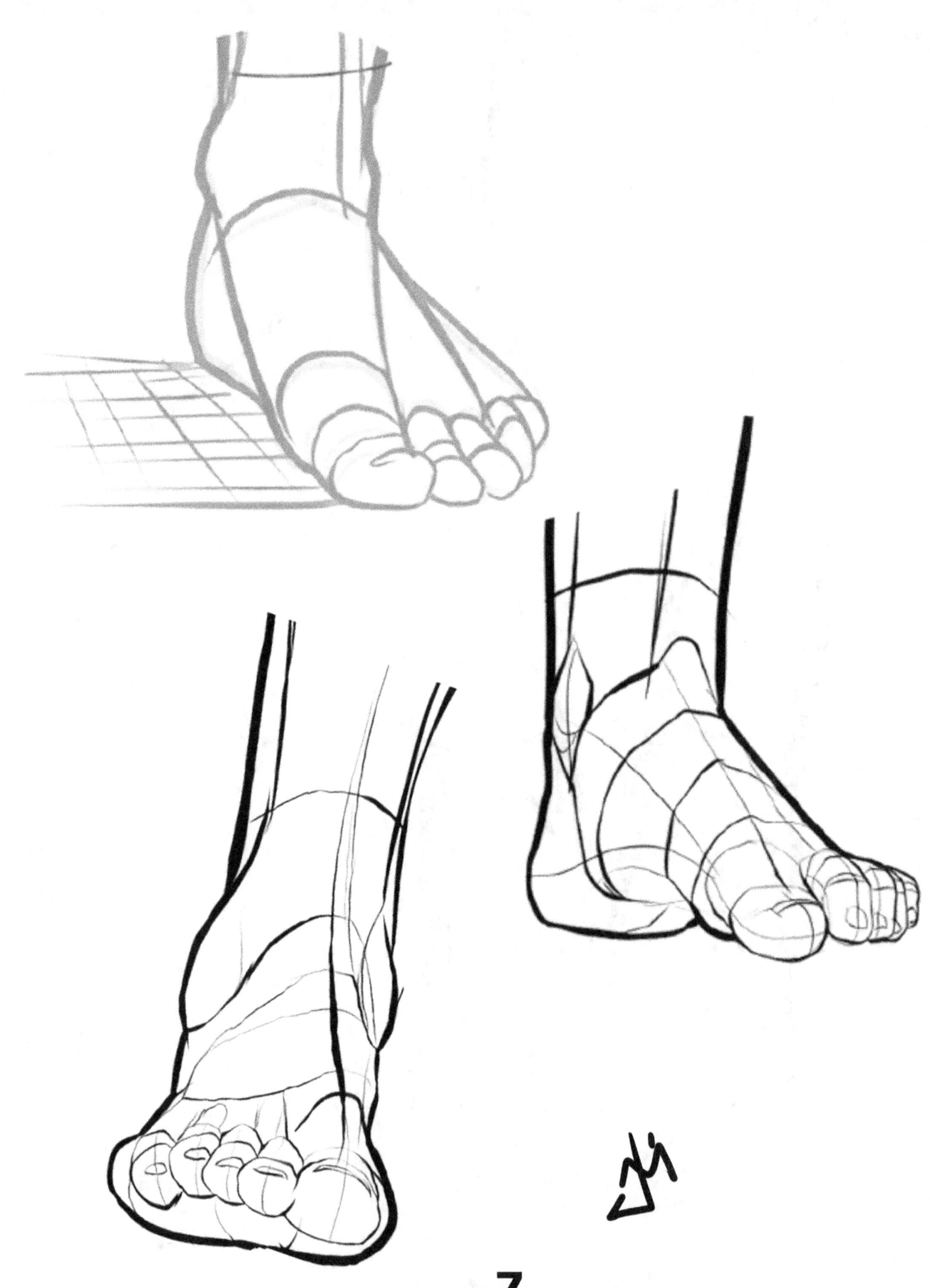

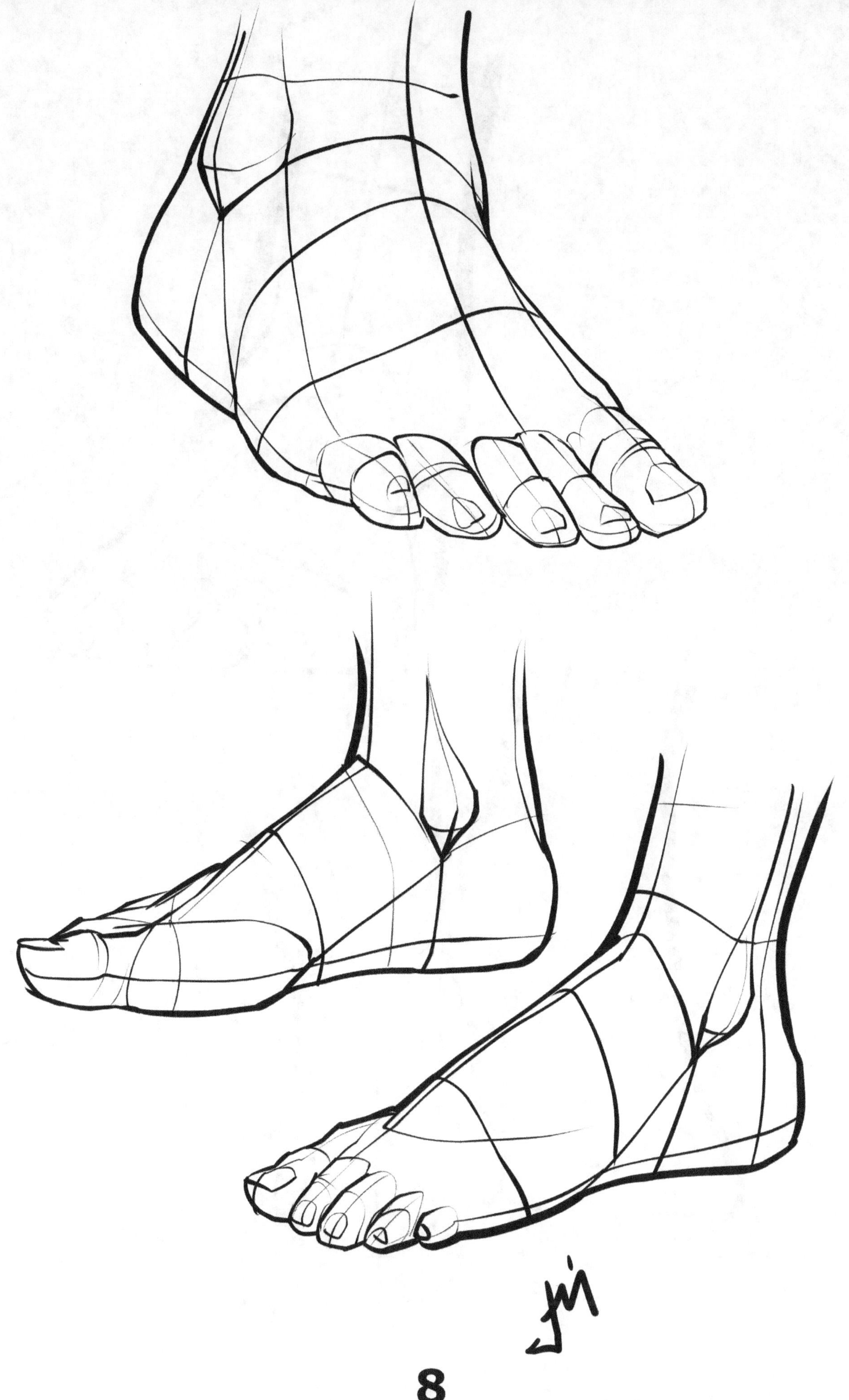

8

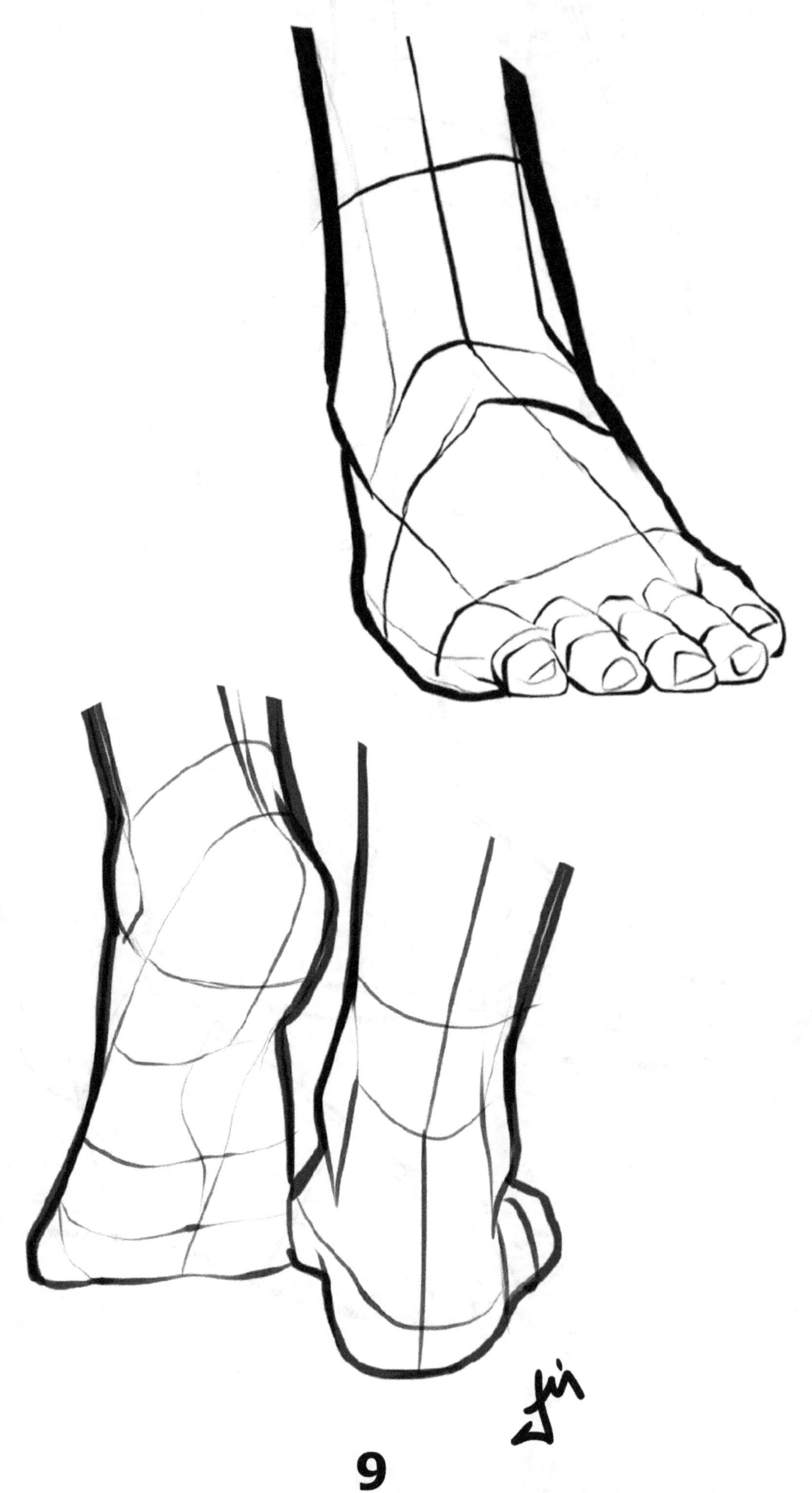

9

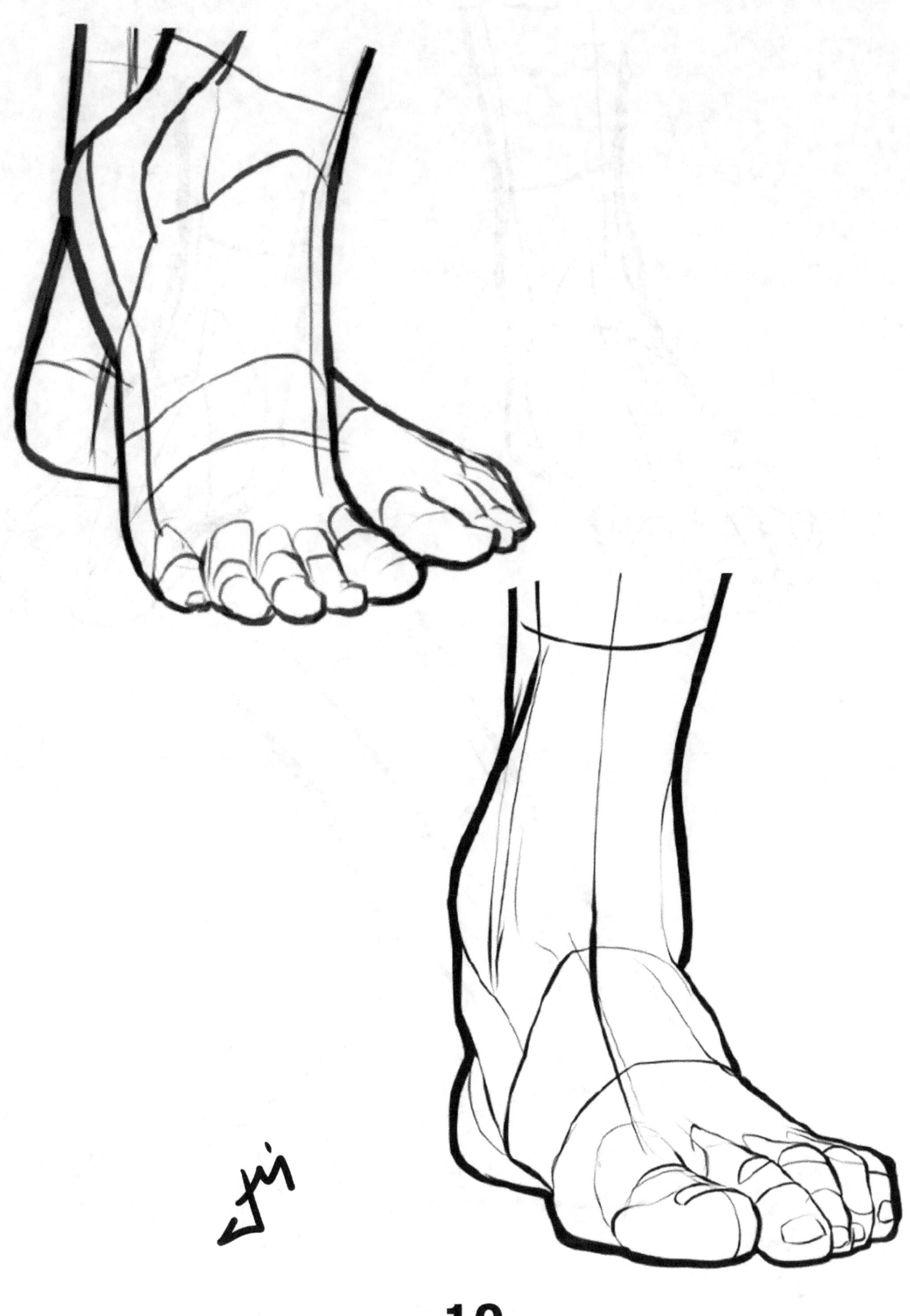

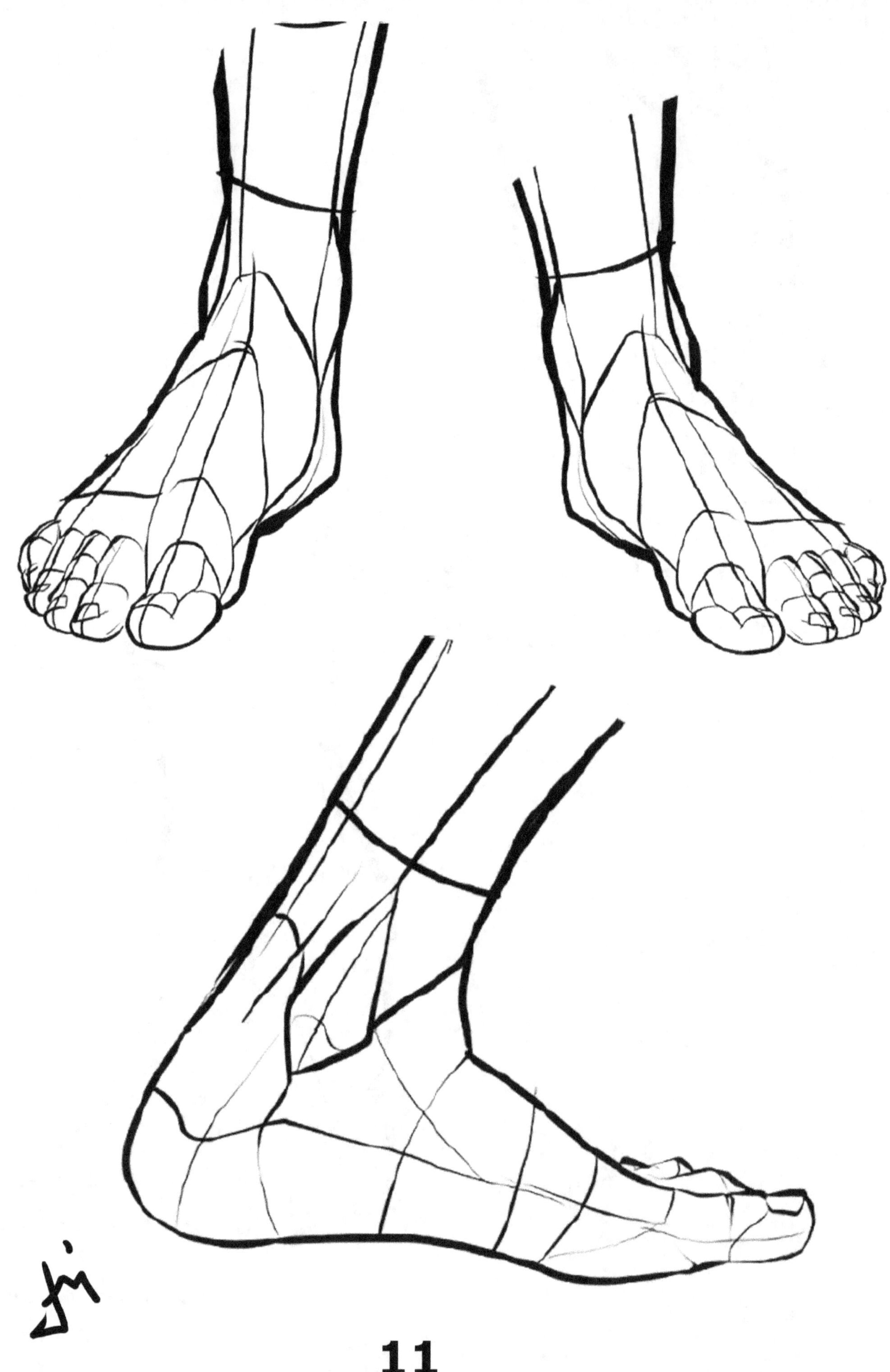

11

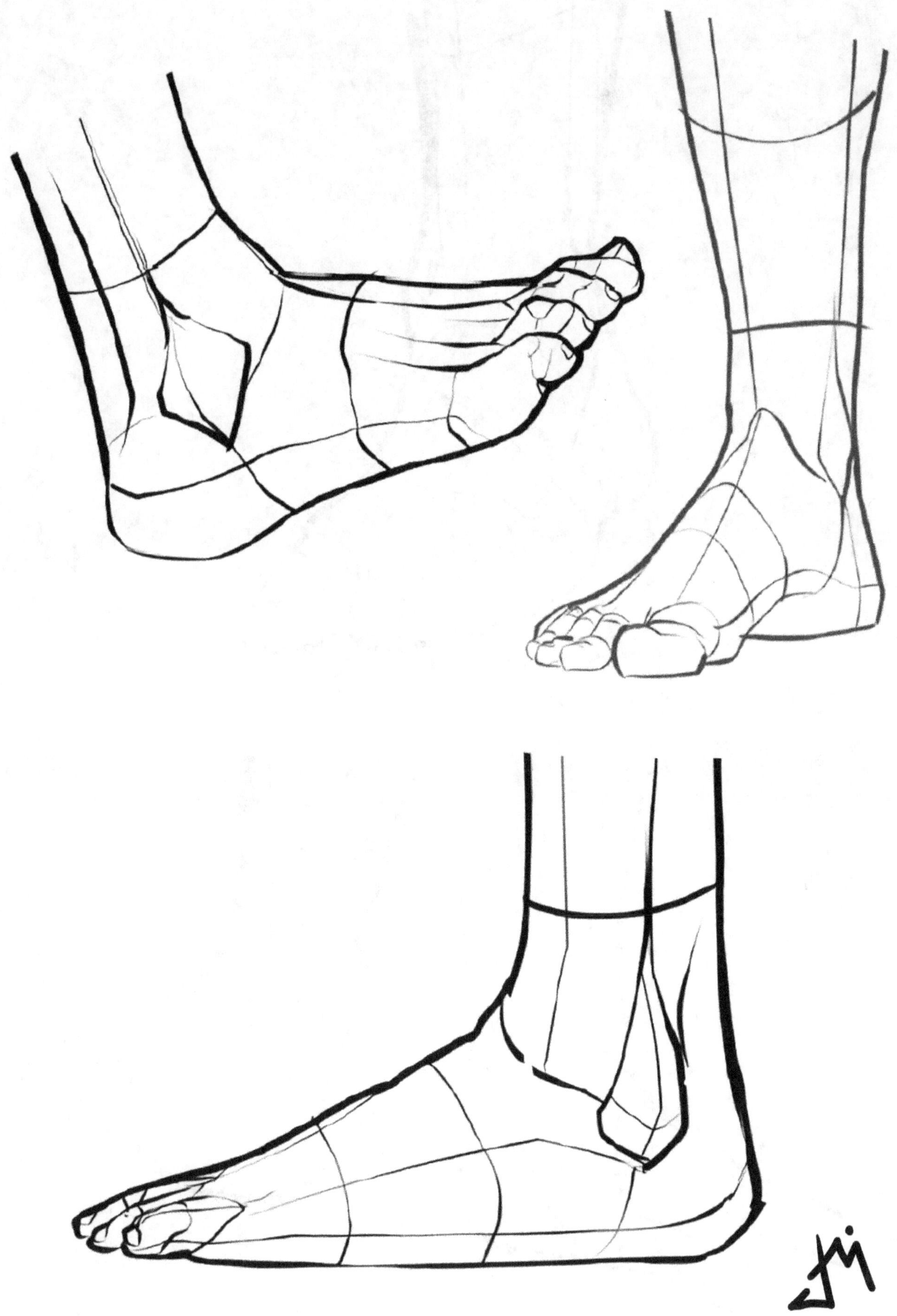

12

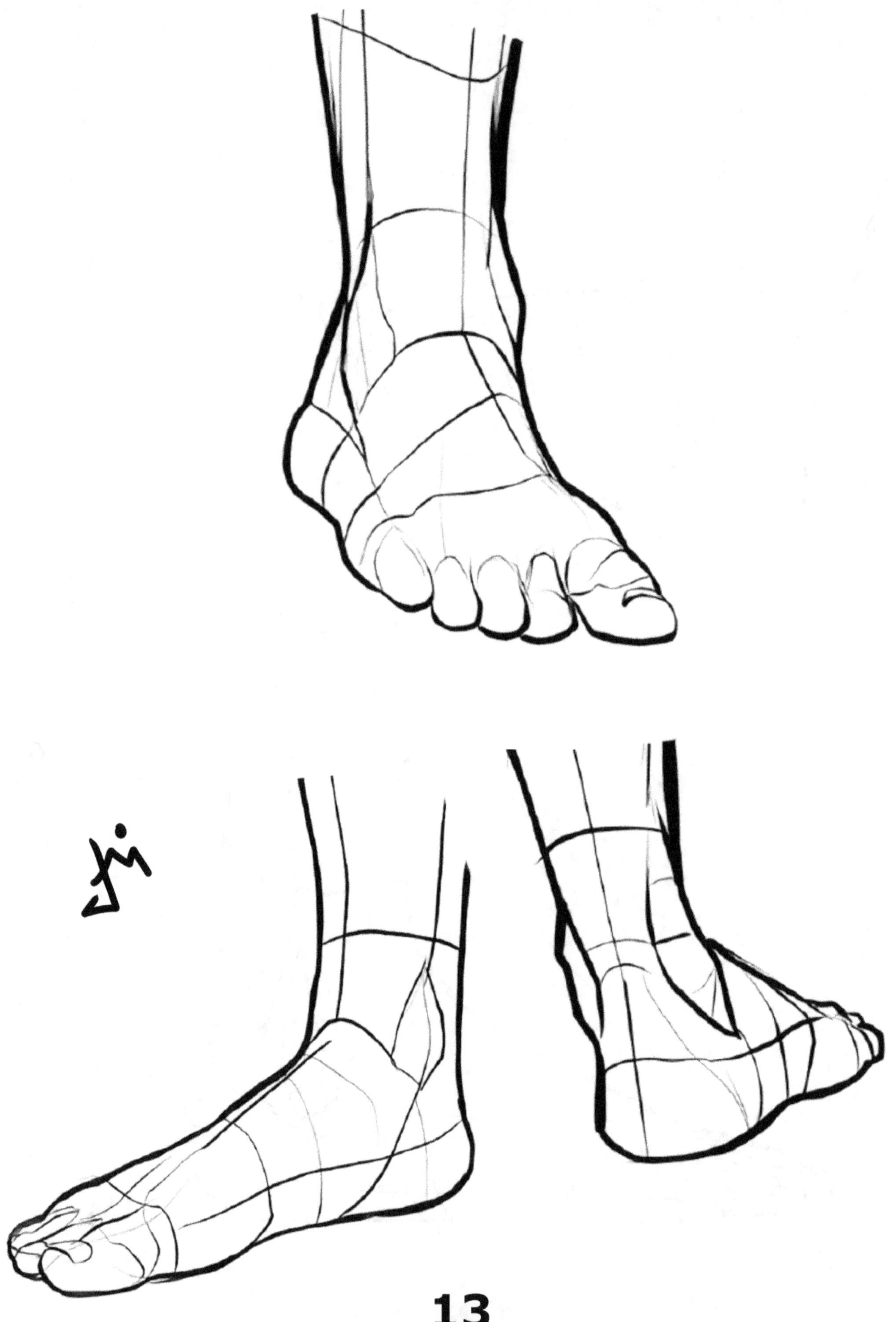

13

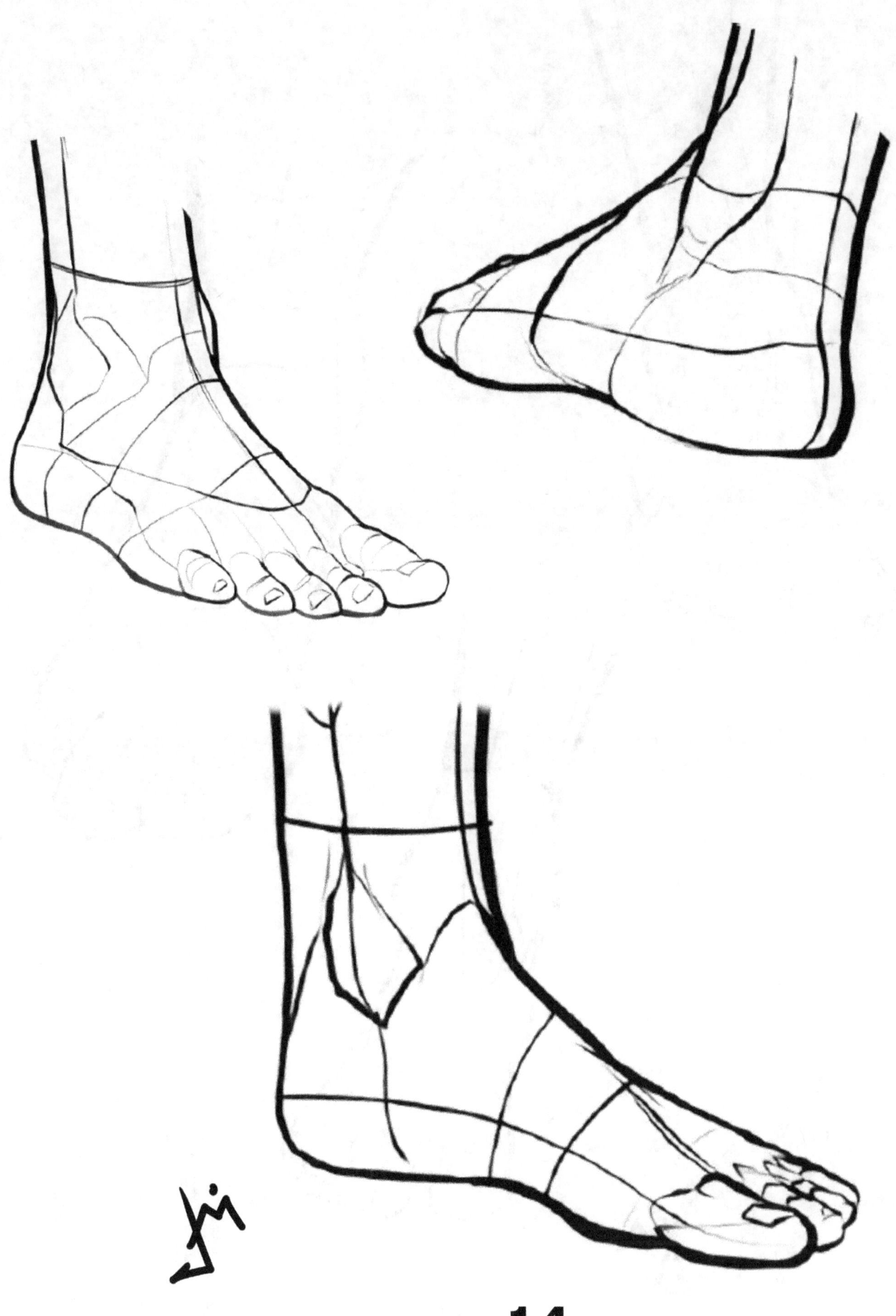

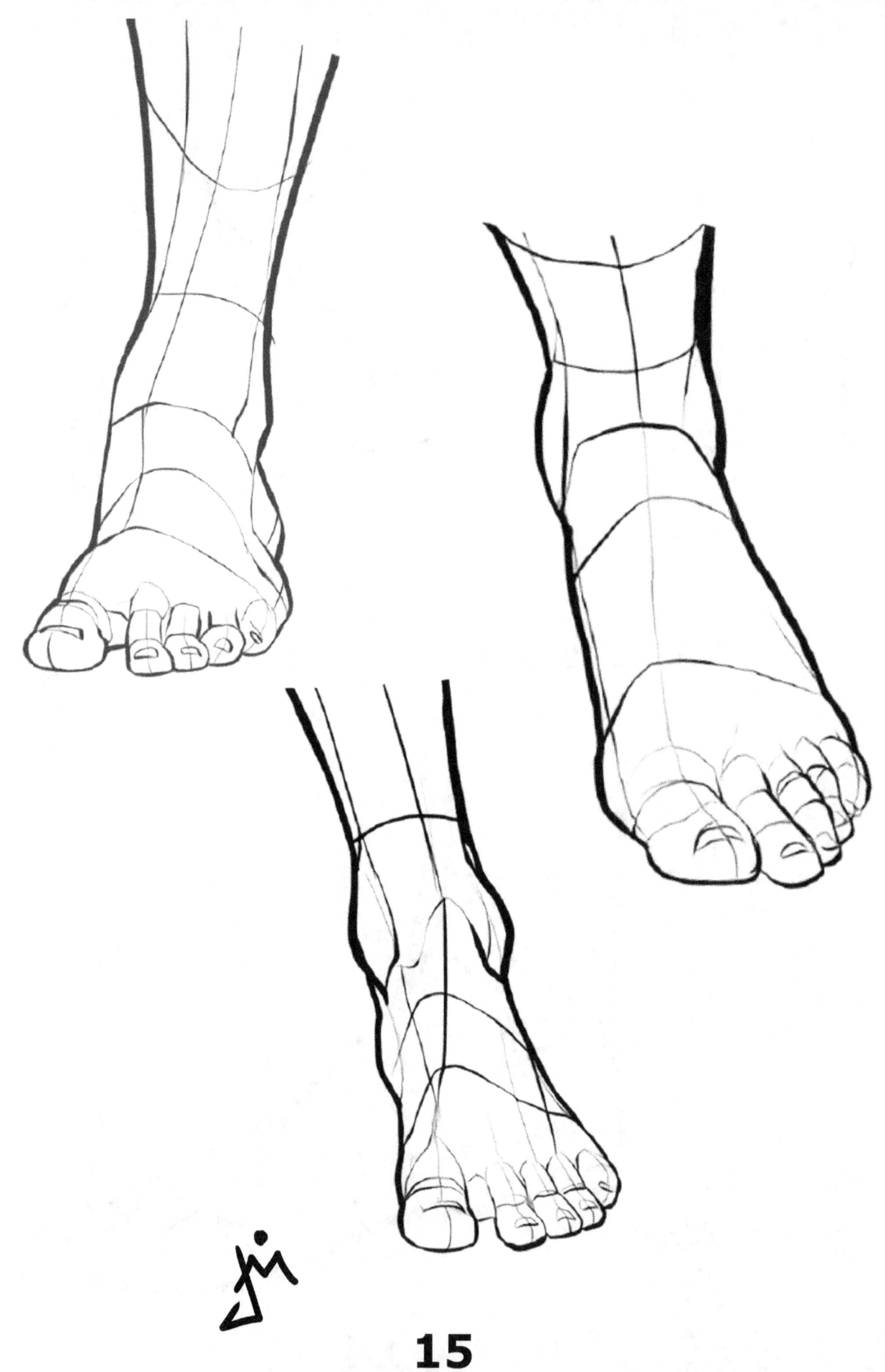

15

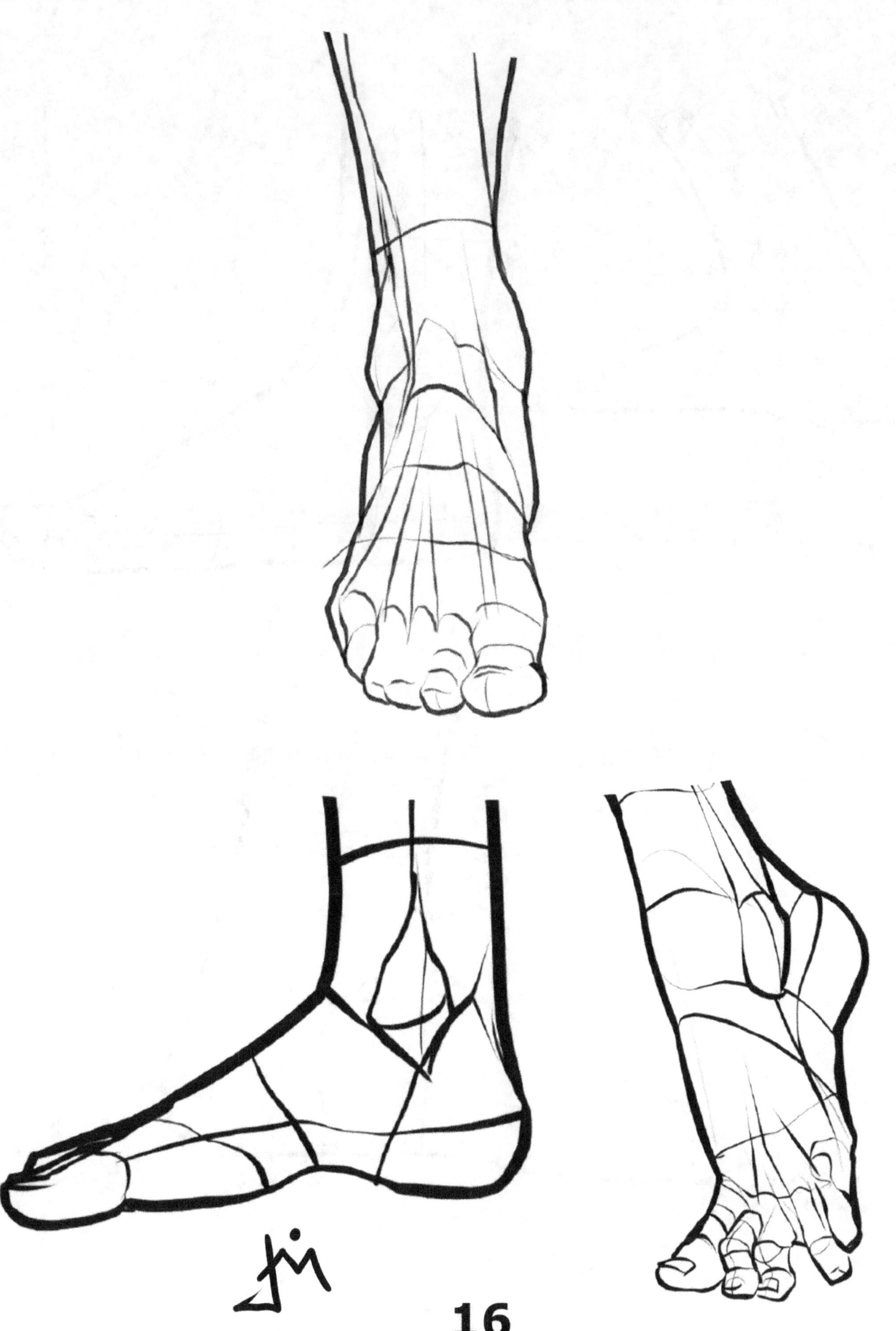

16

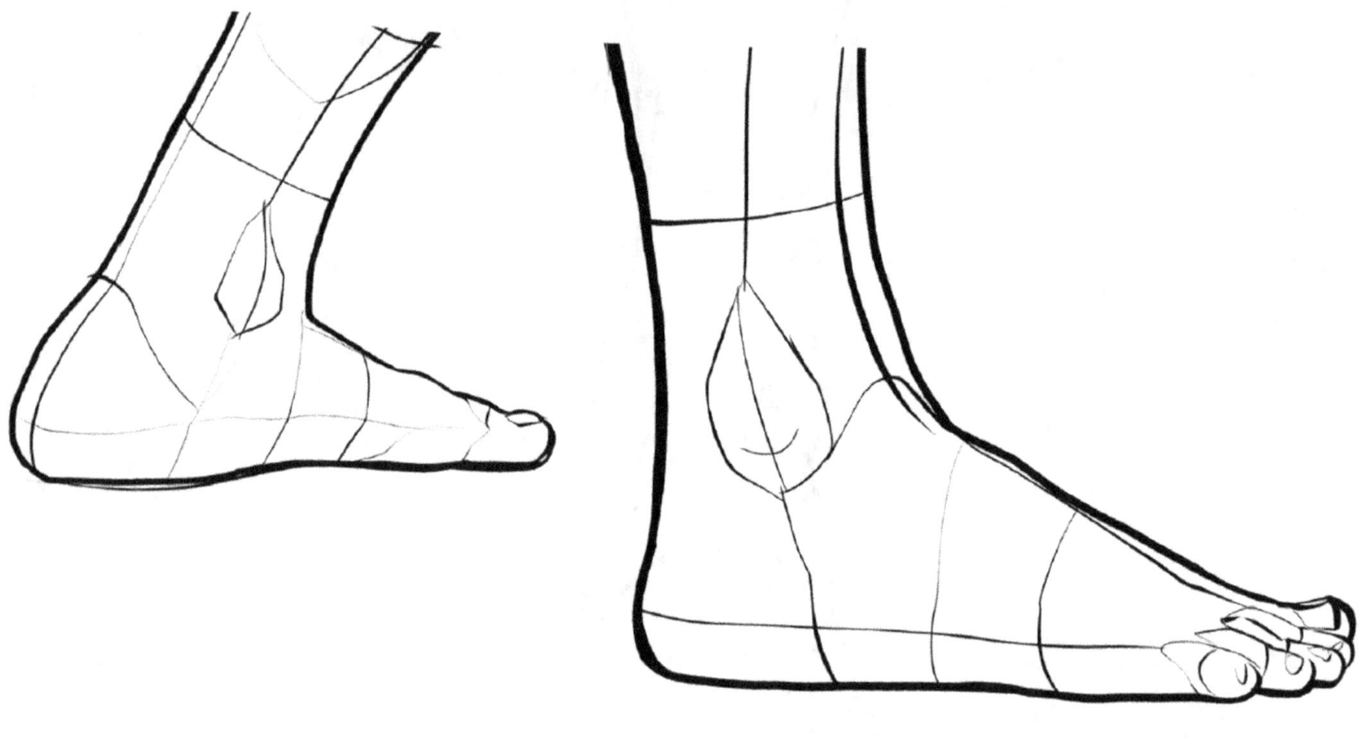

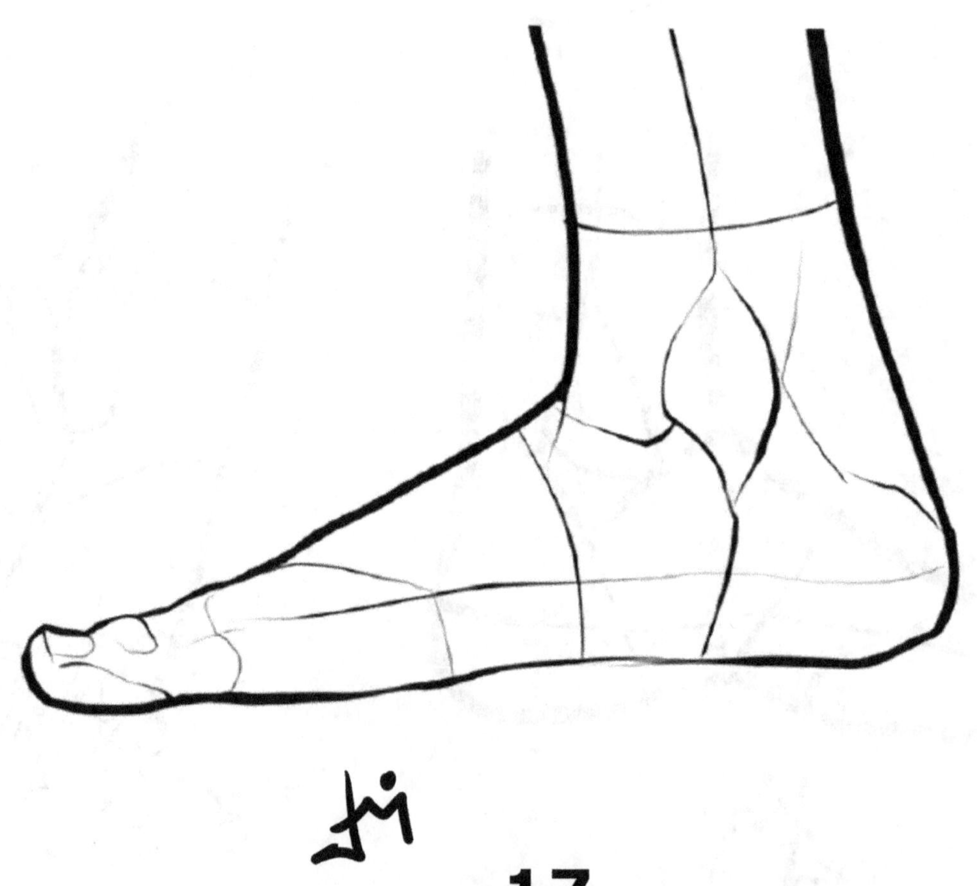

17

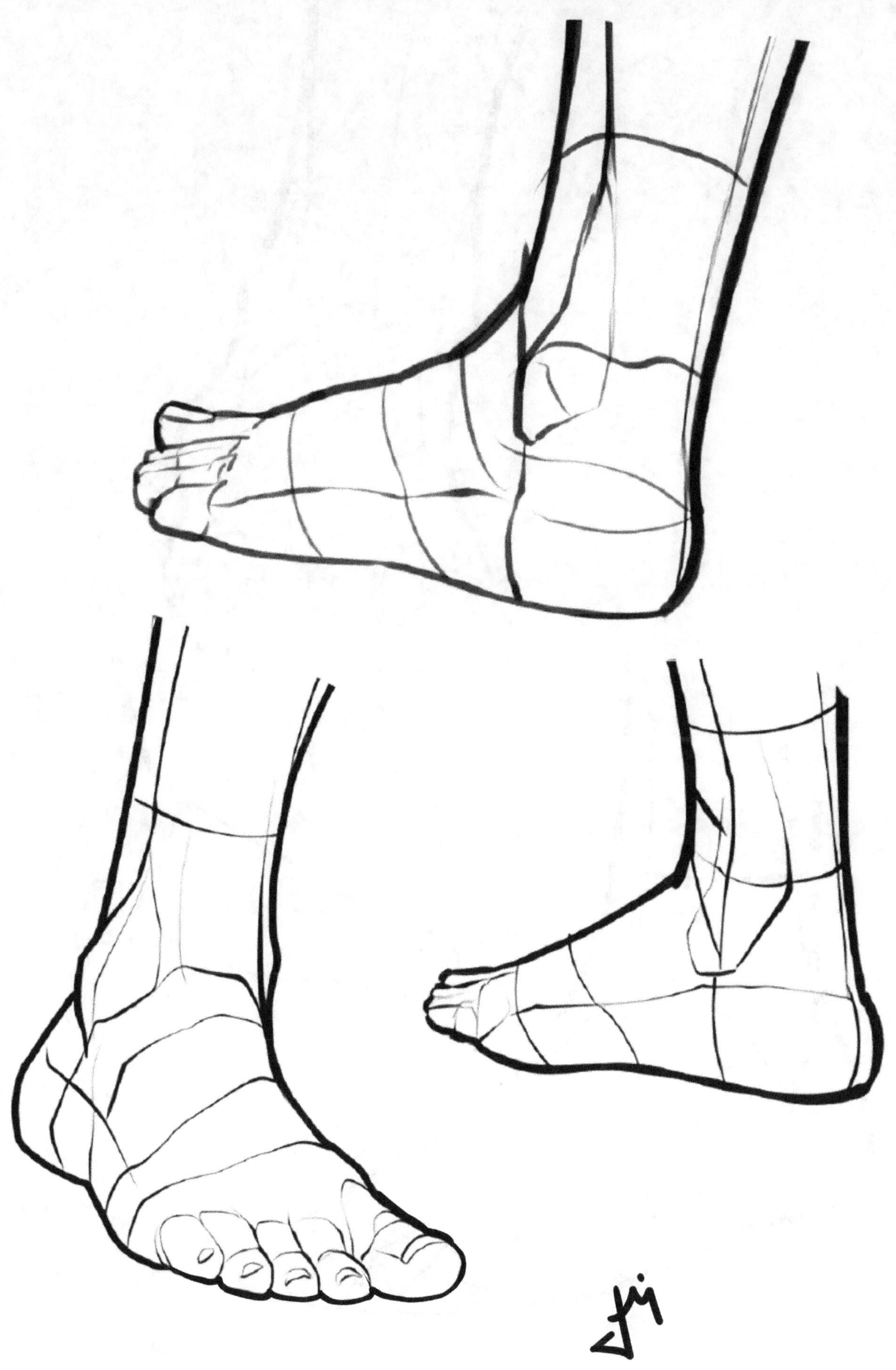

18

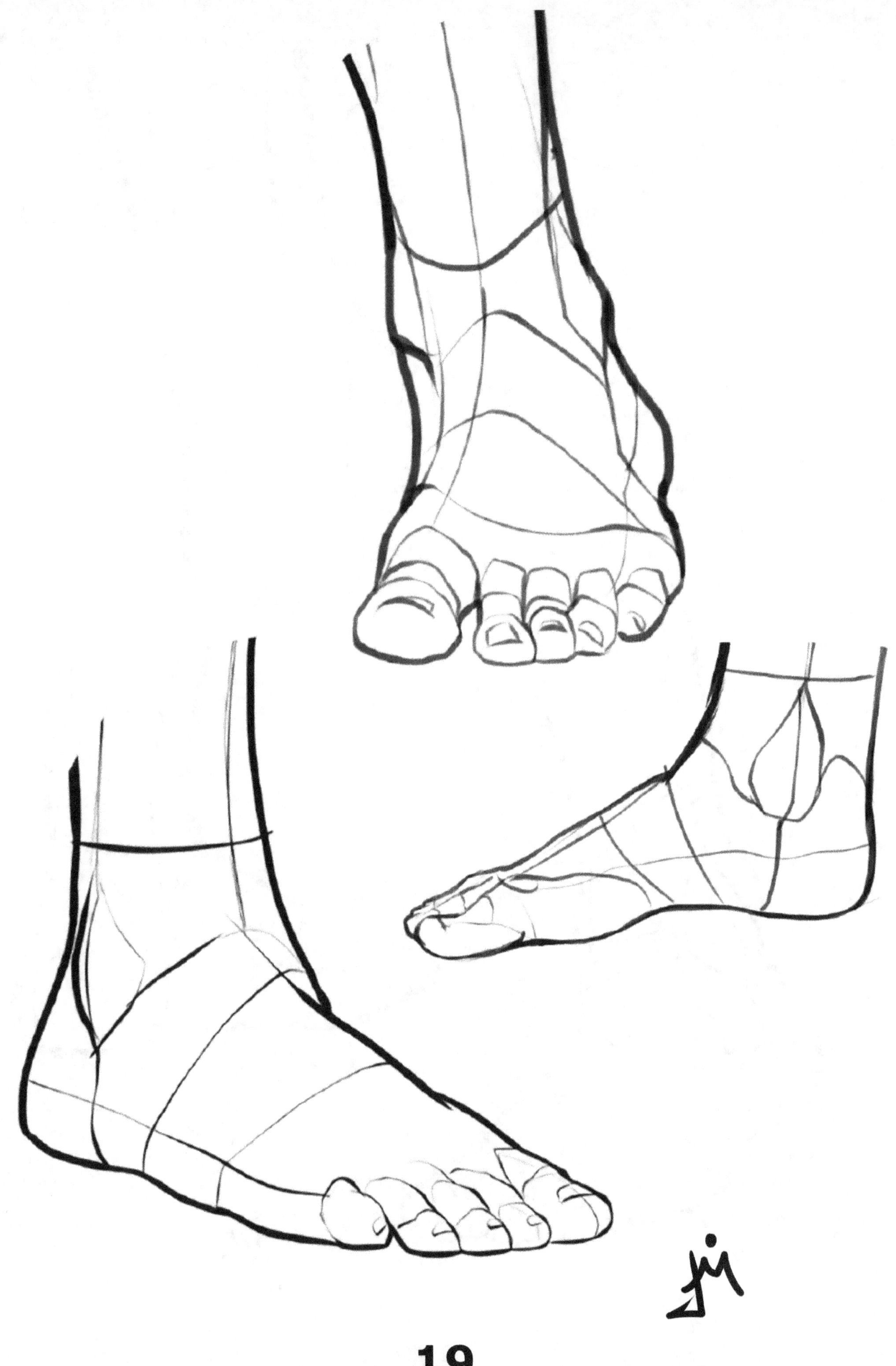

19

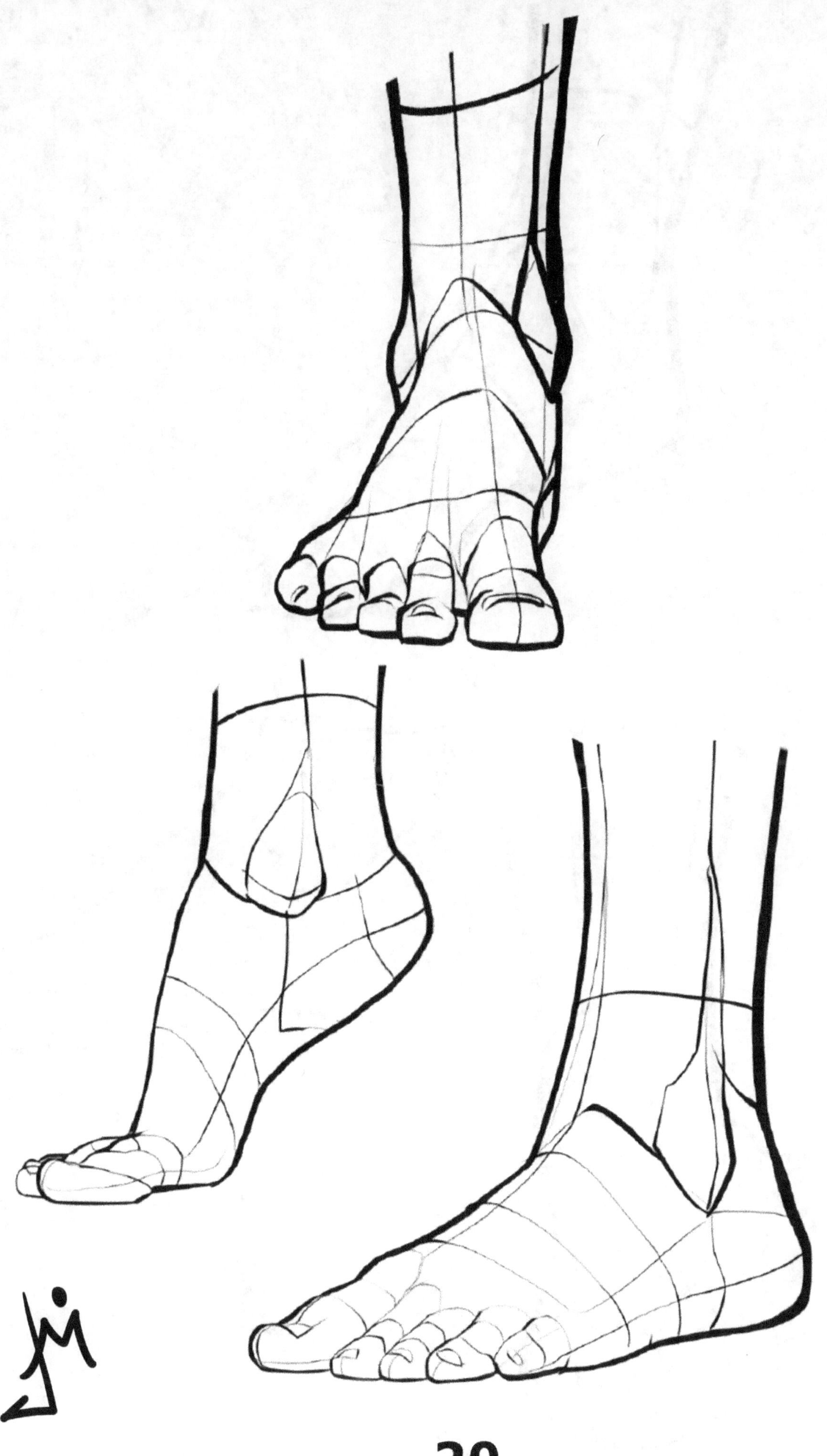

20

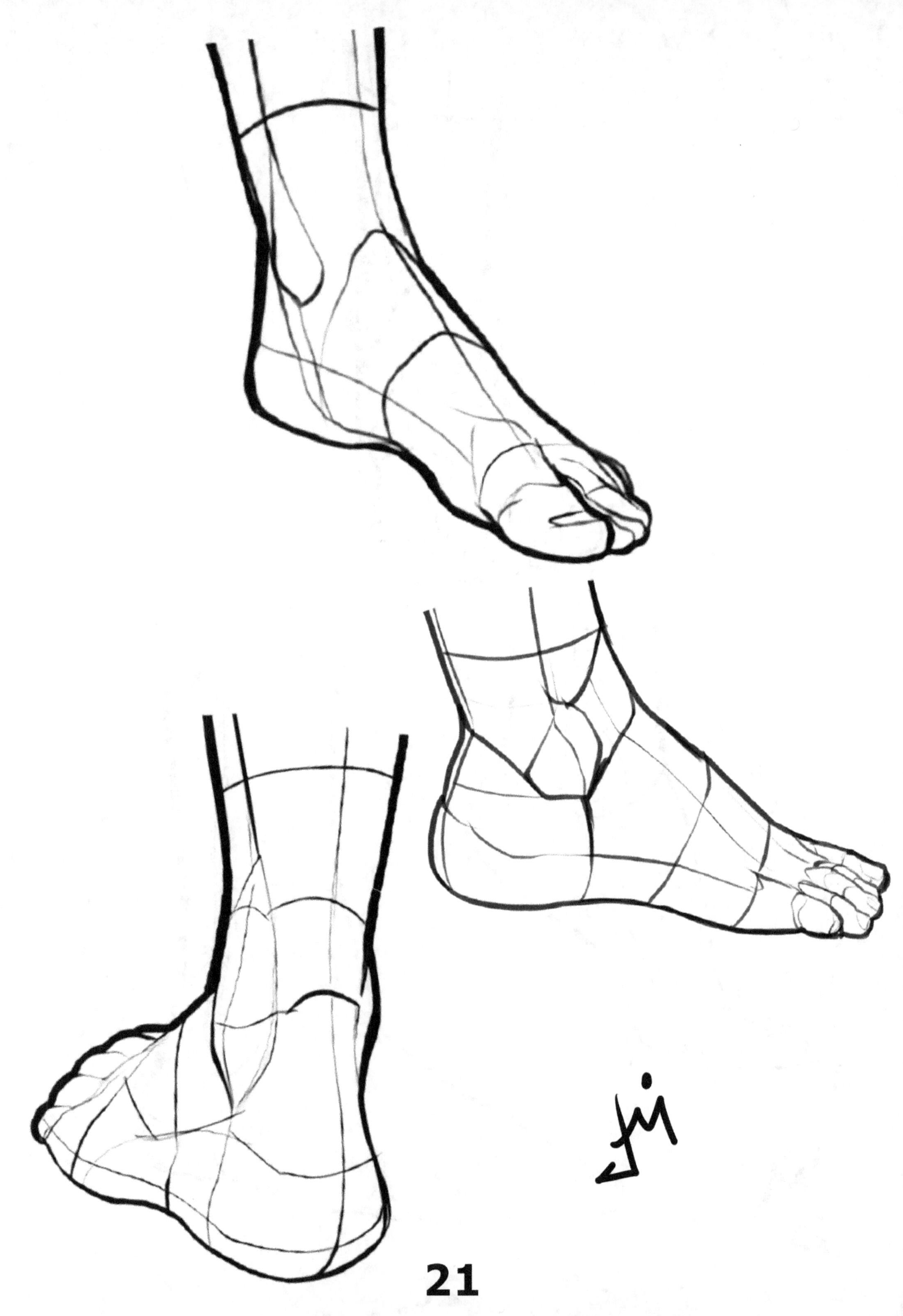

21

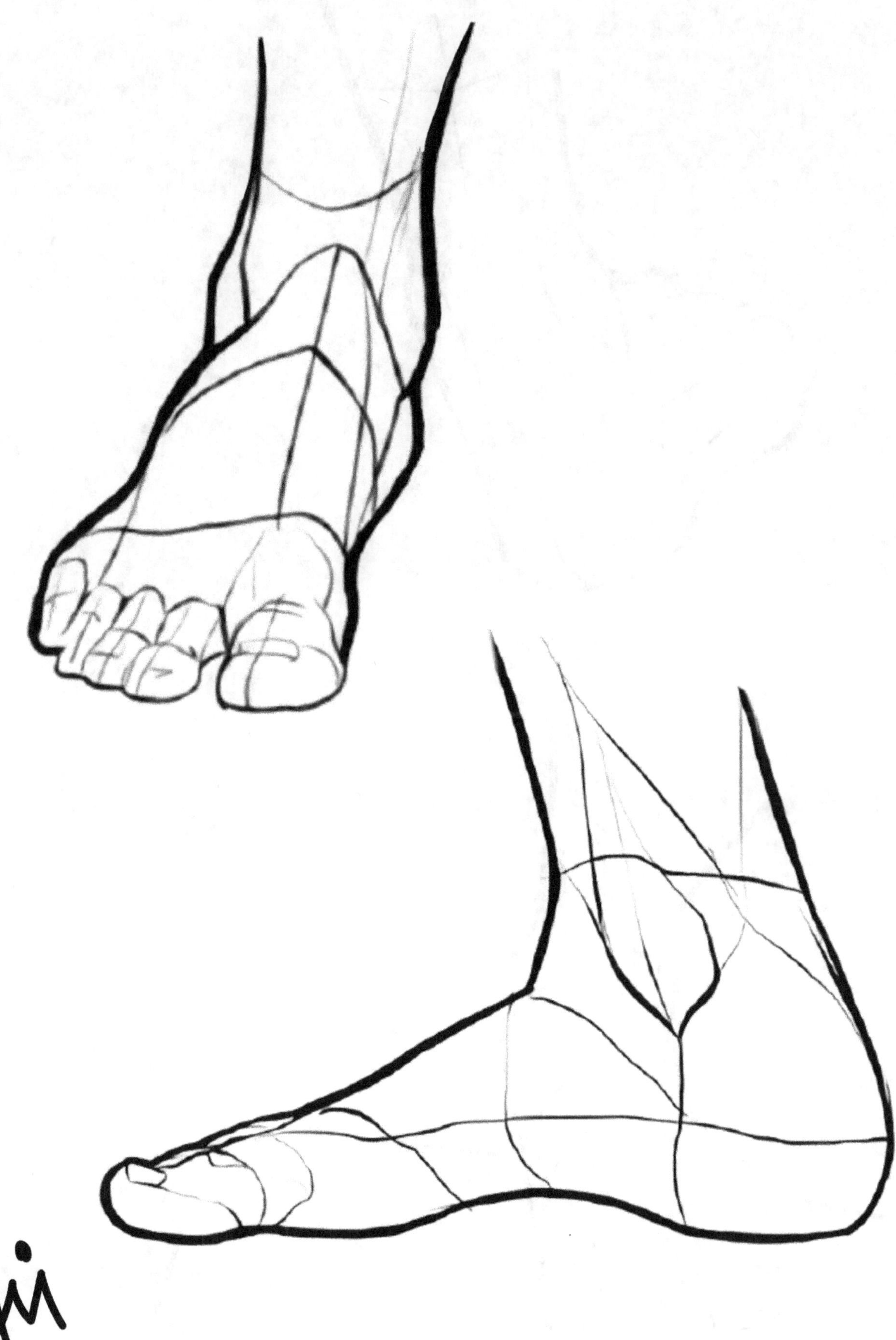

22

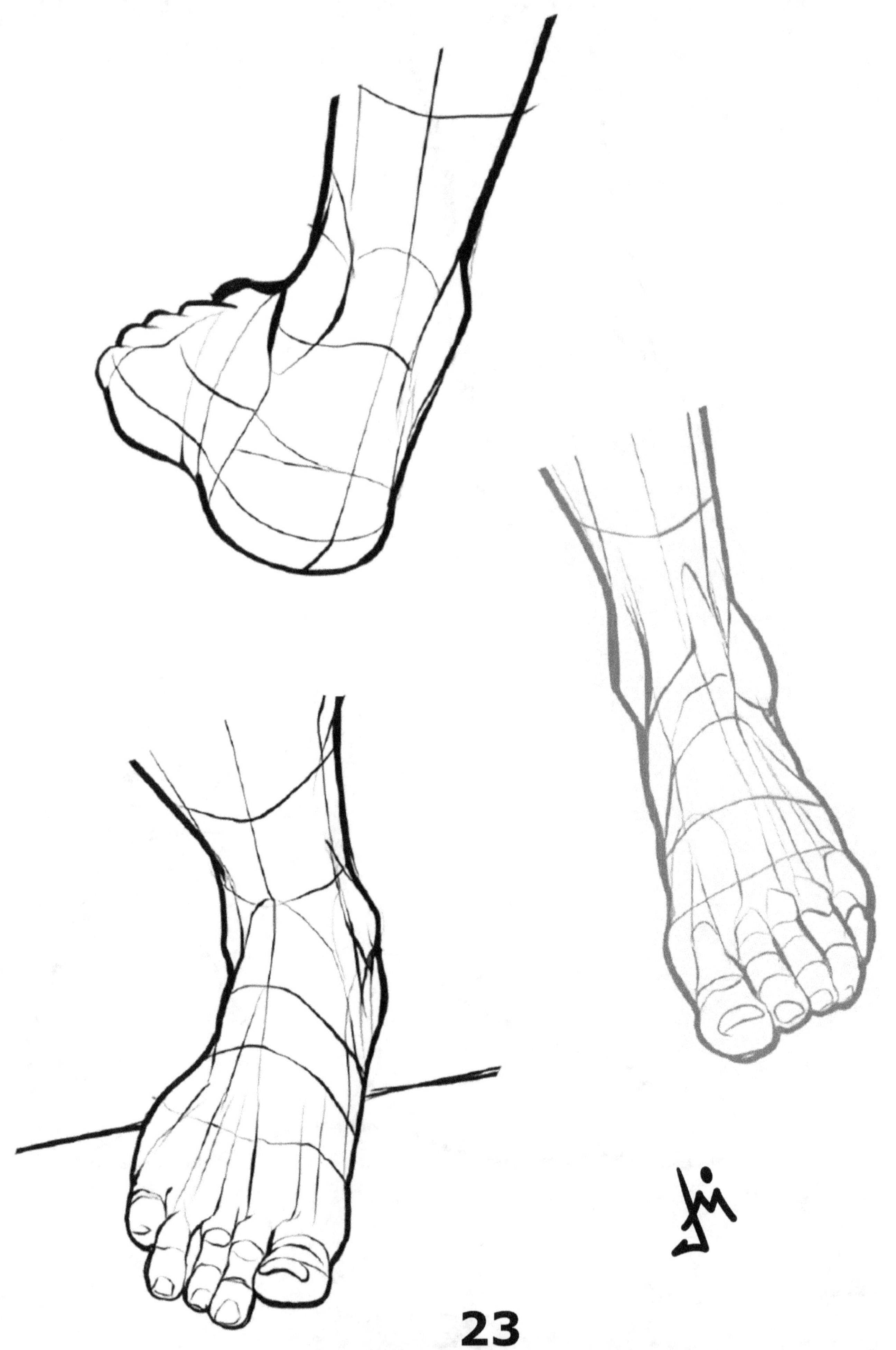

23

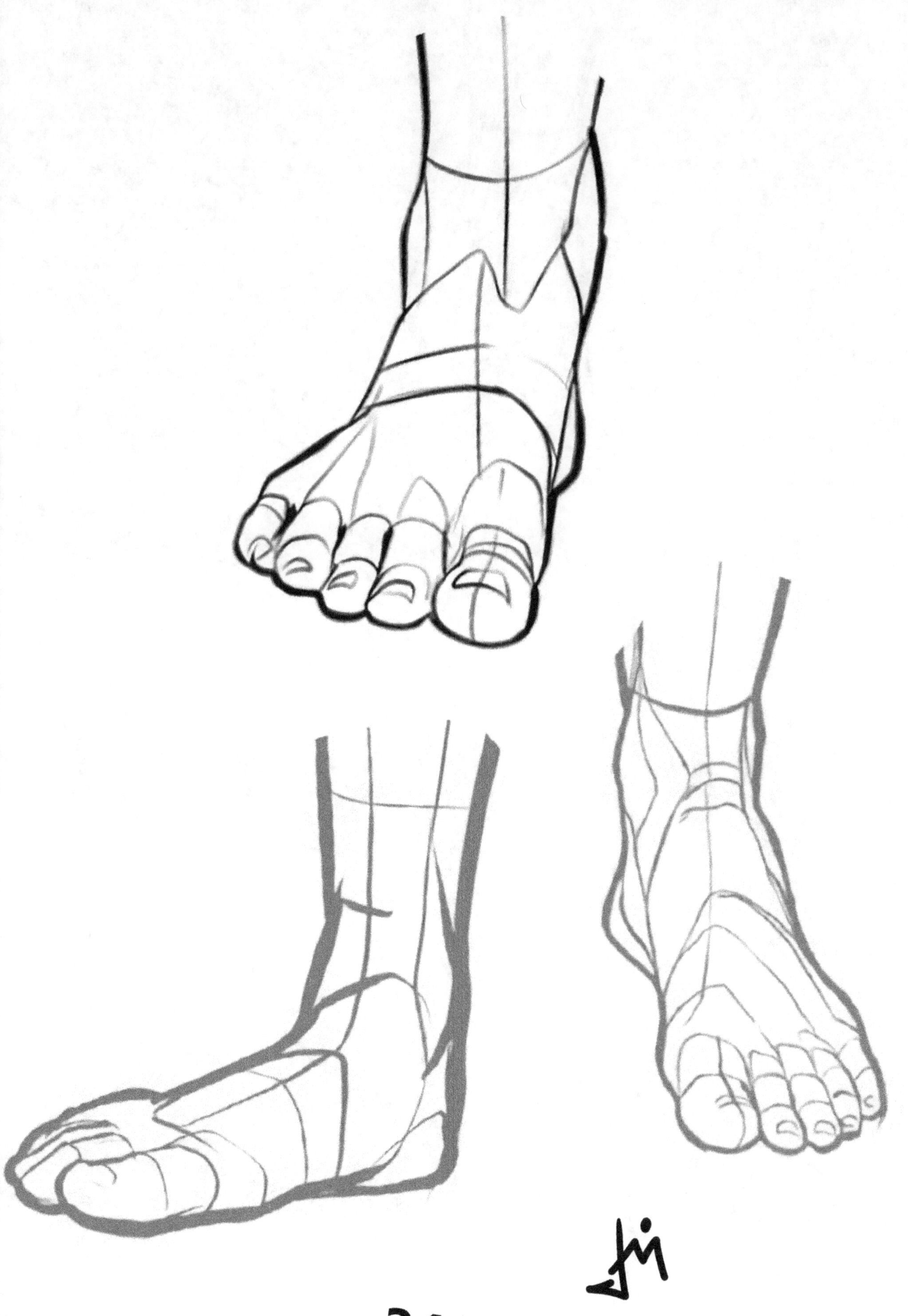

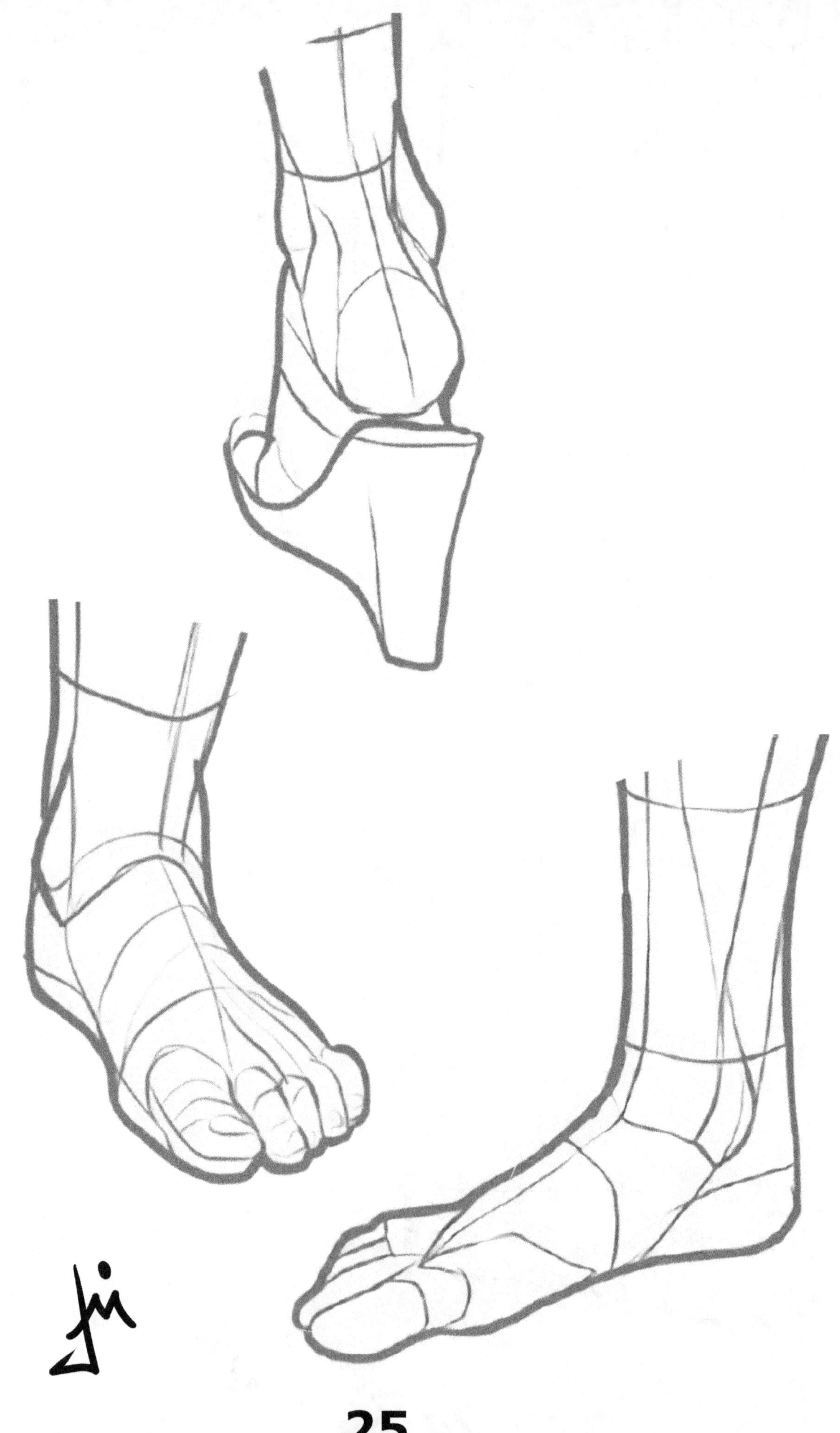

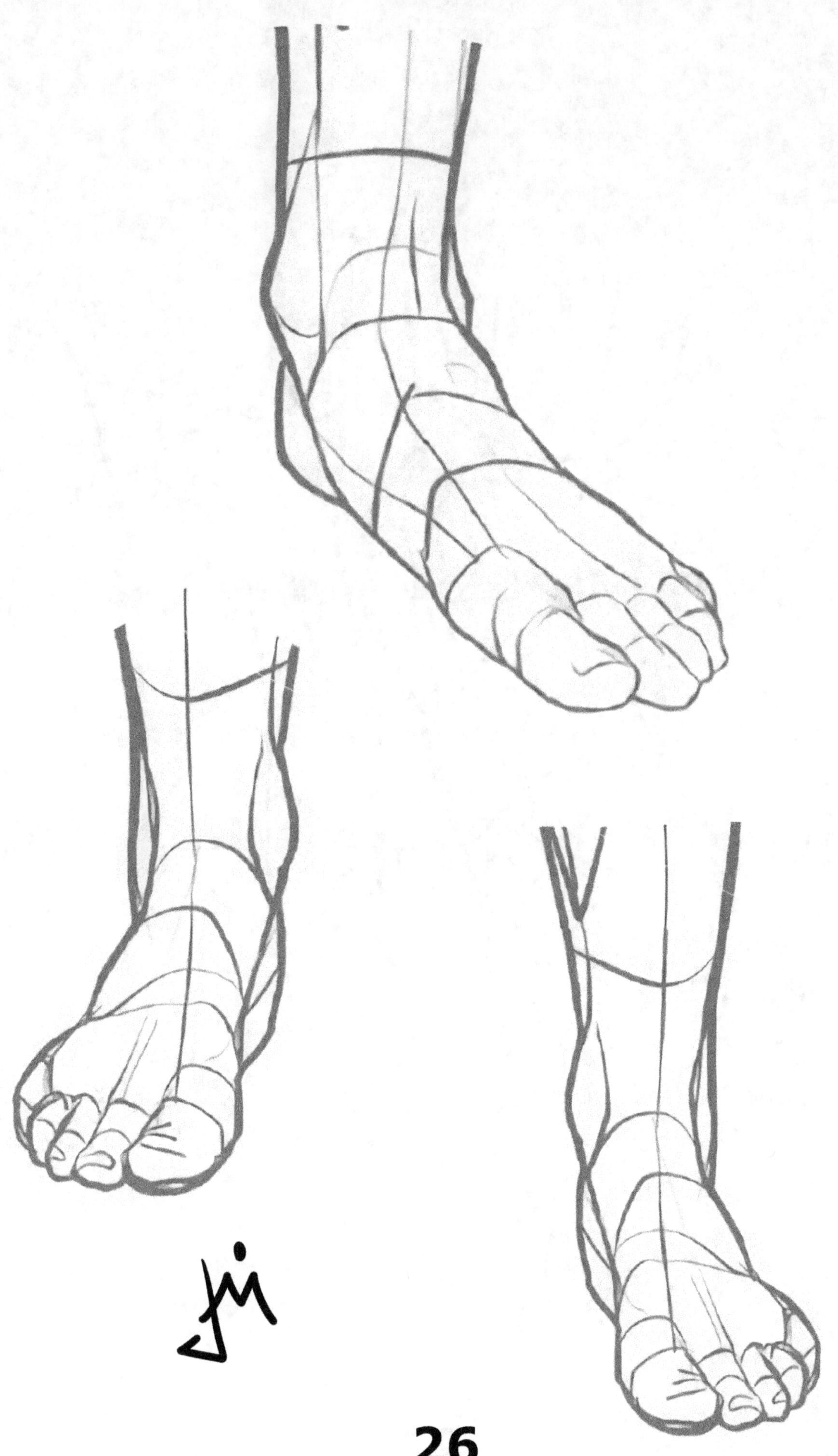

26

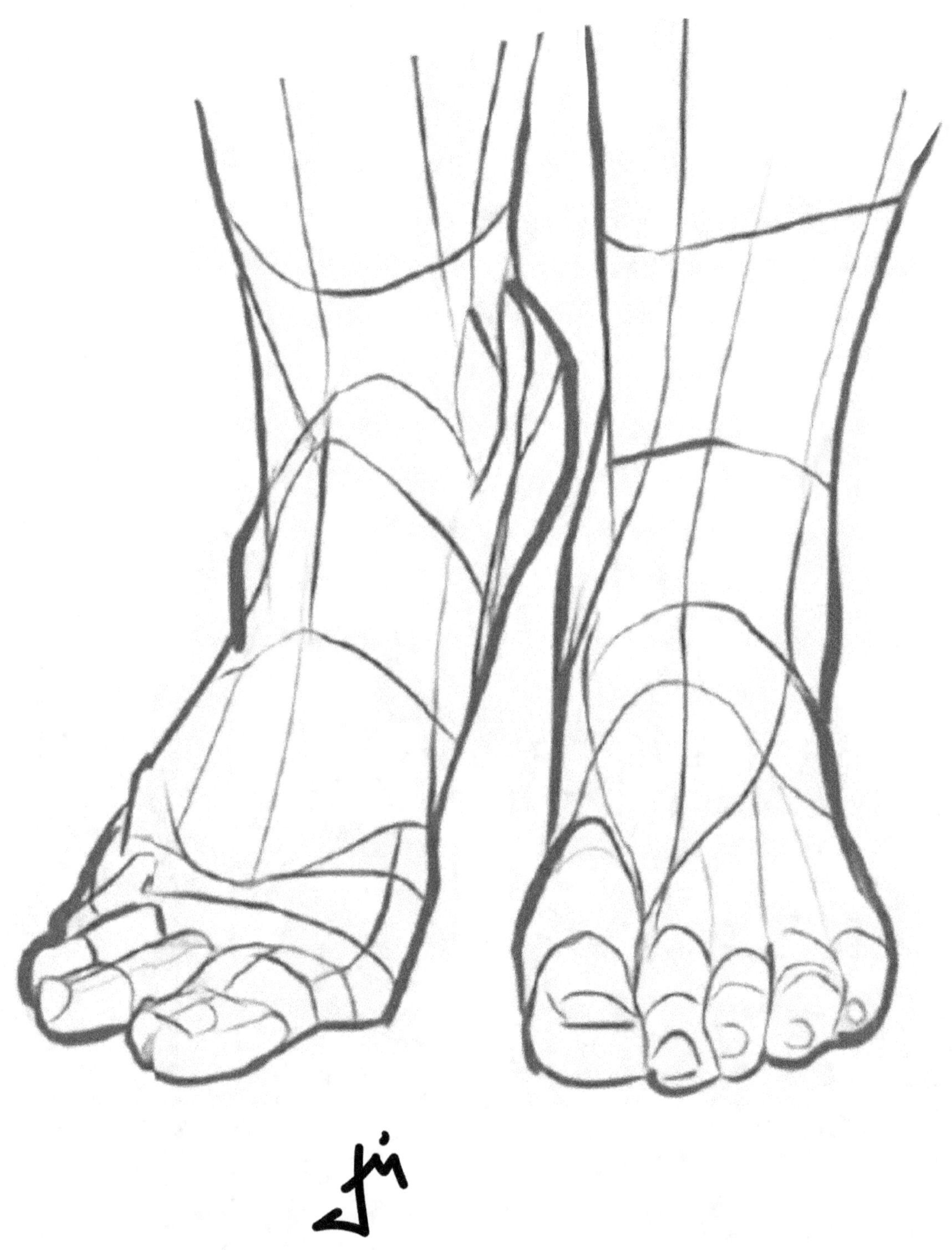

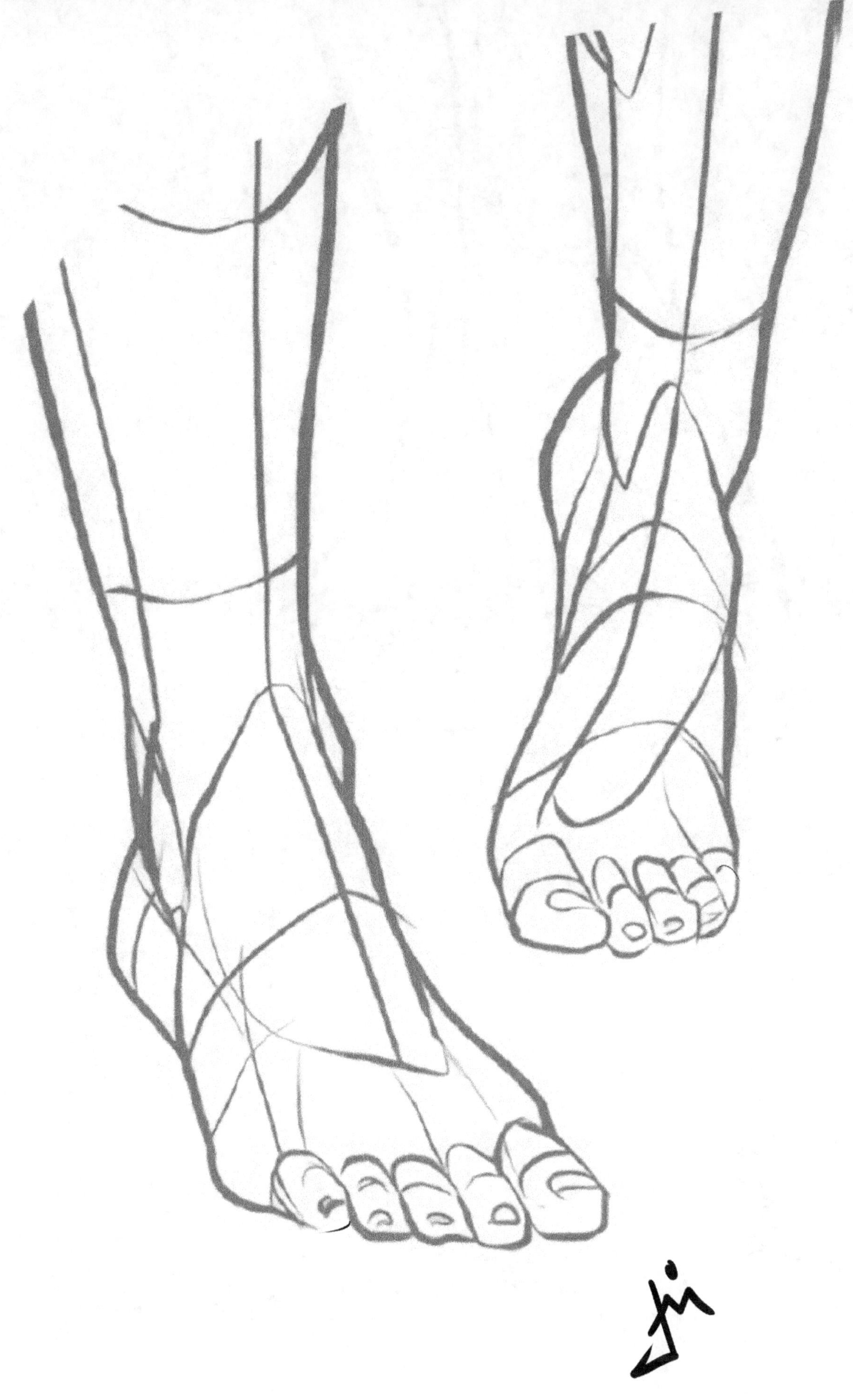

28

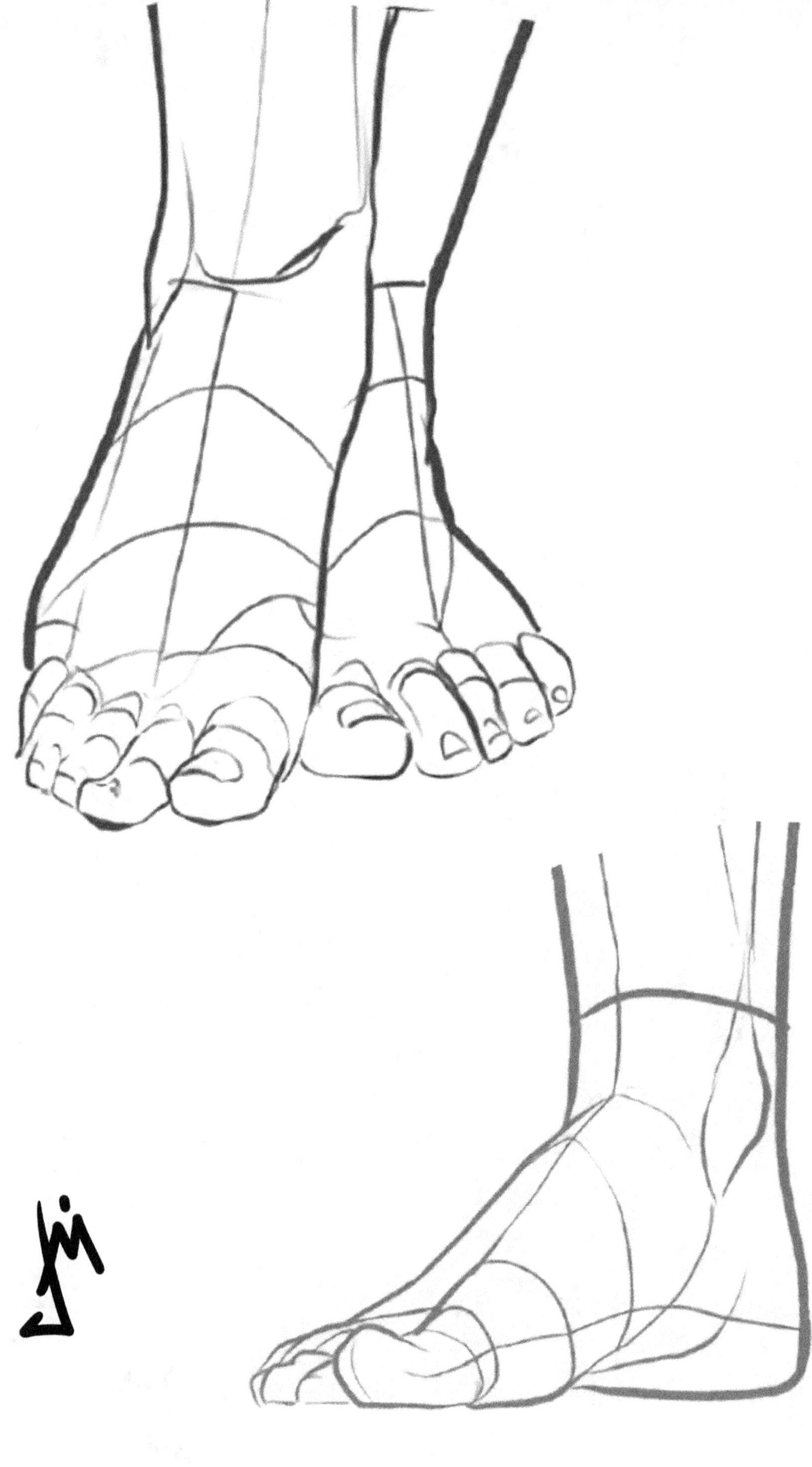

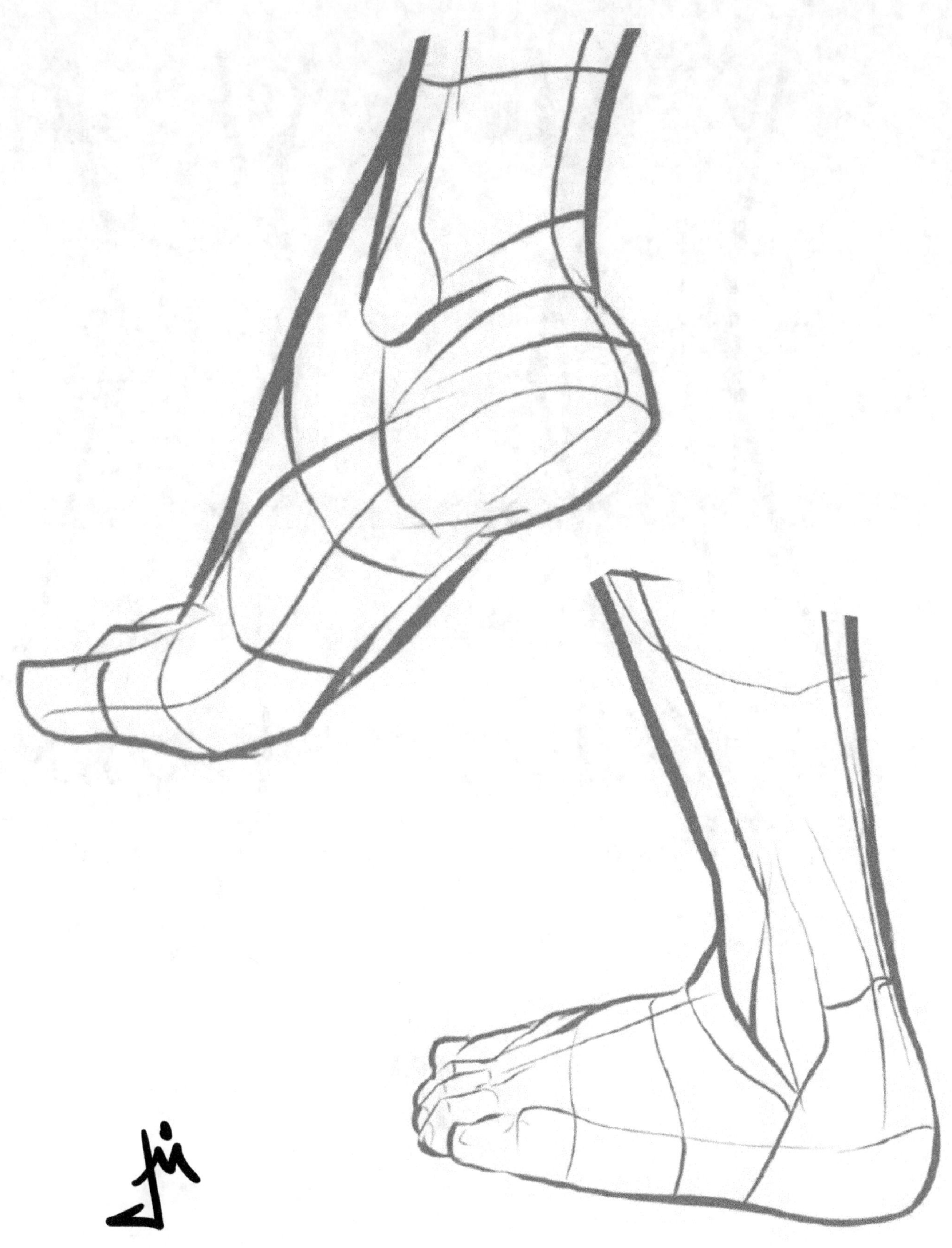

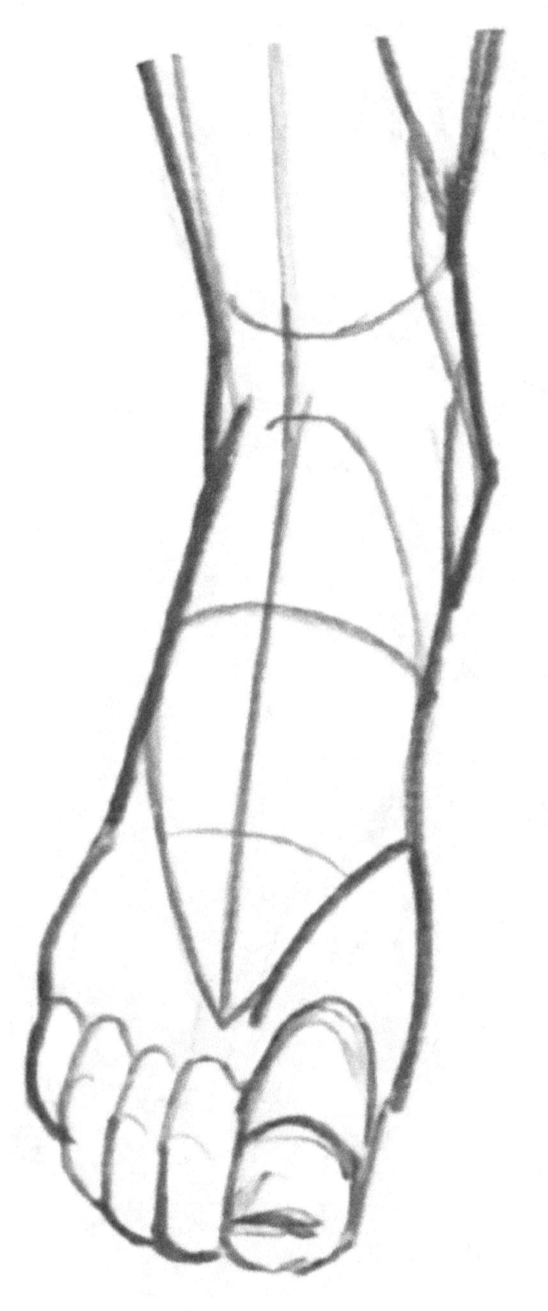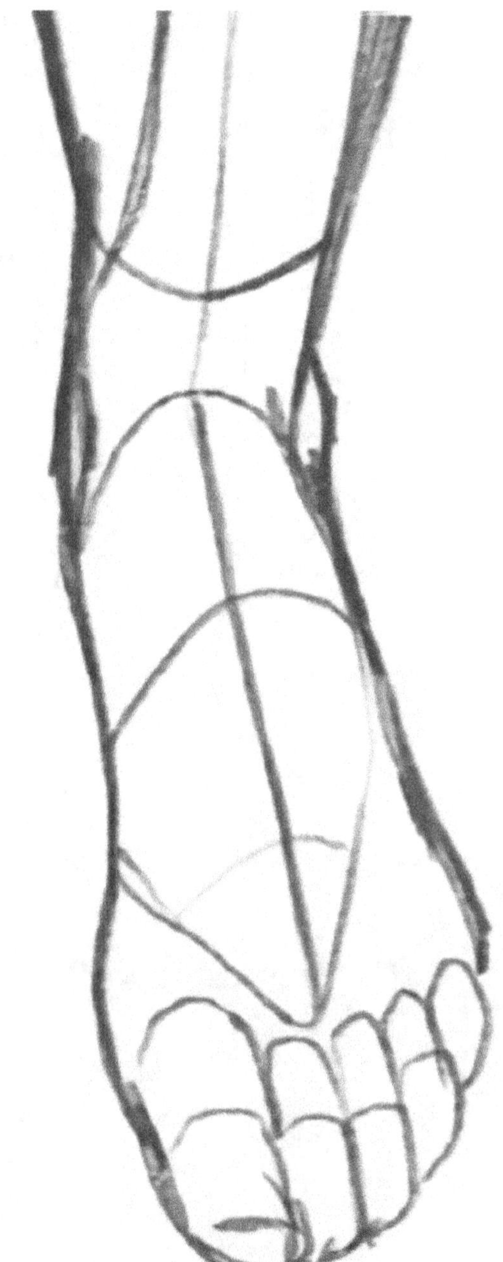

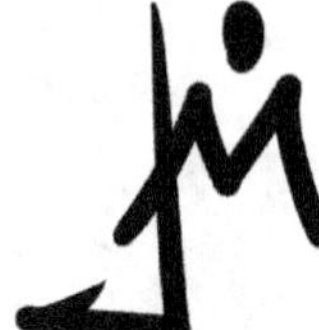

31

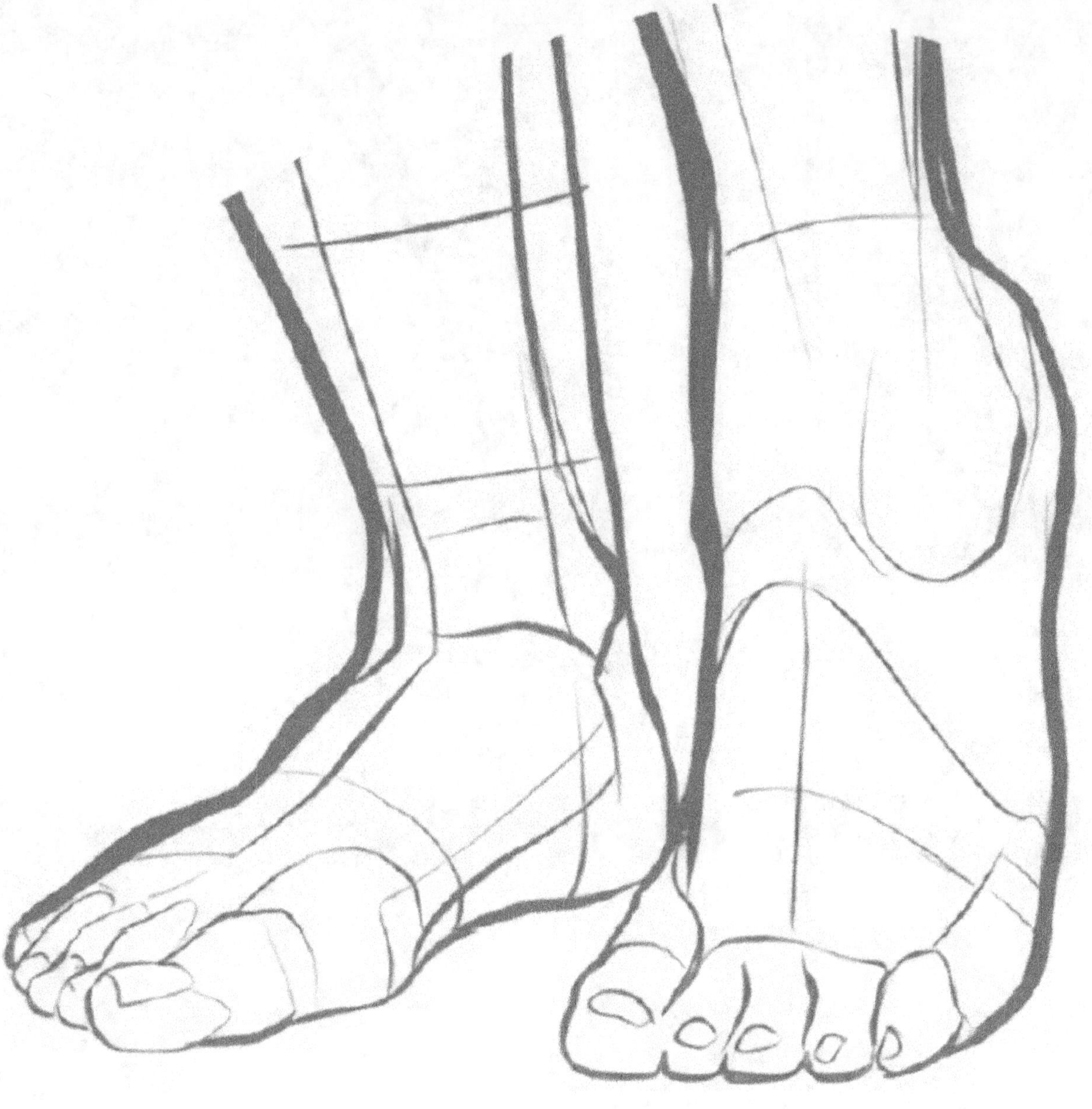

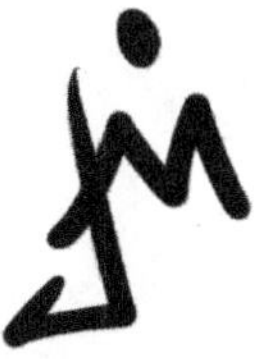

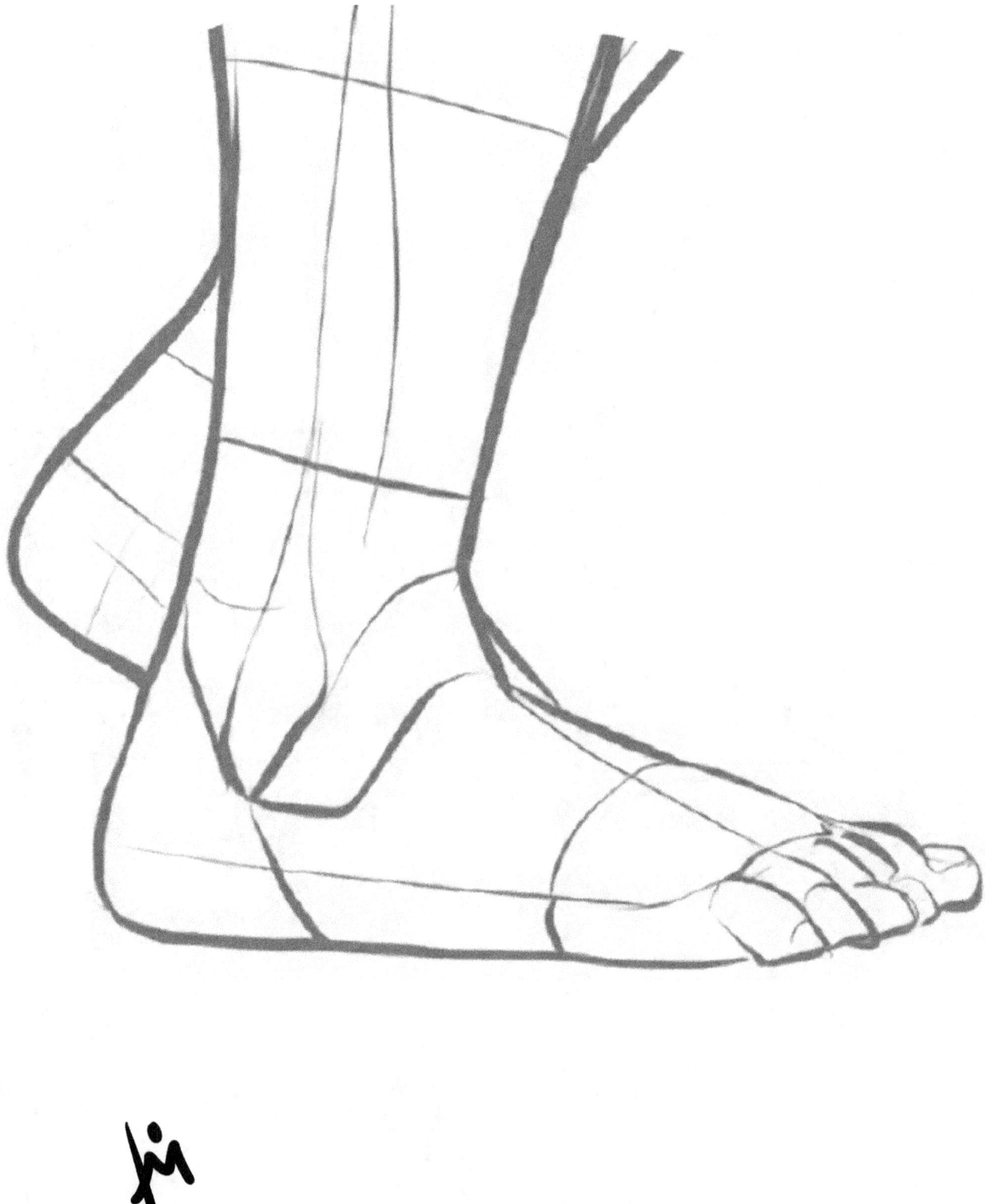

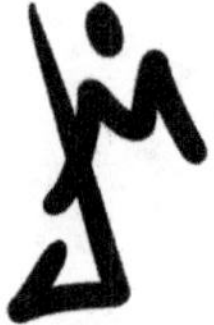

33

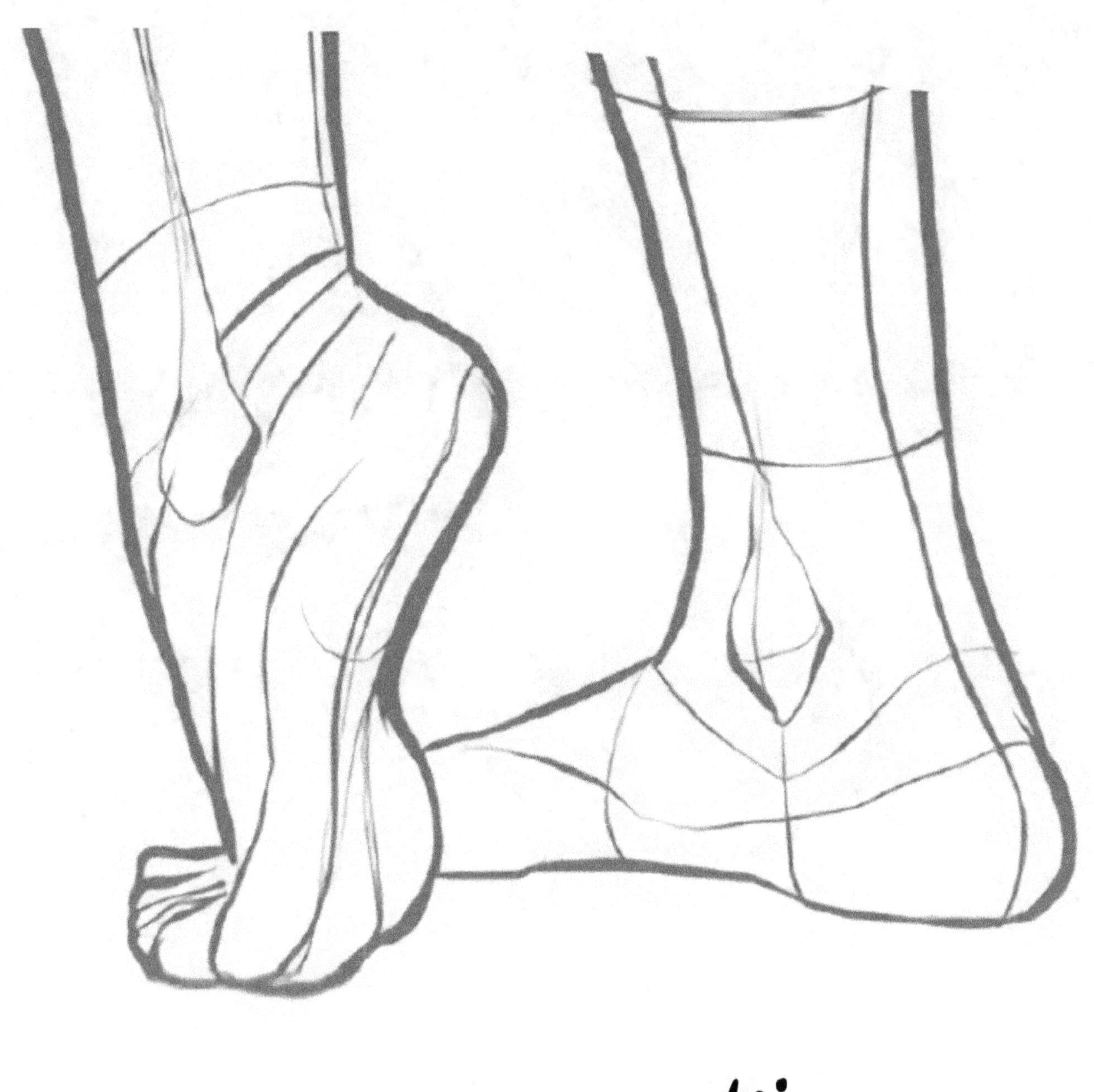

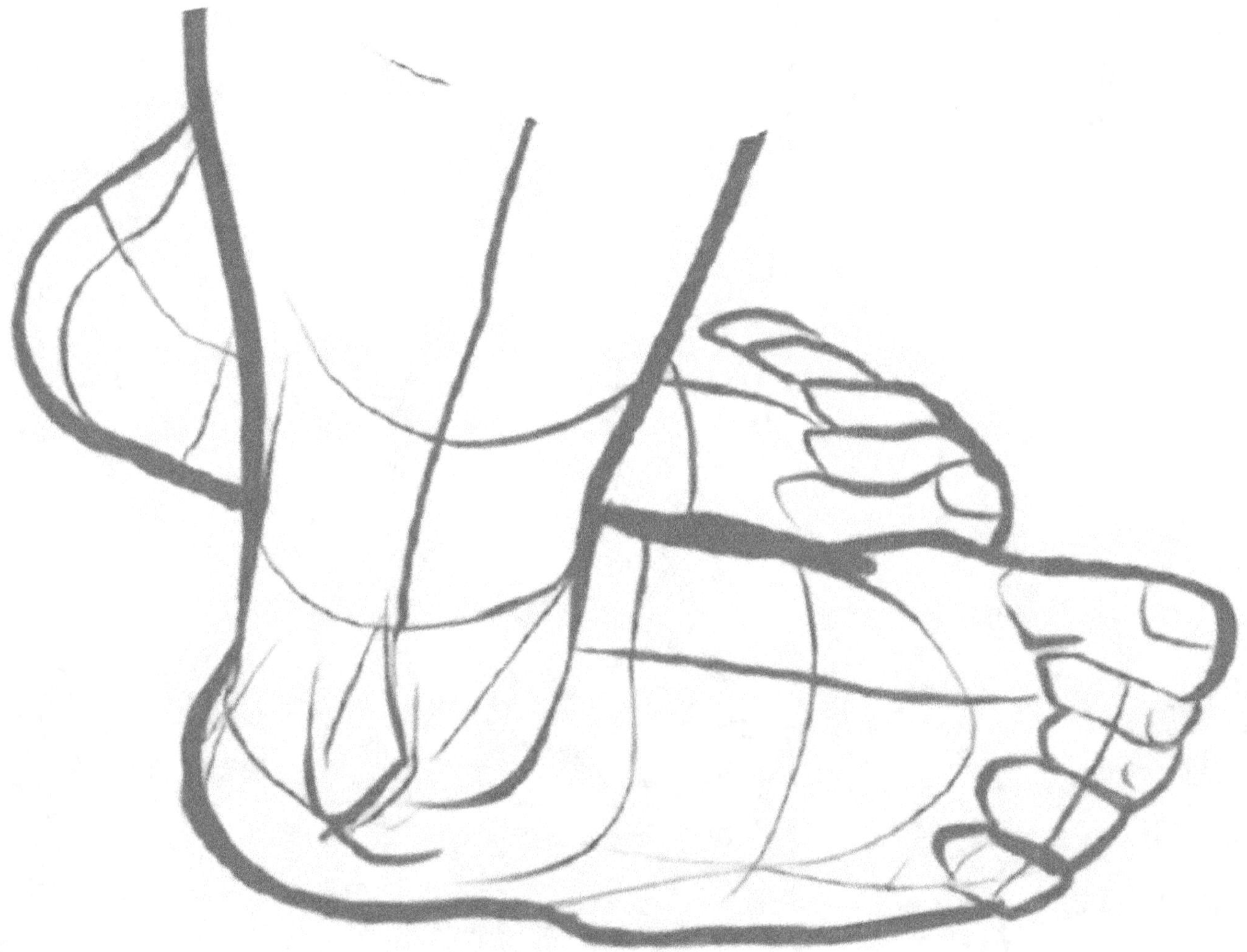

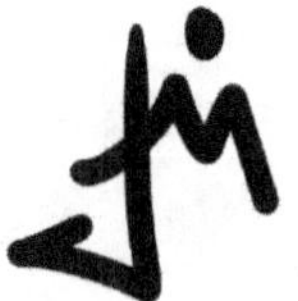

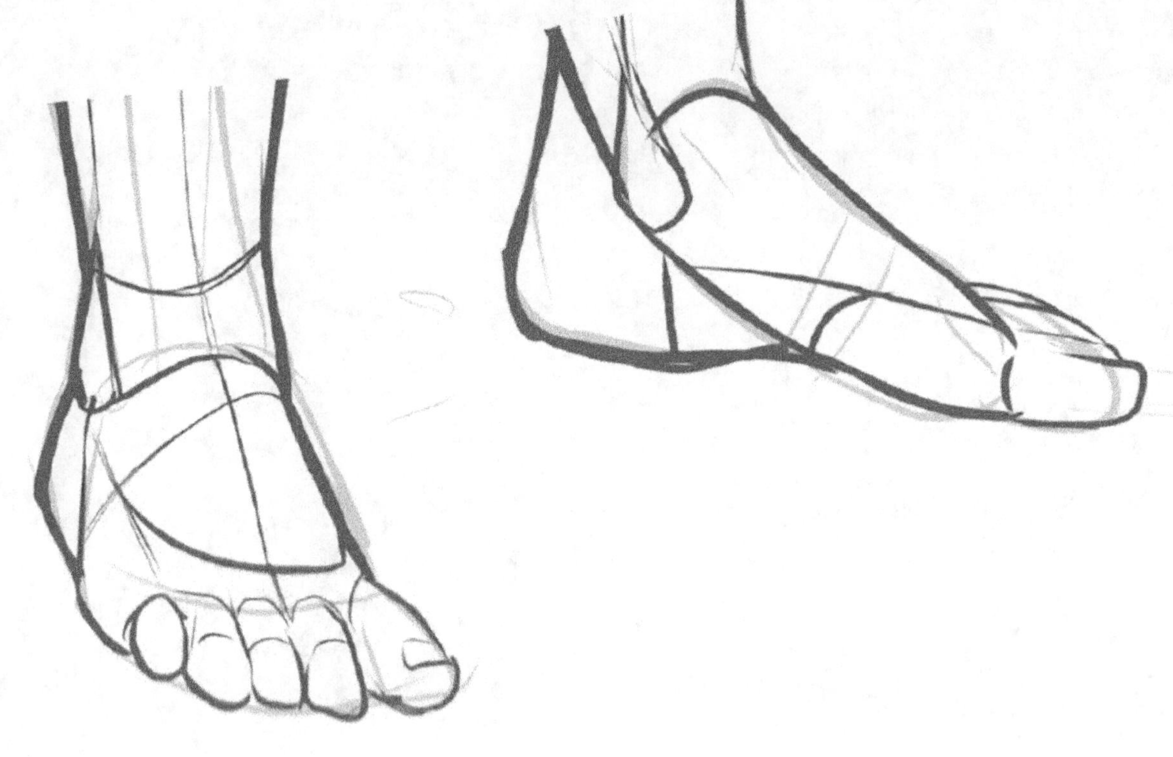

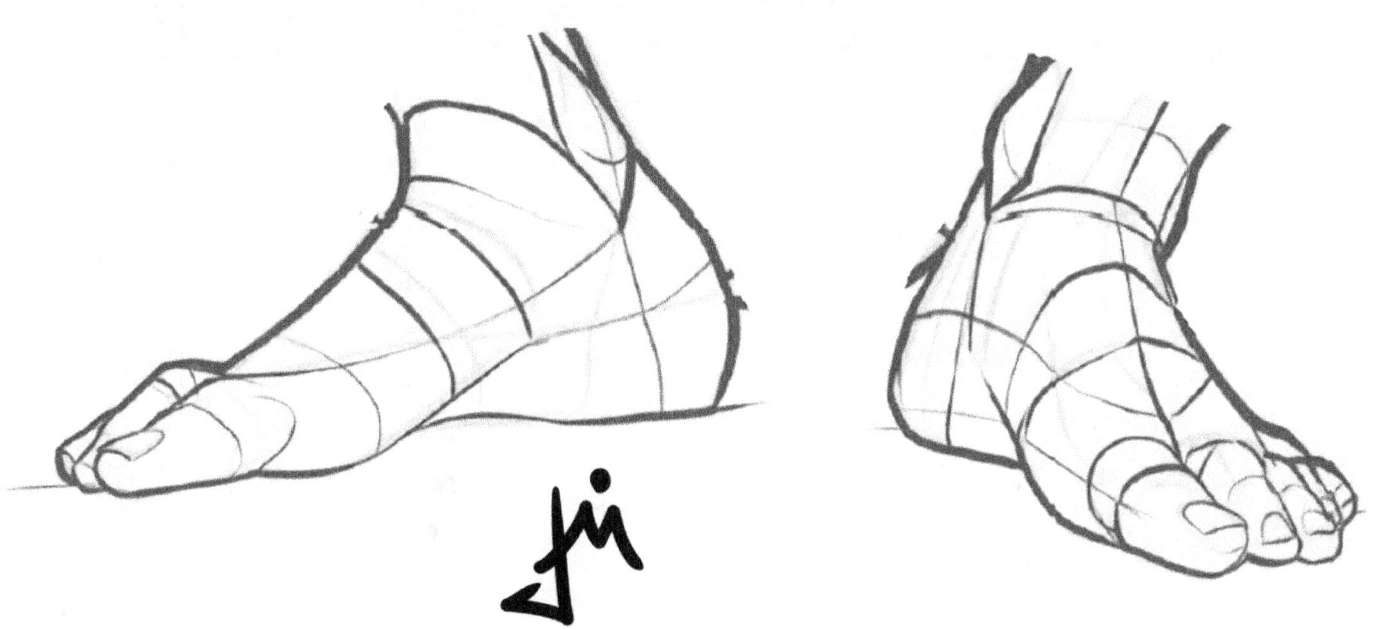

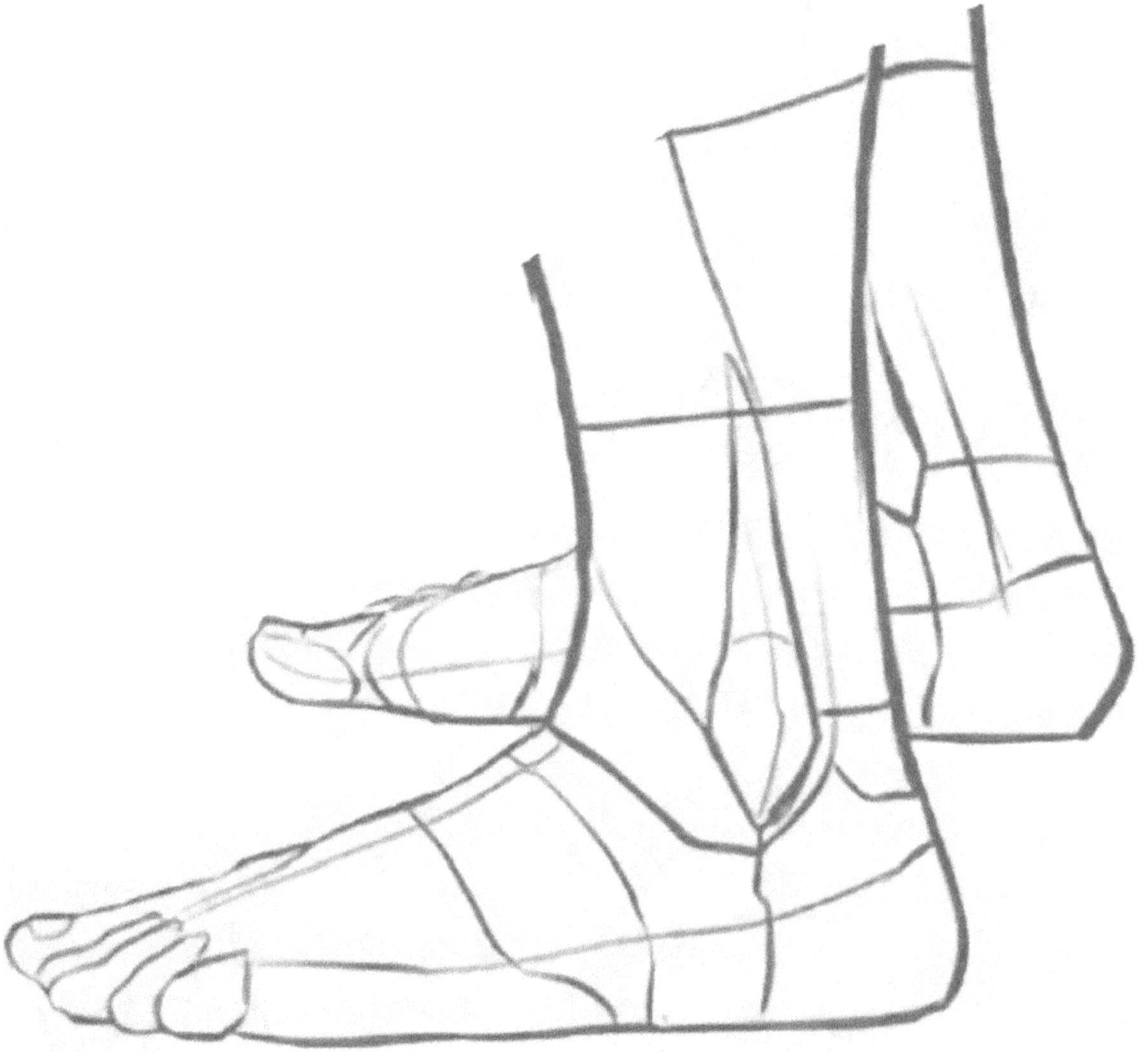

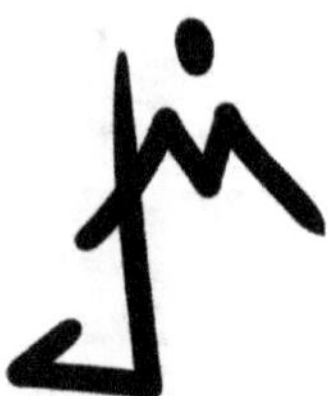

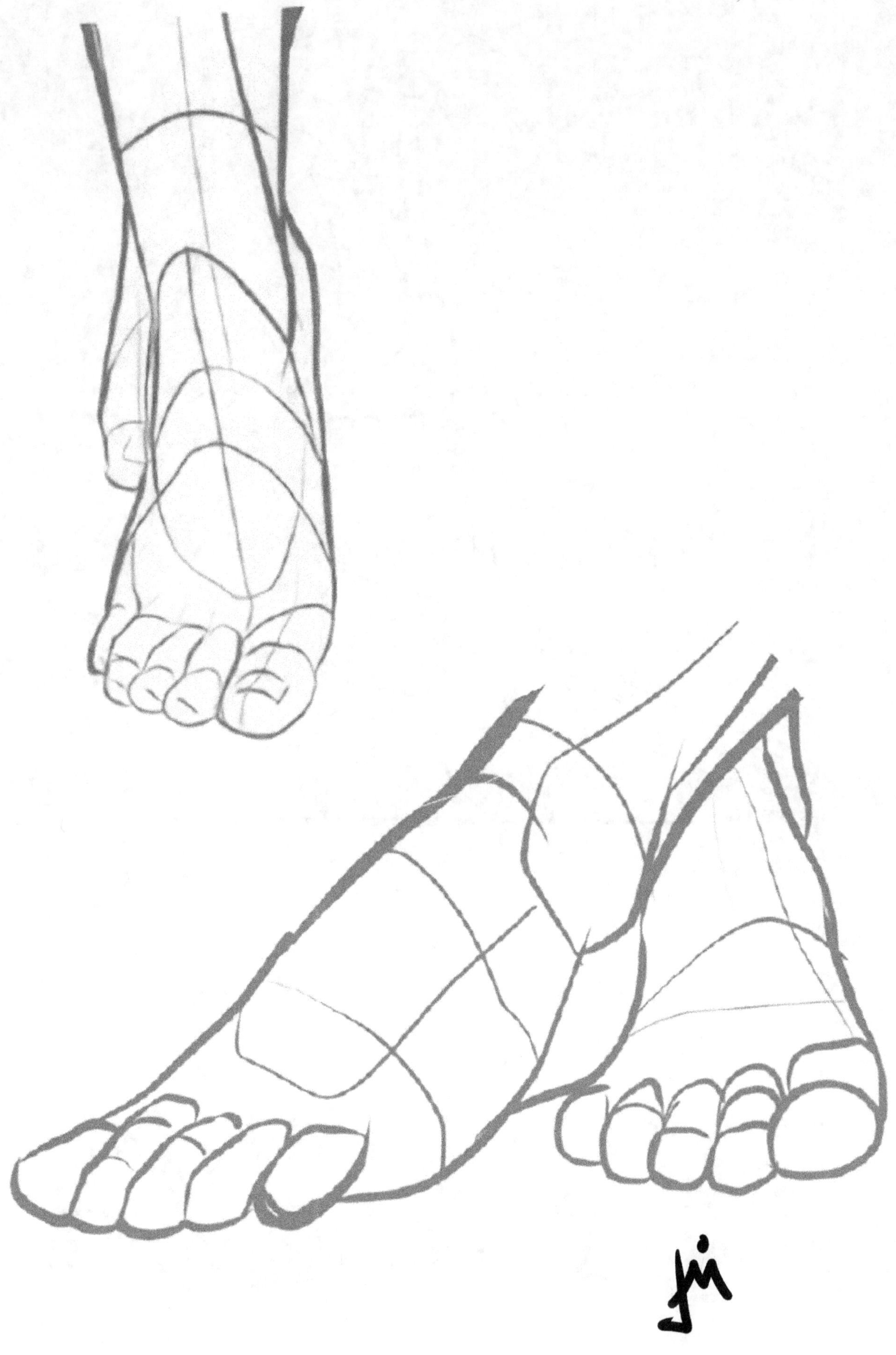

38

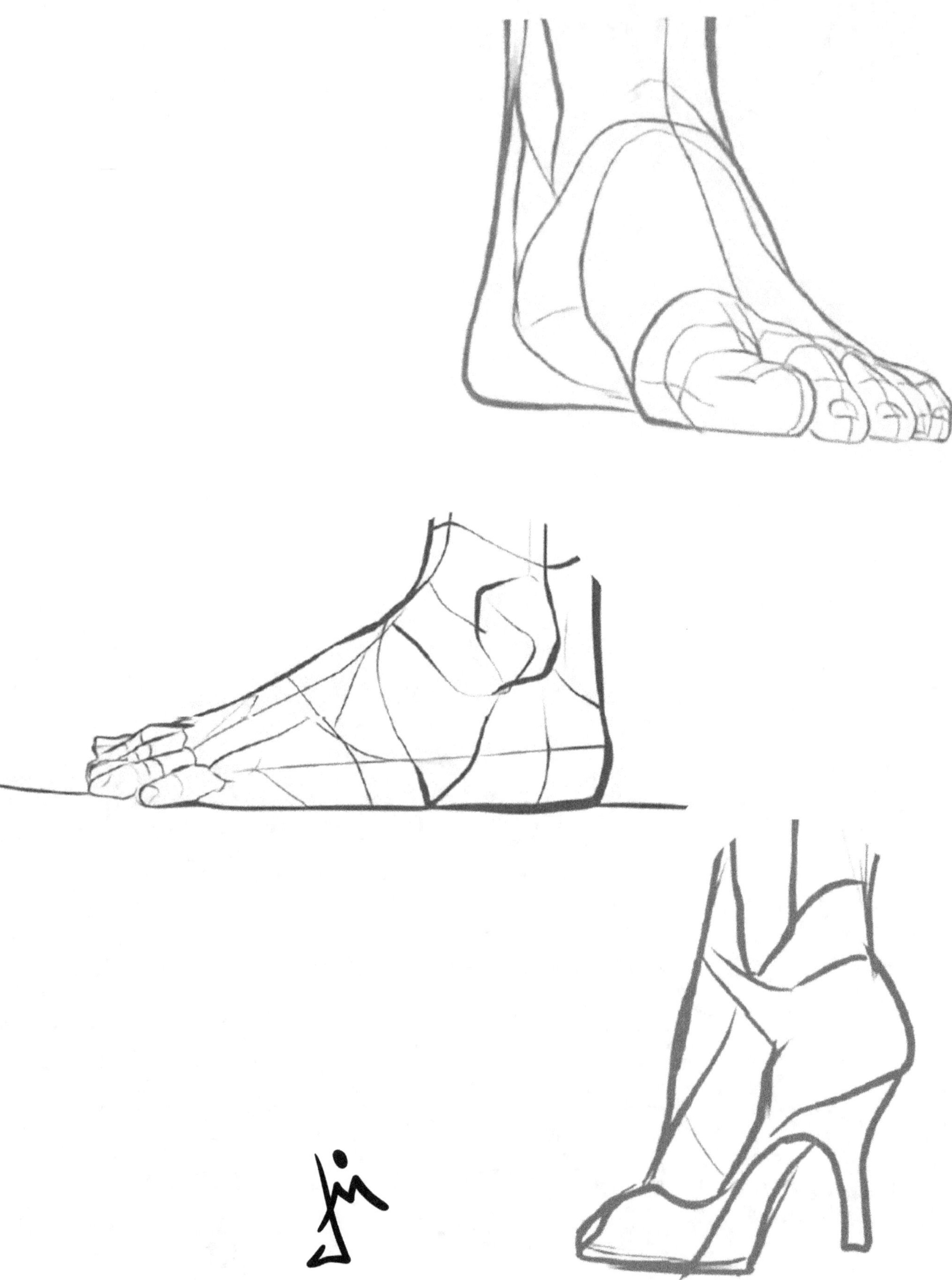

39

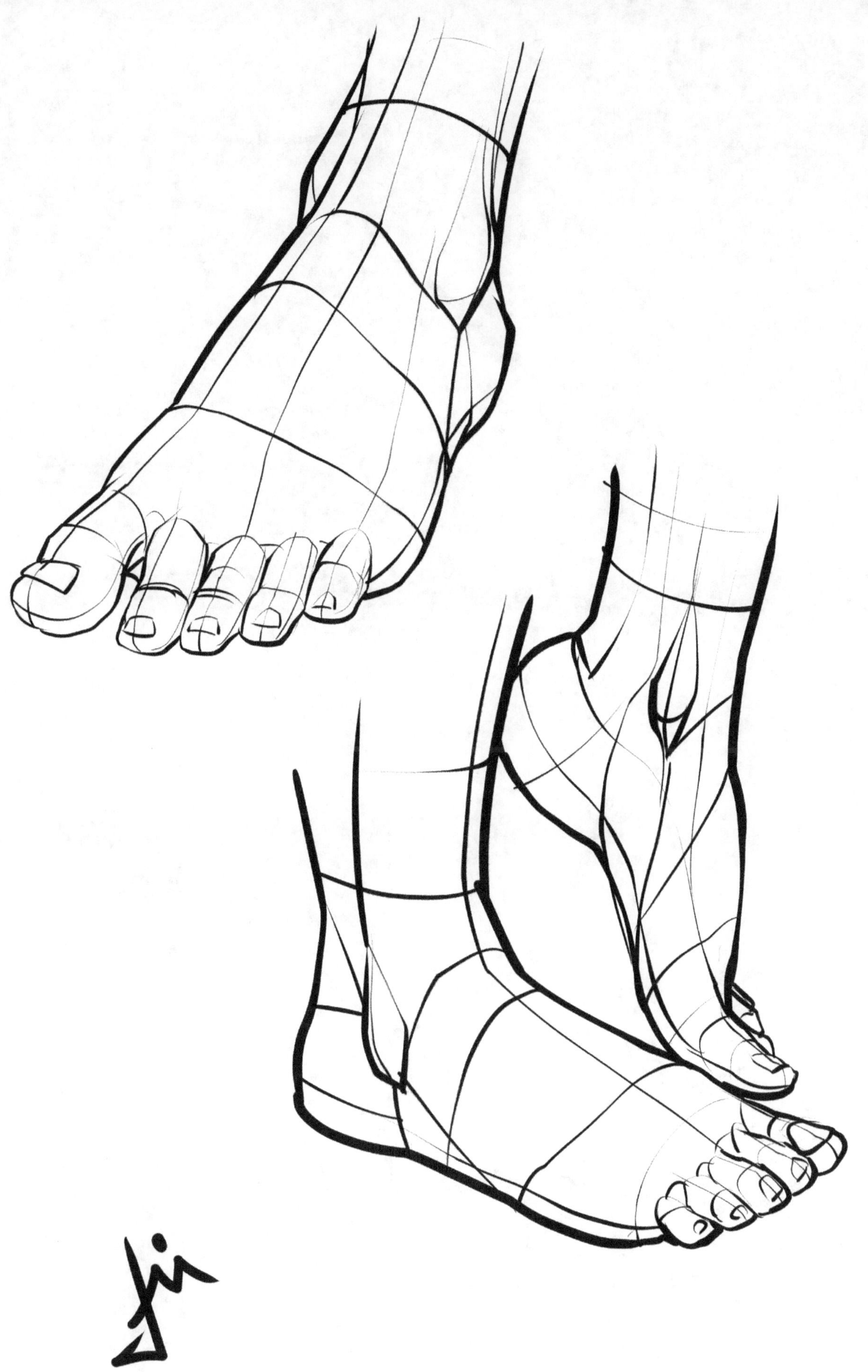

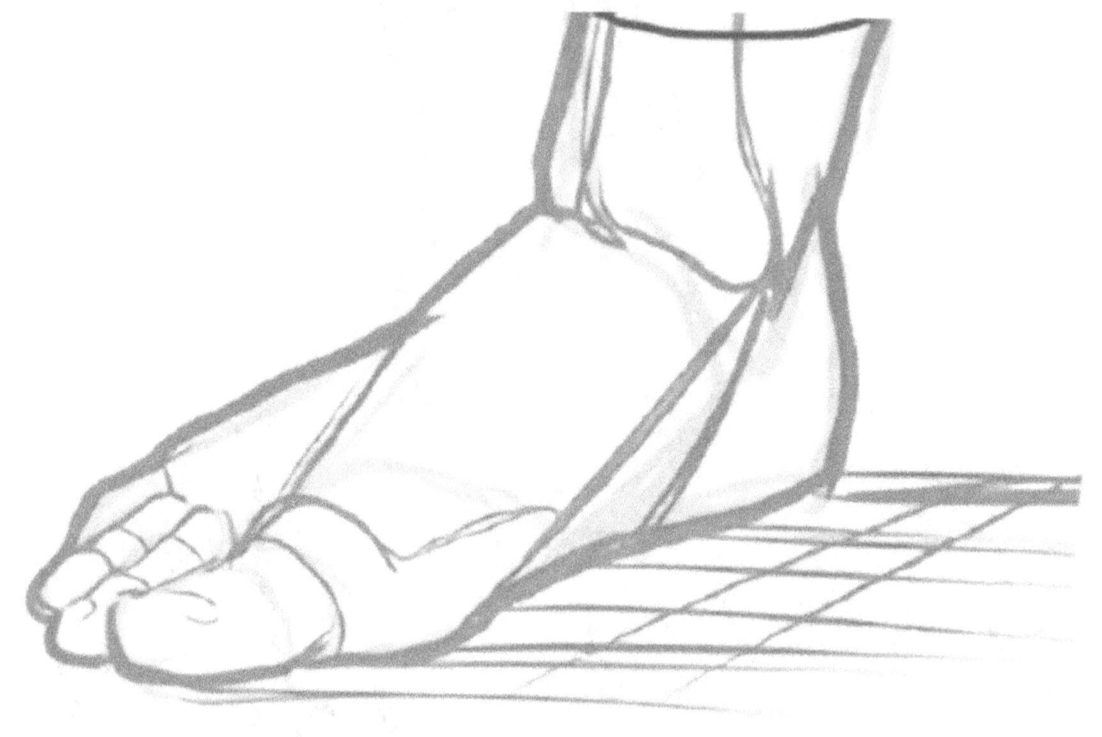

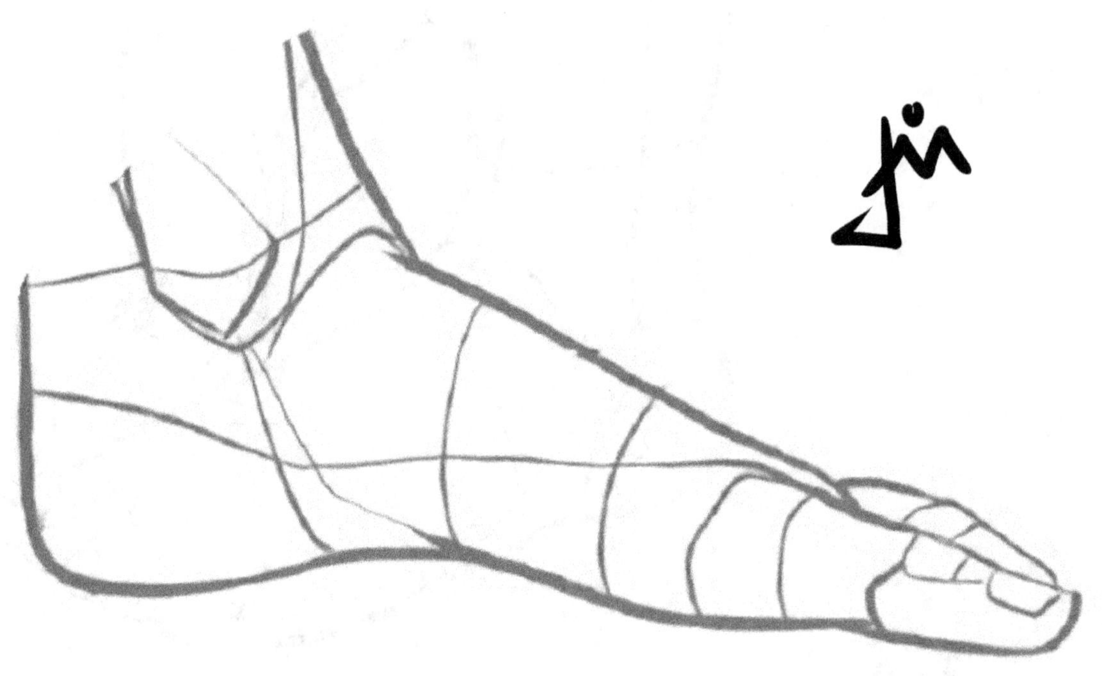

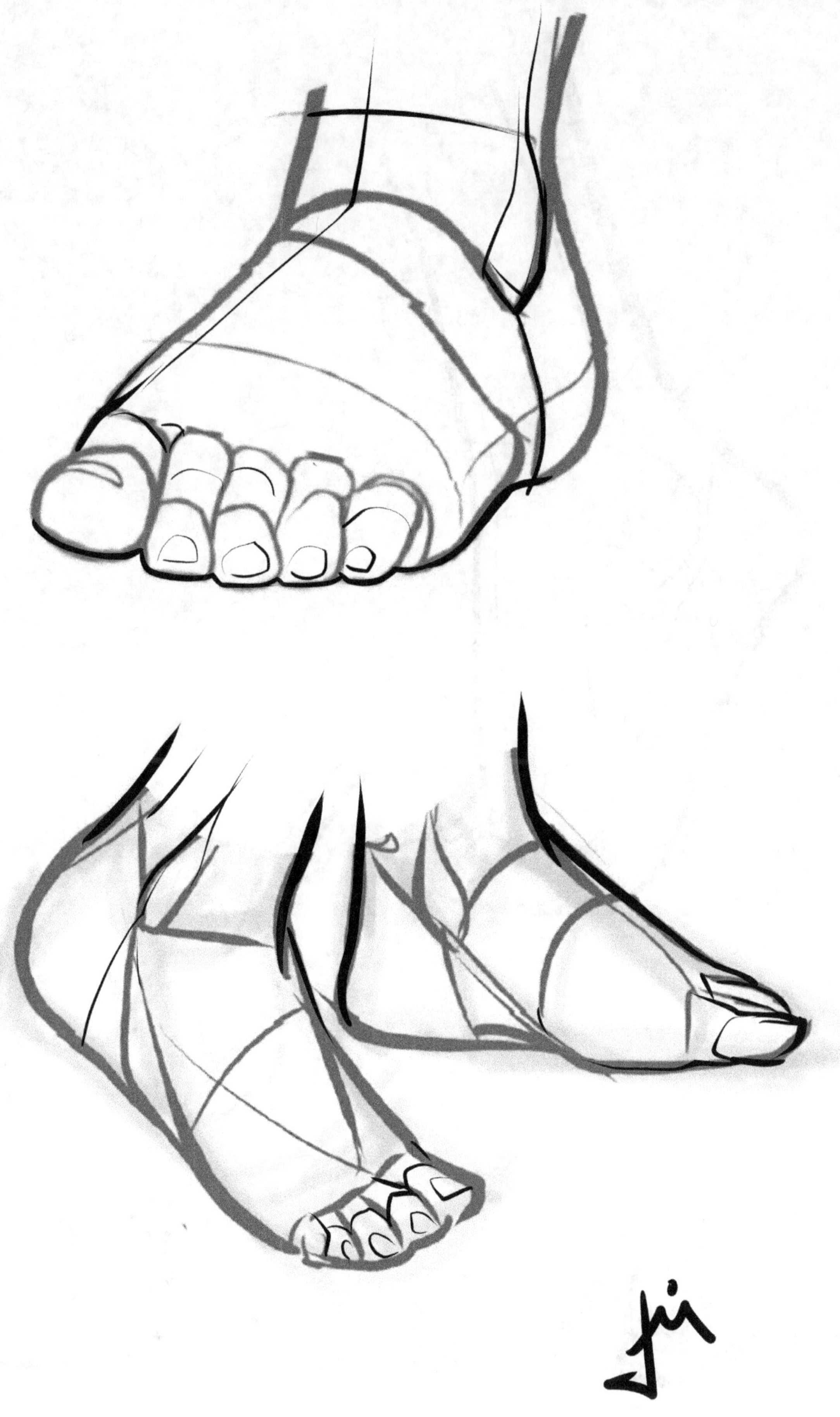

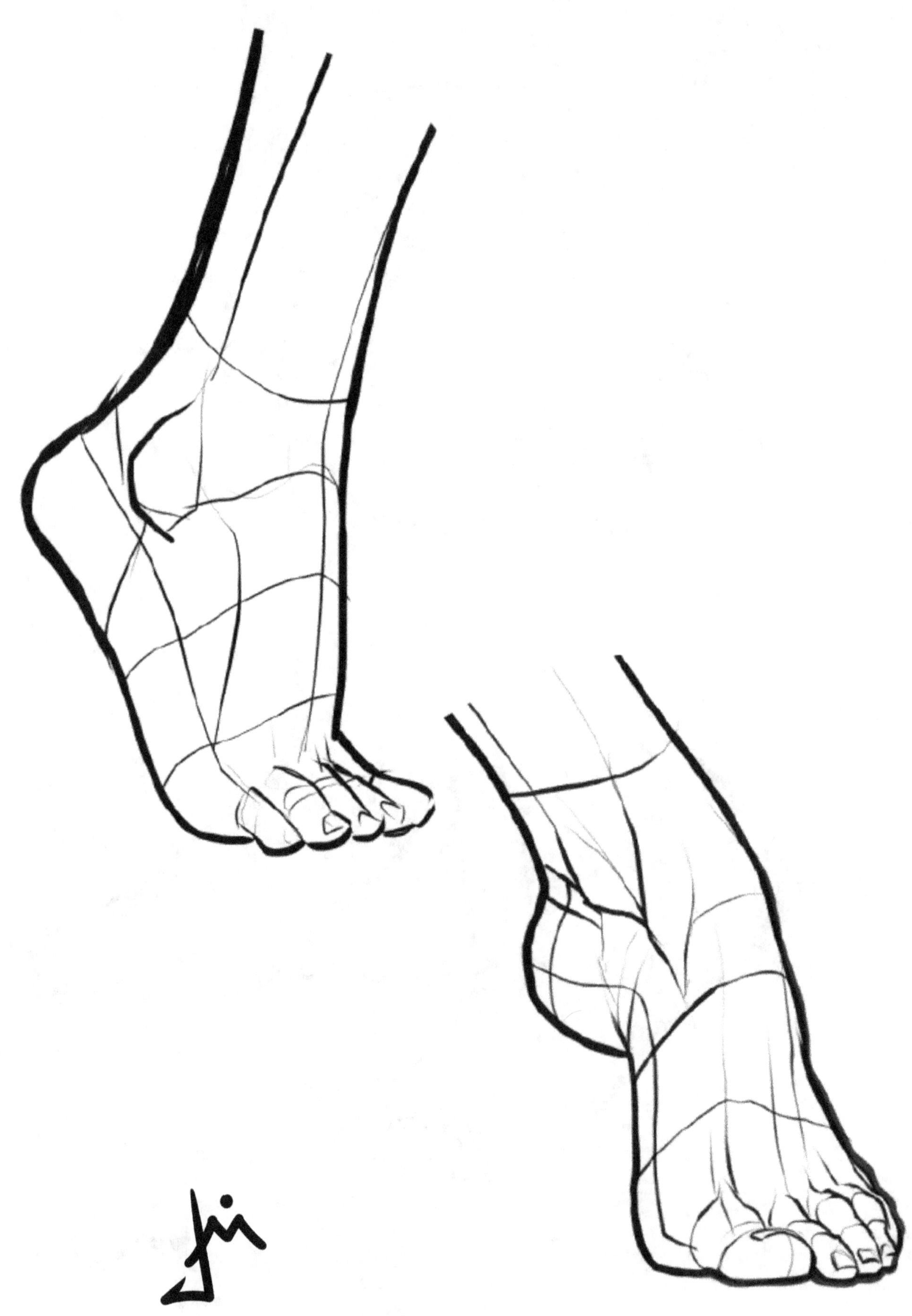

43

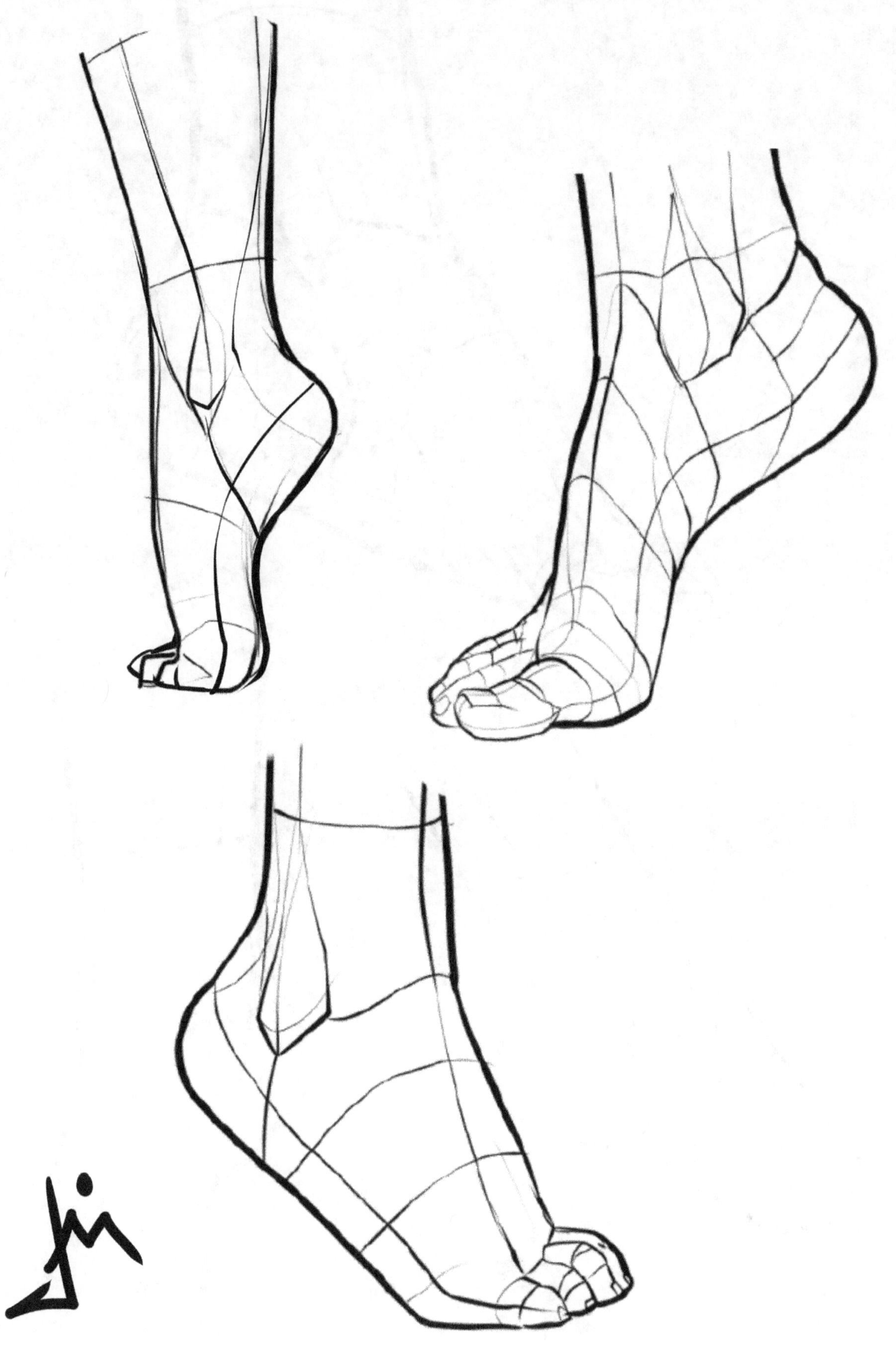

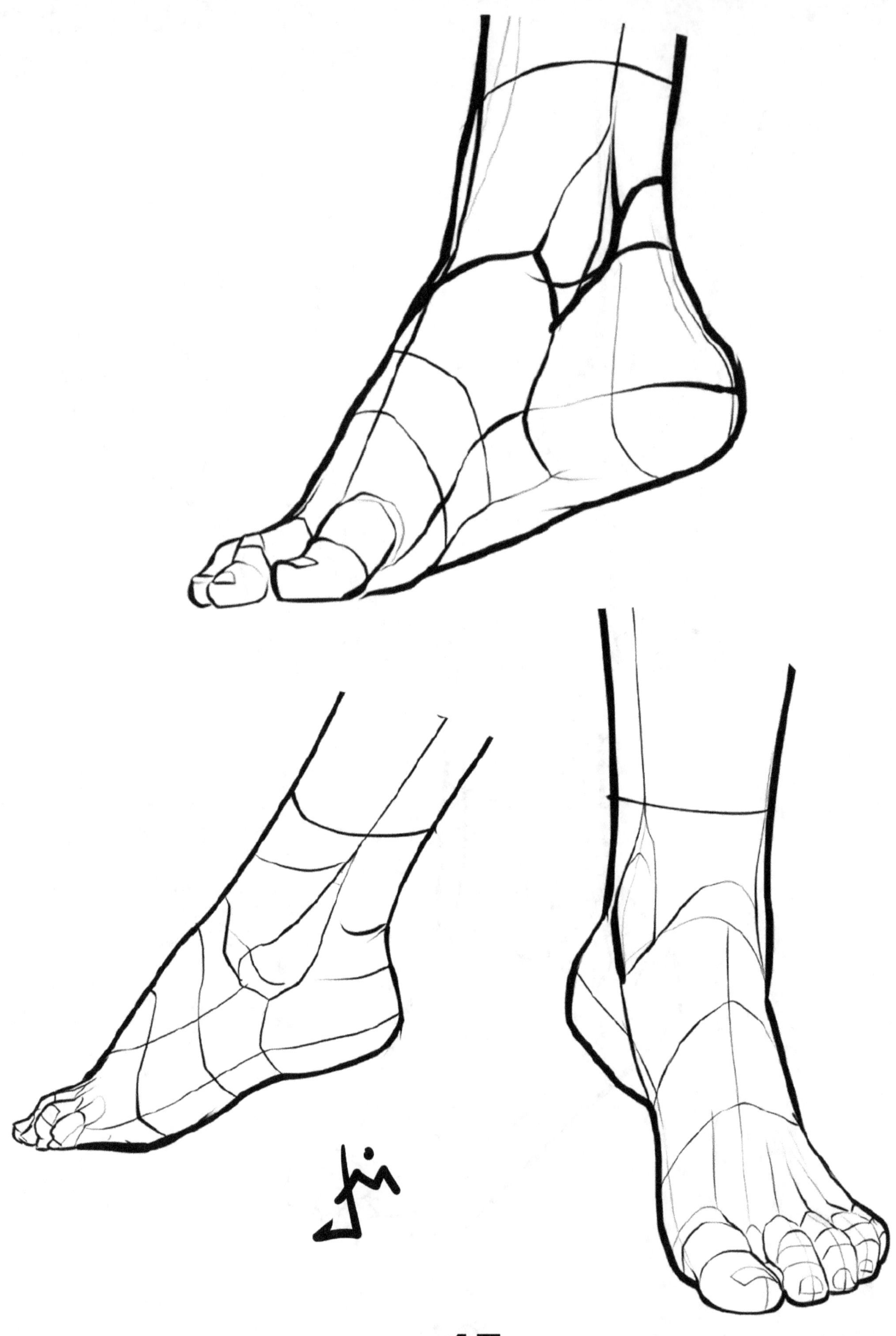

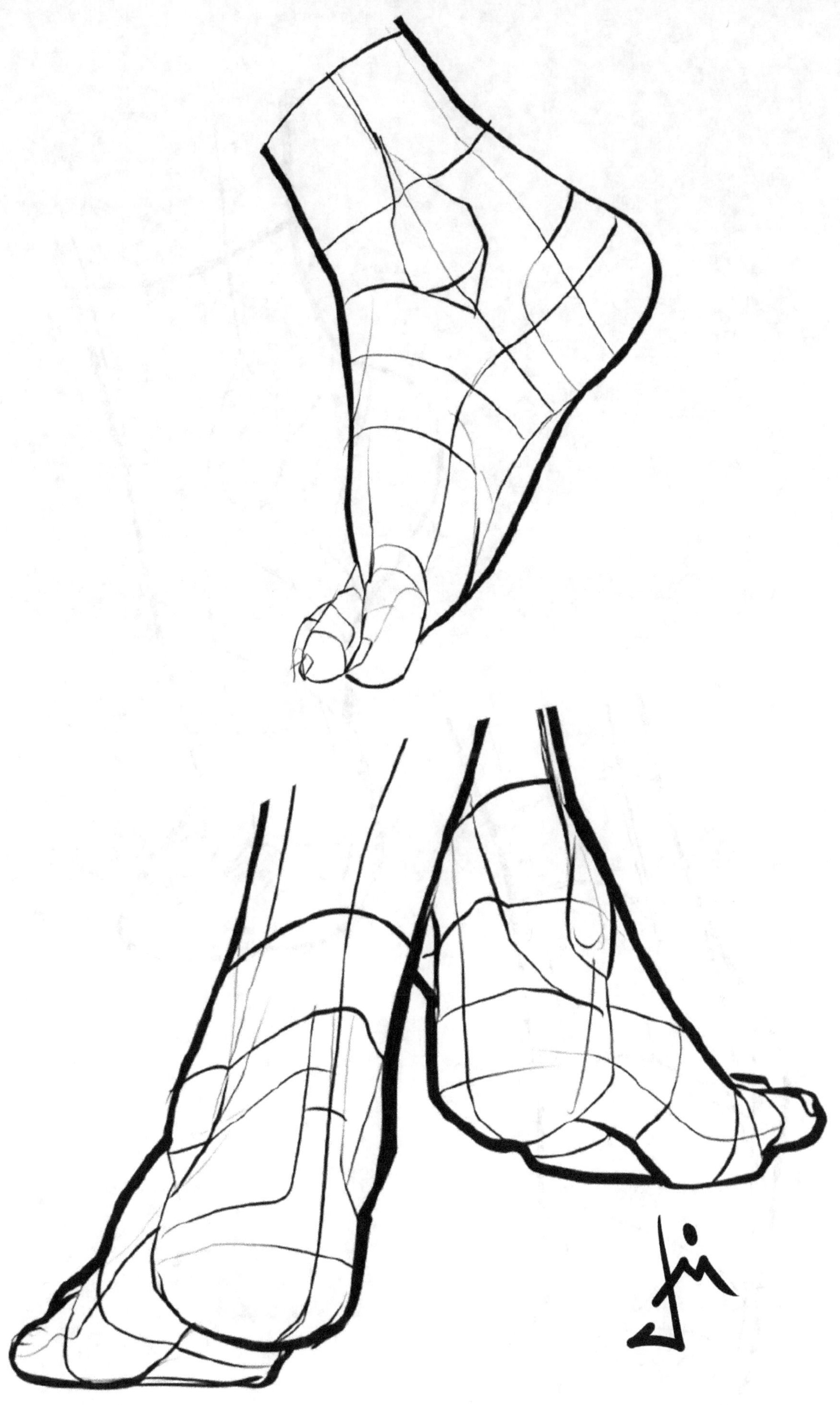

46

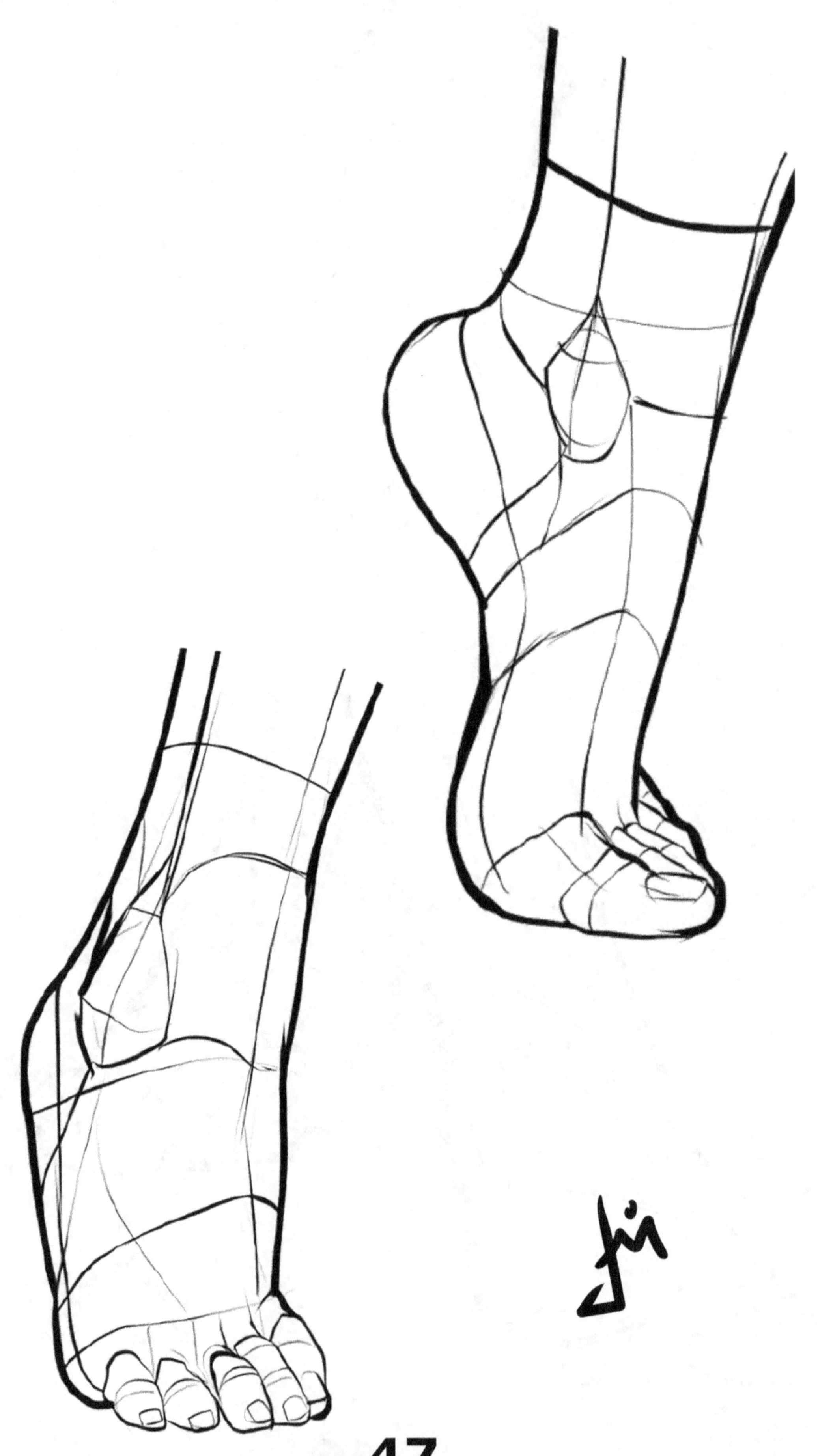

47

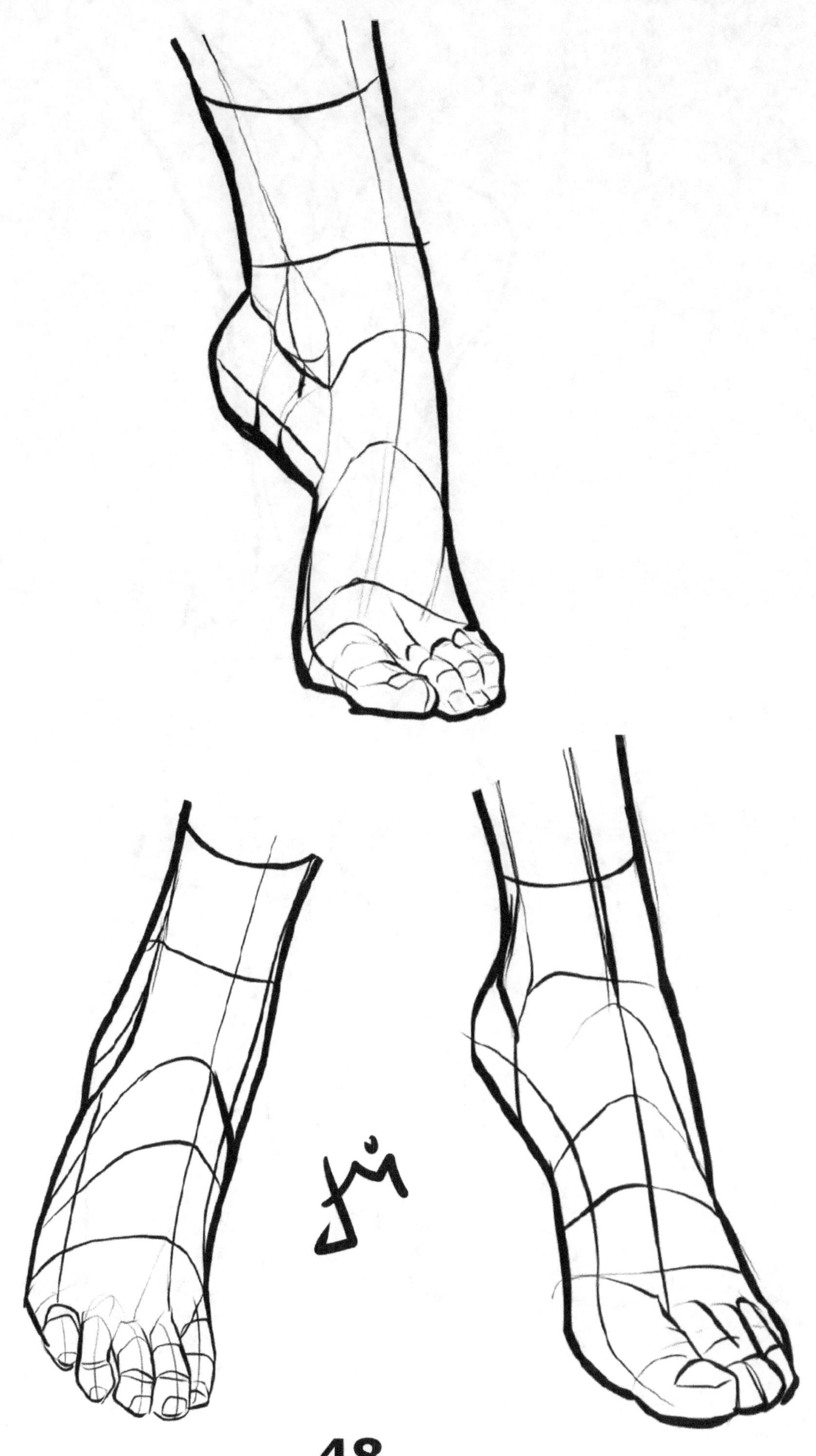

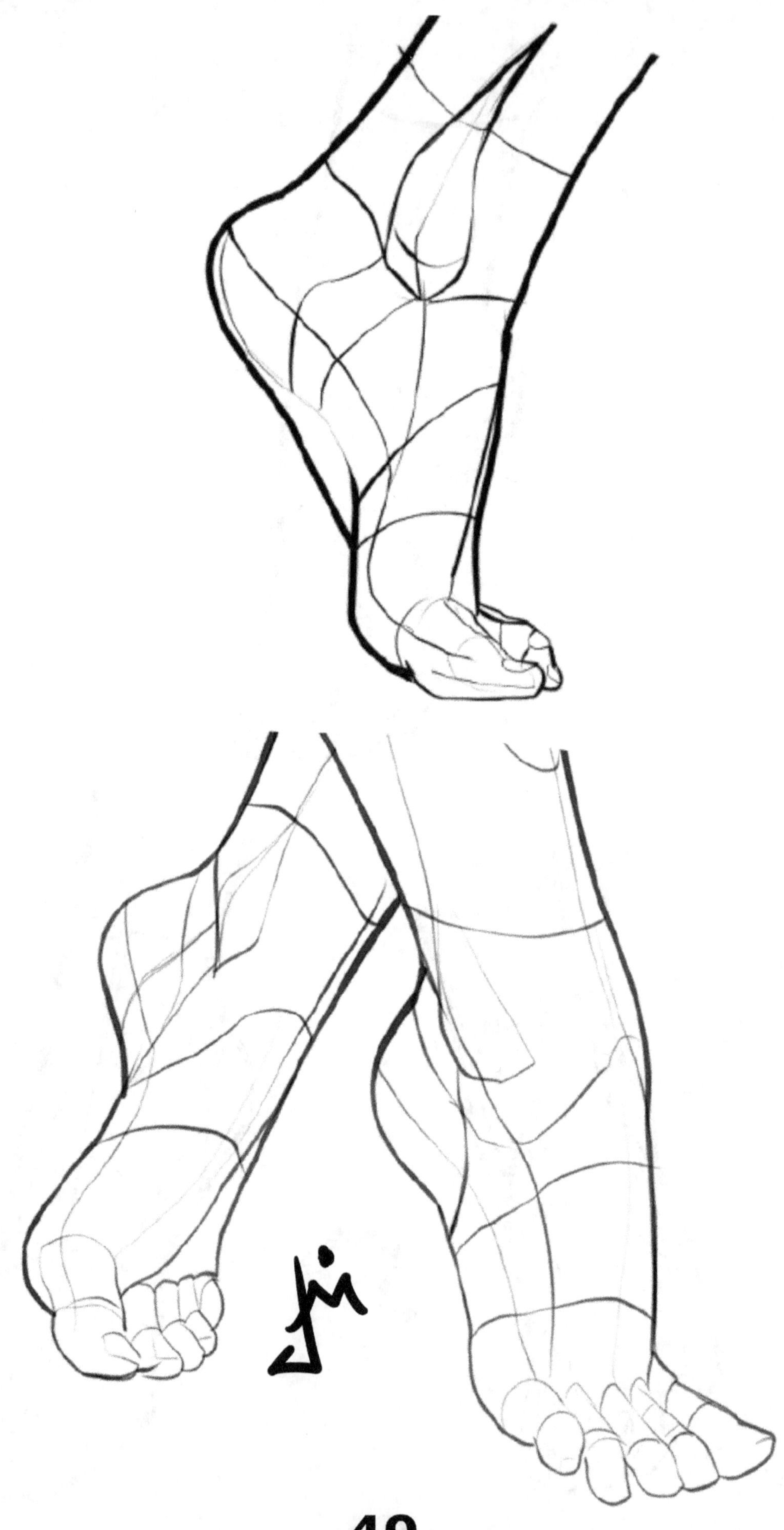

49

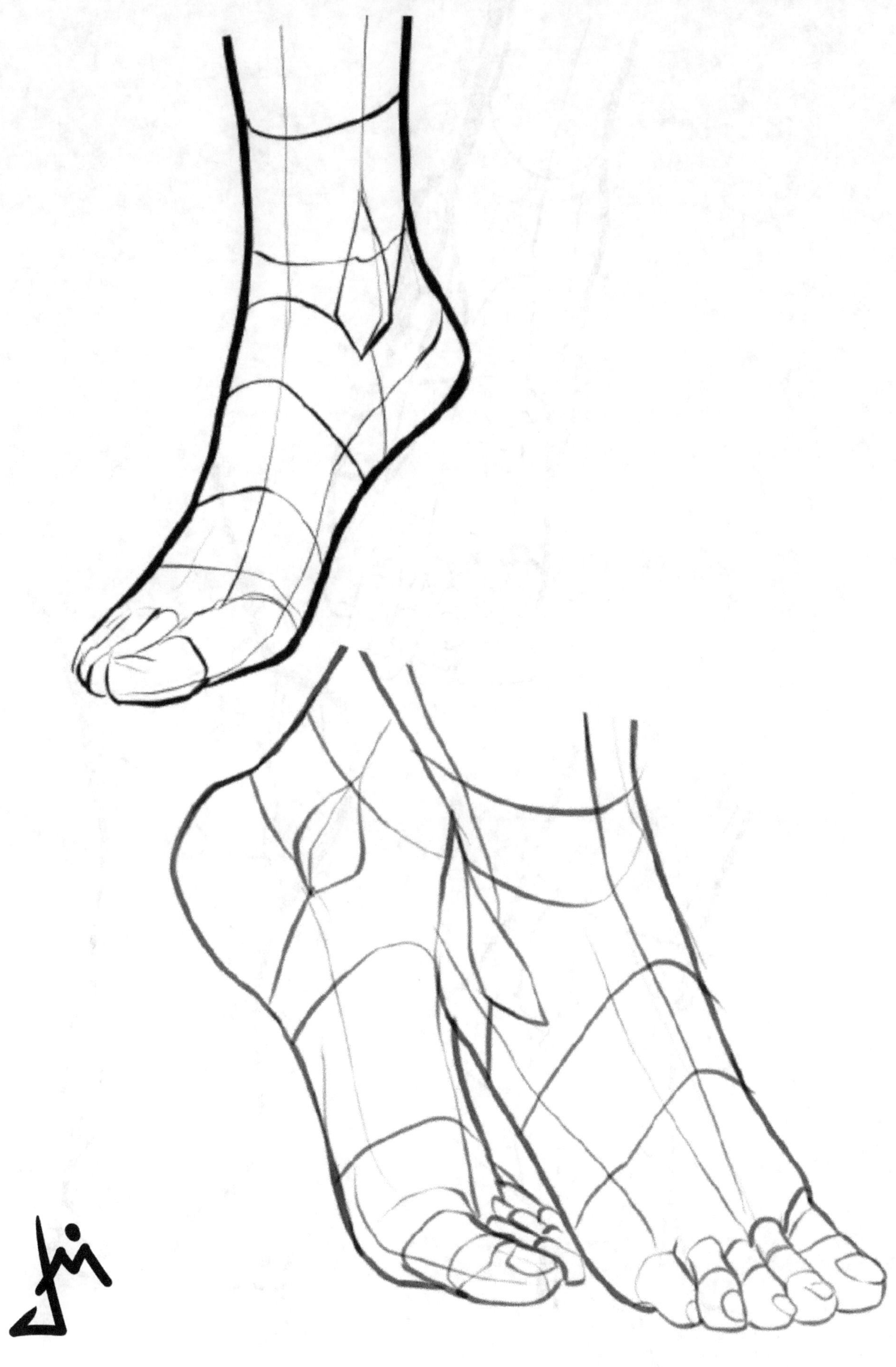

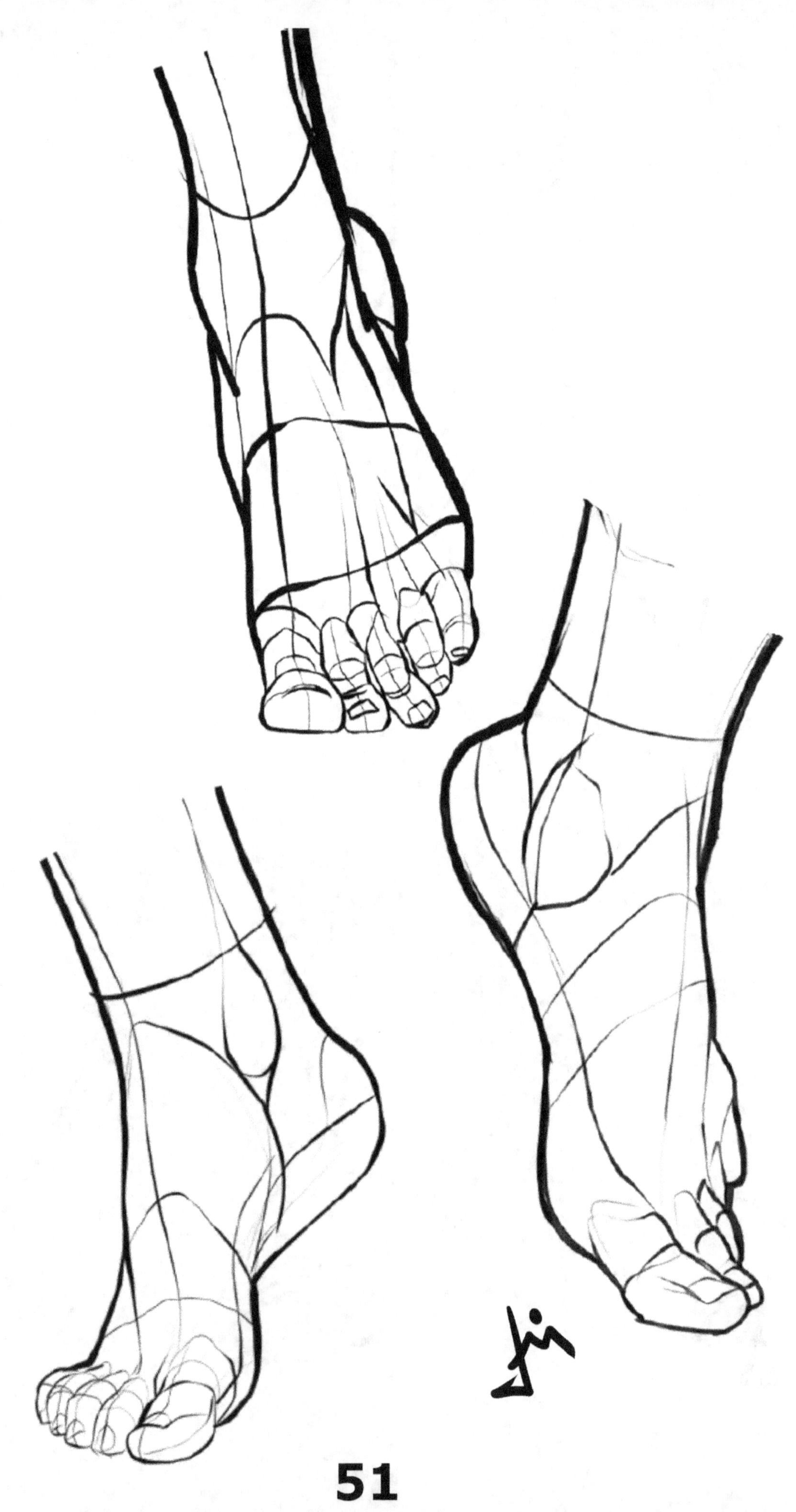

51

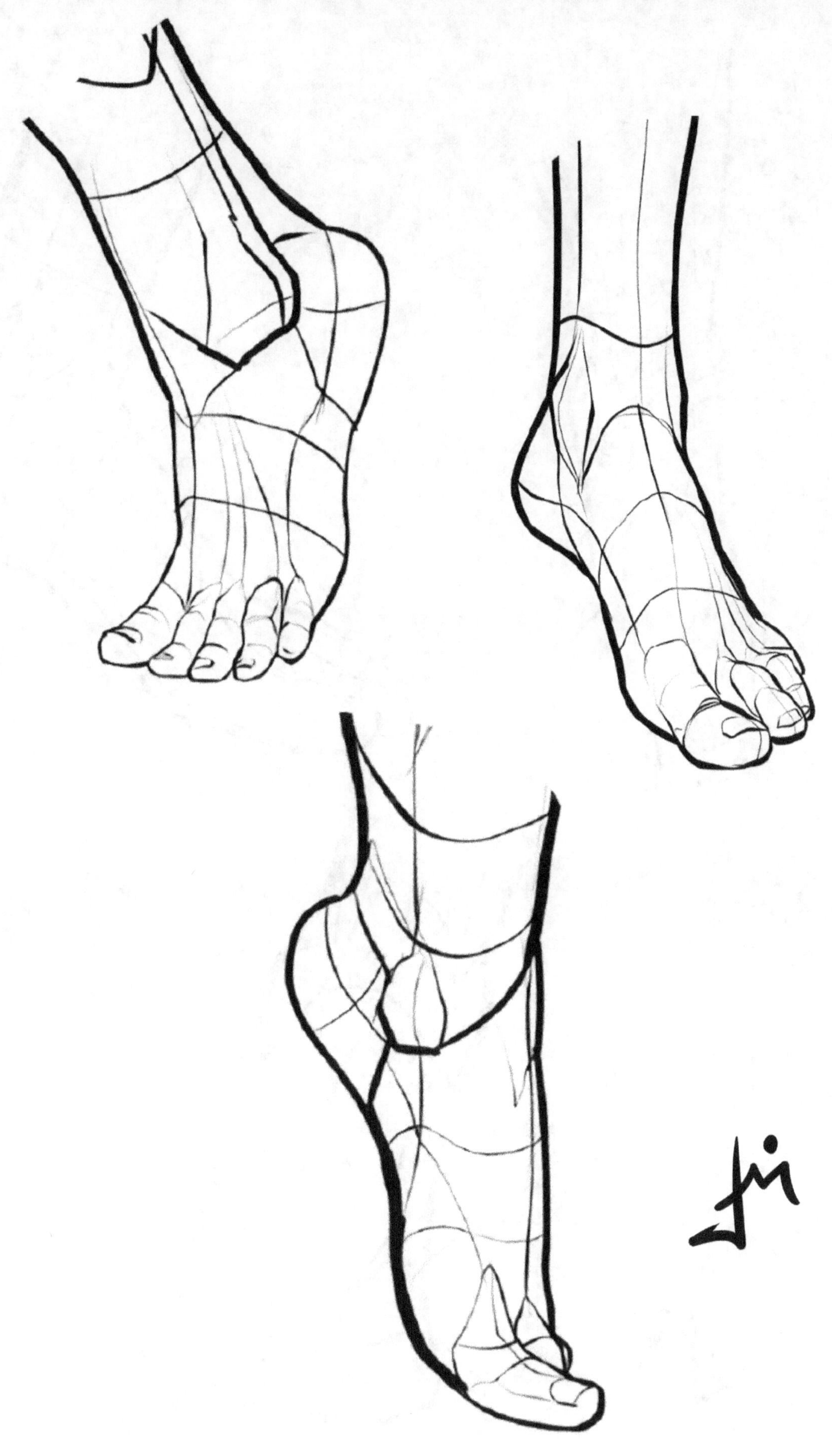

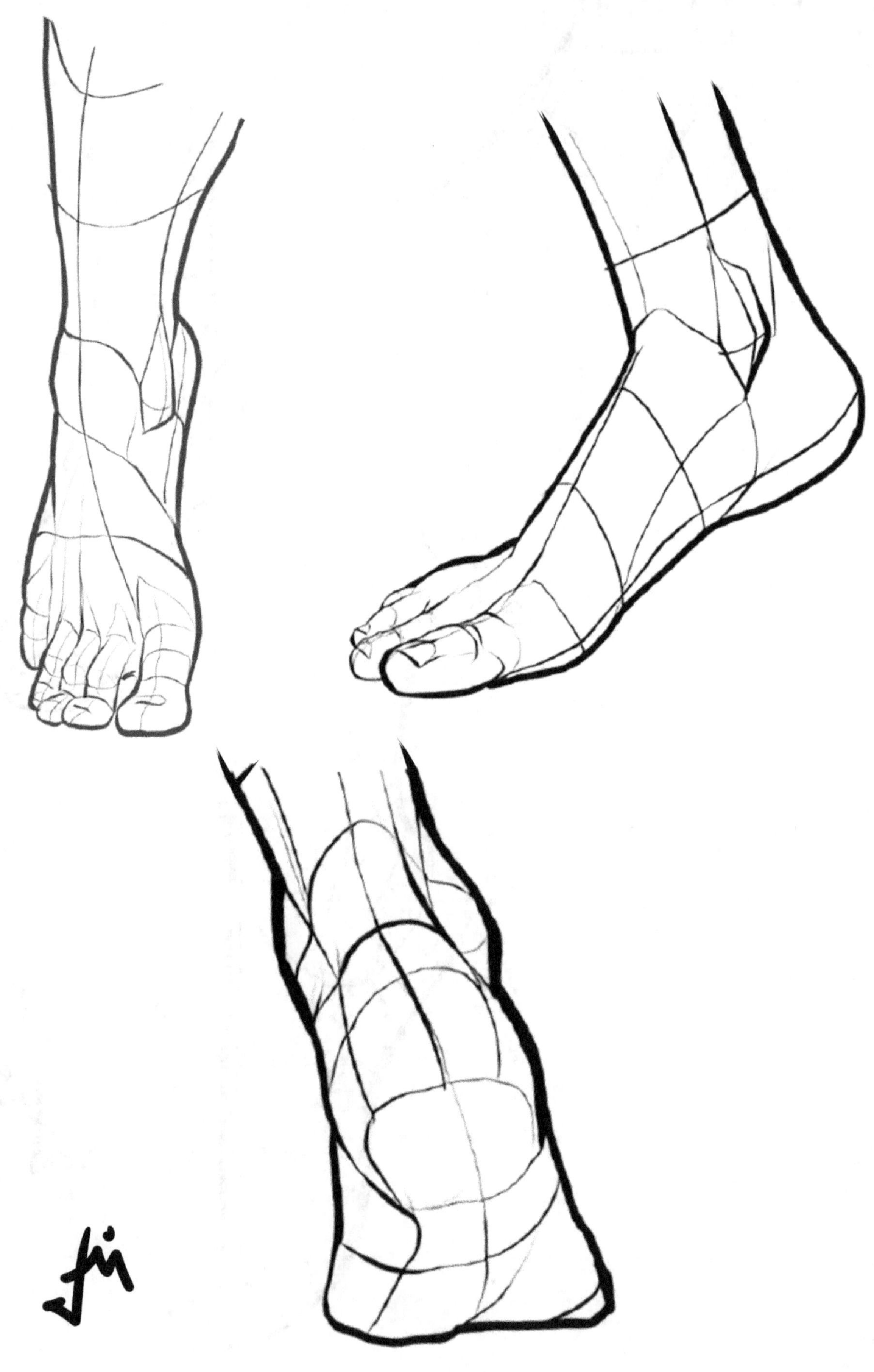

53

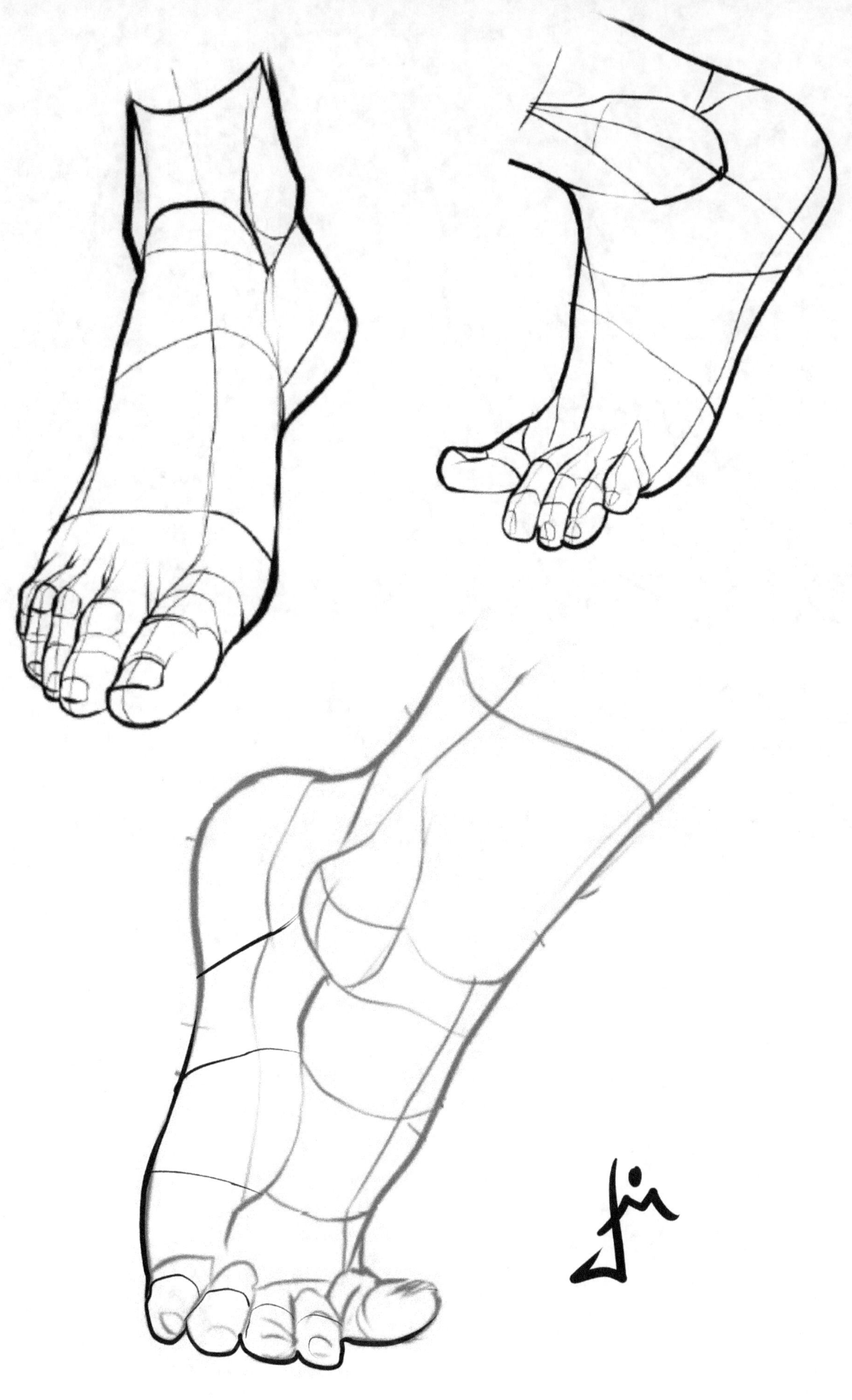

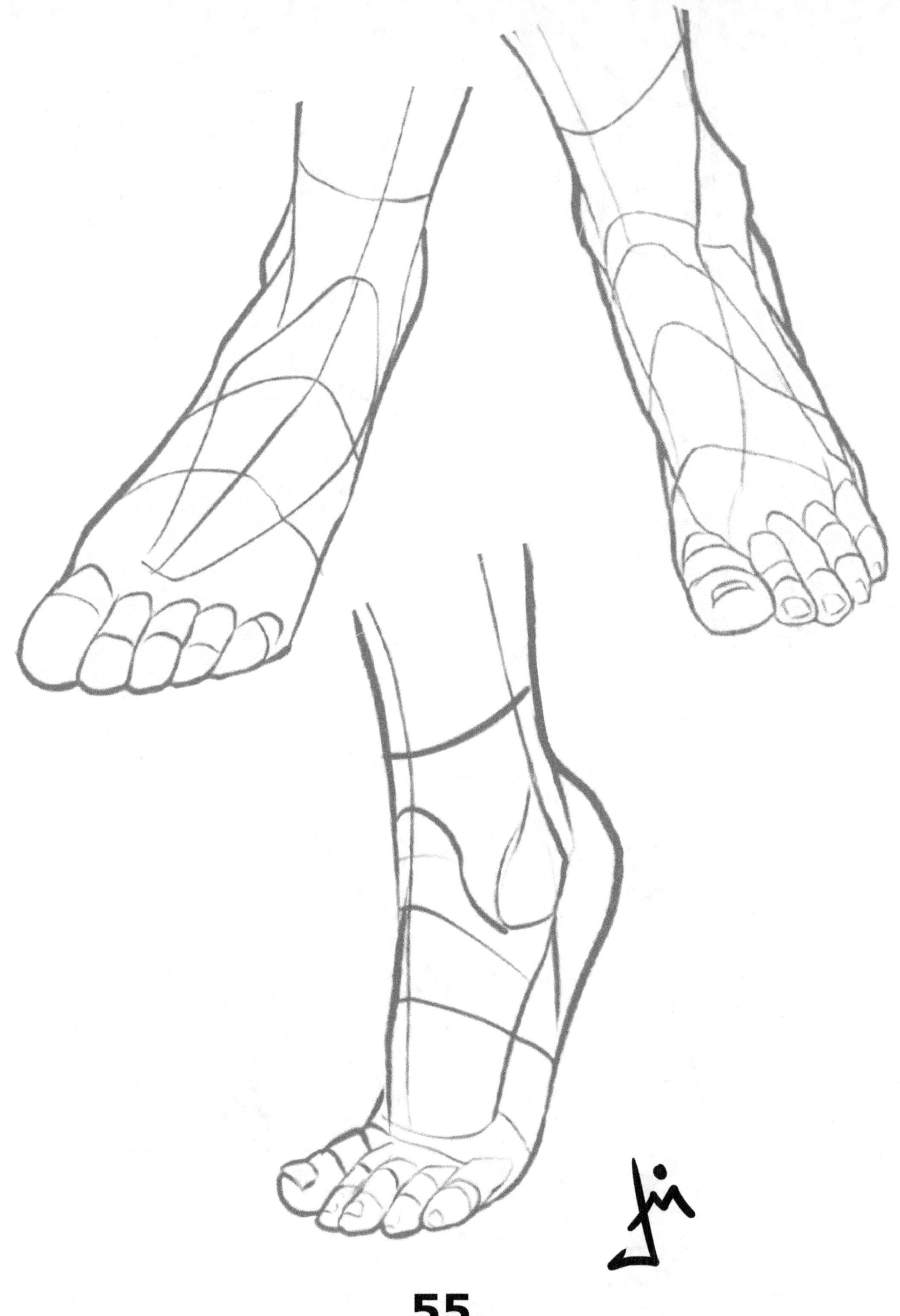

55

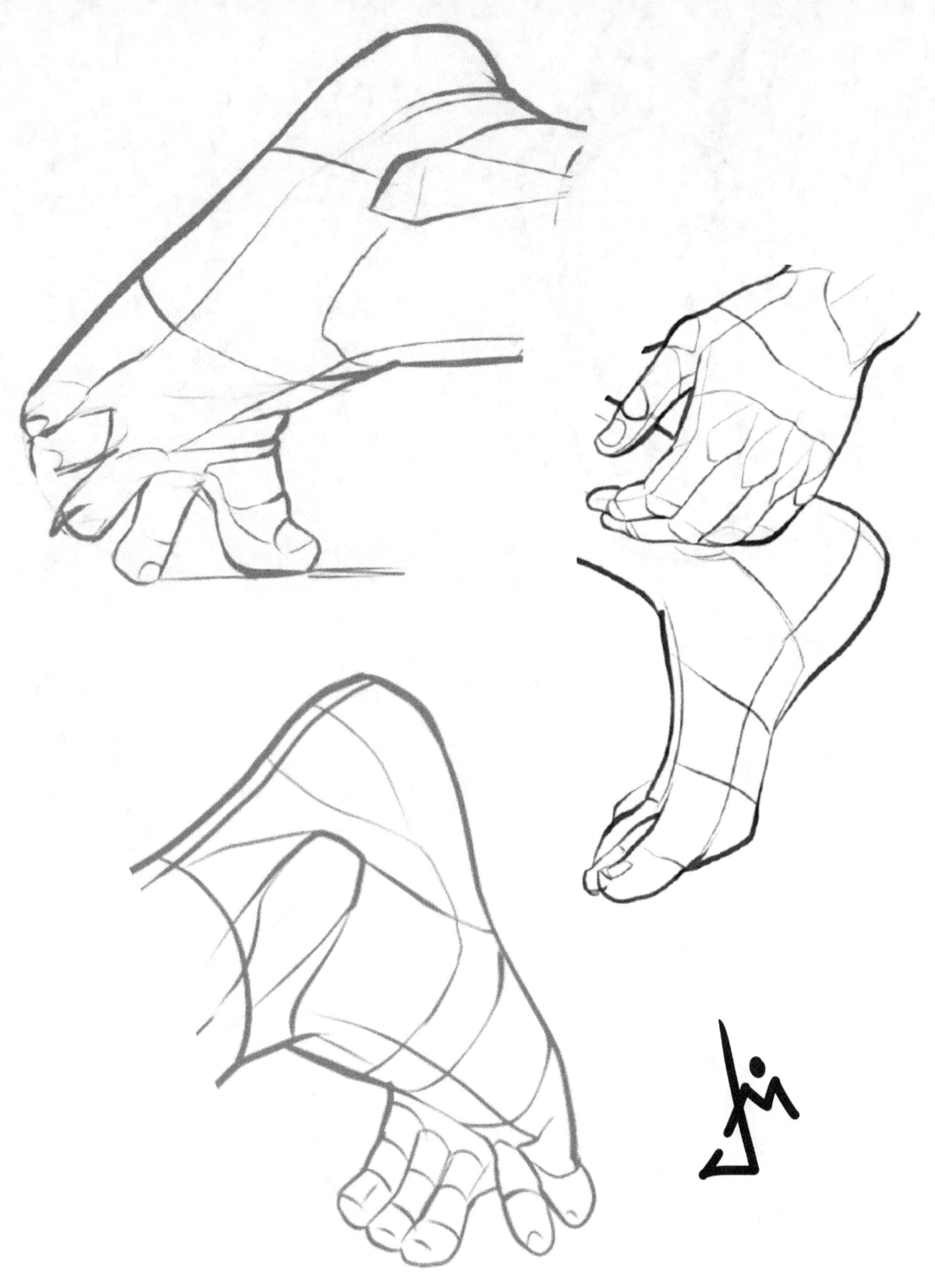

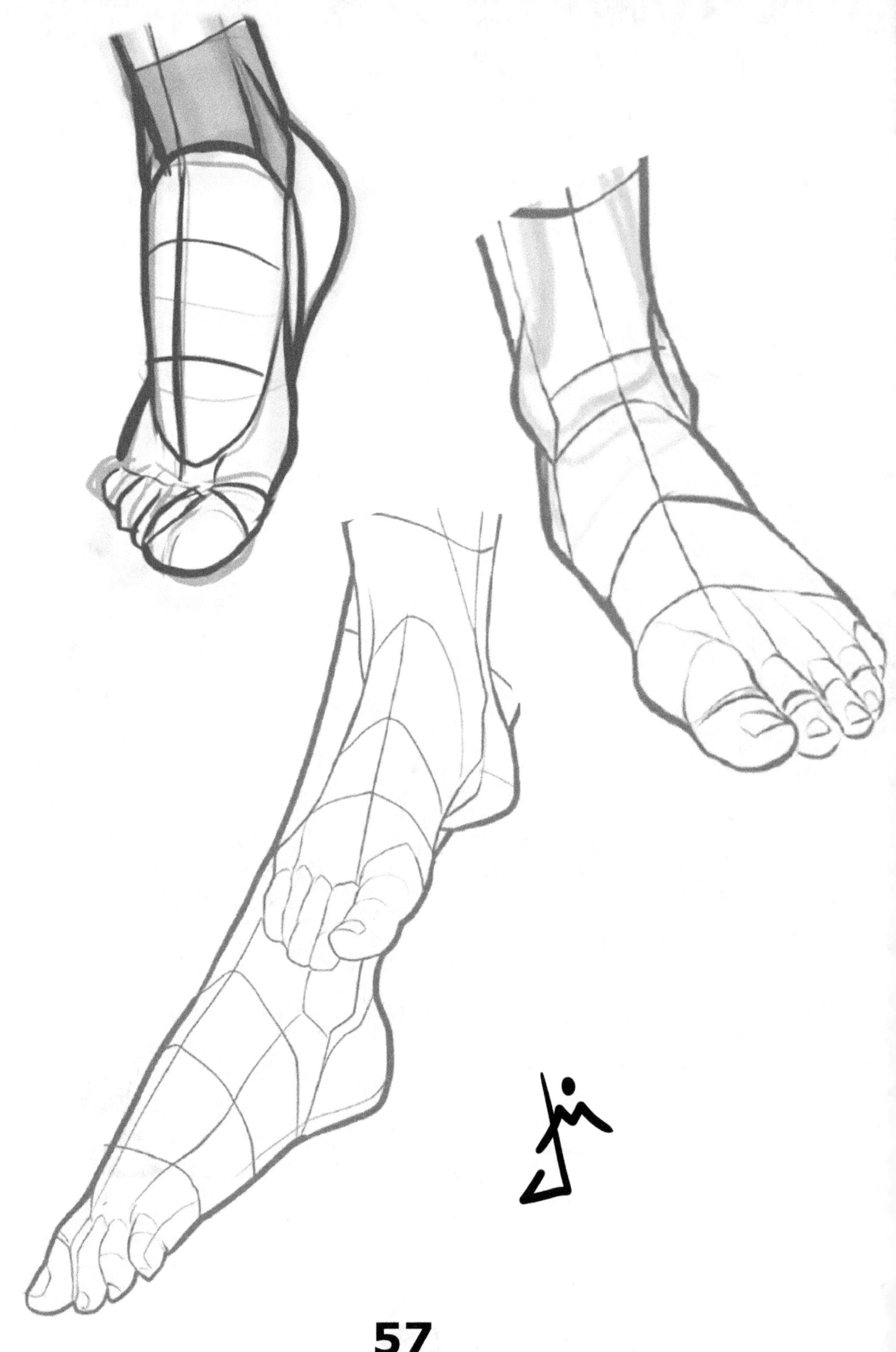

57

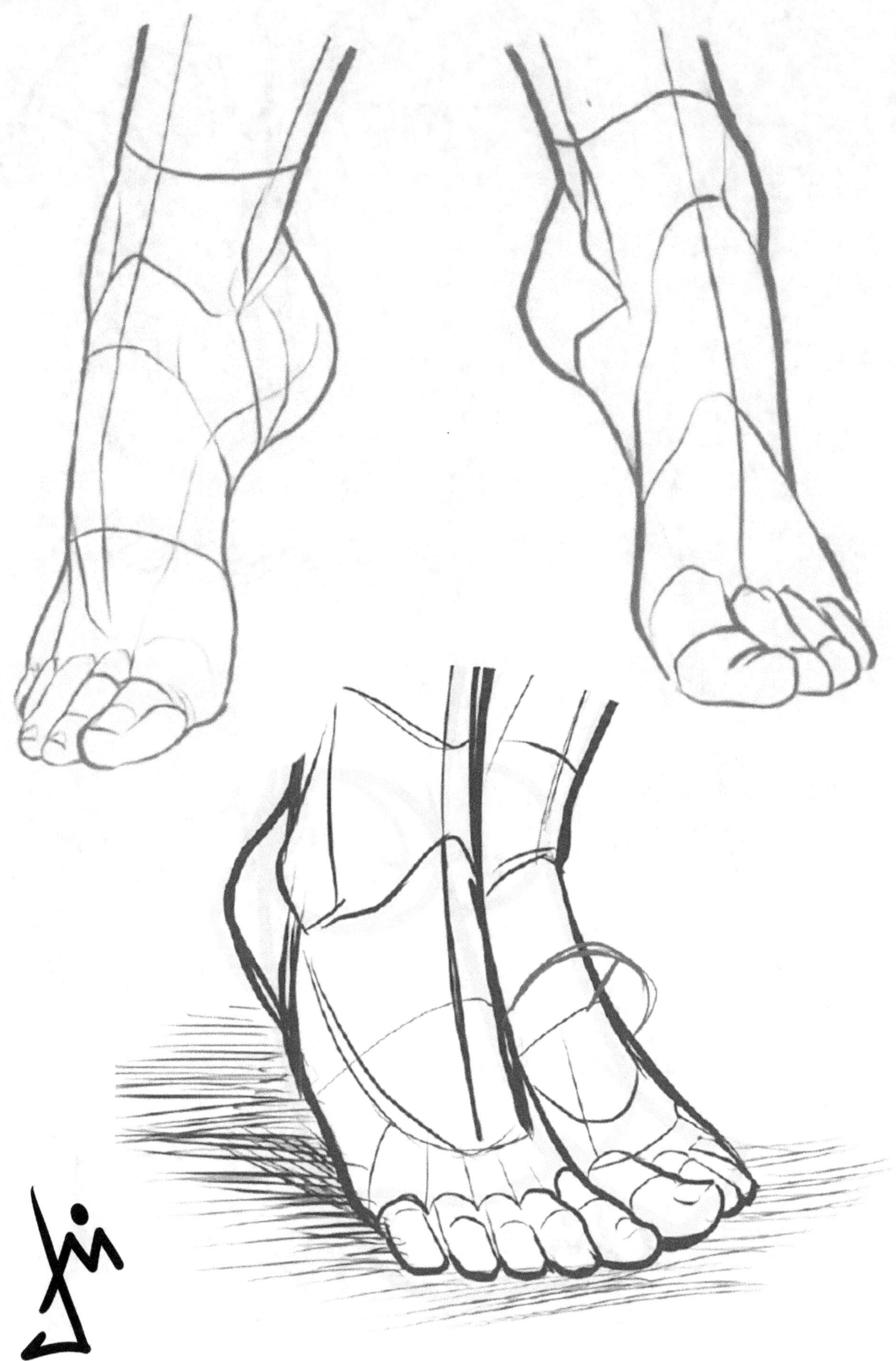

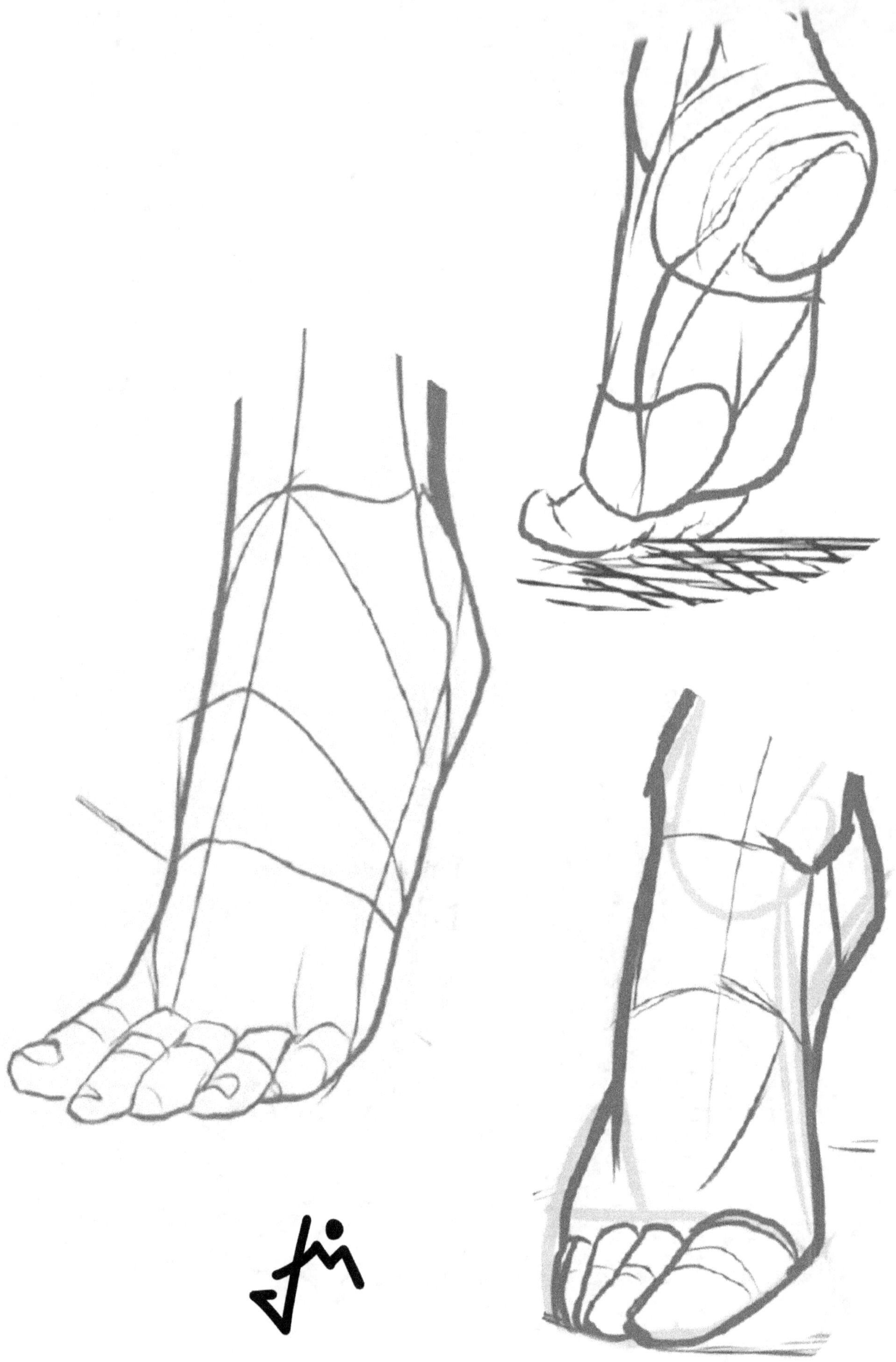

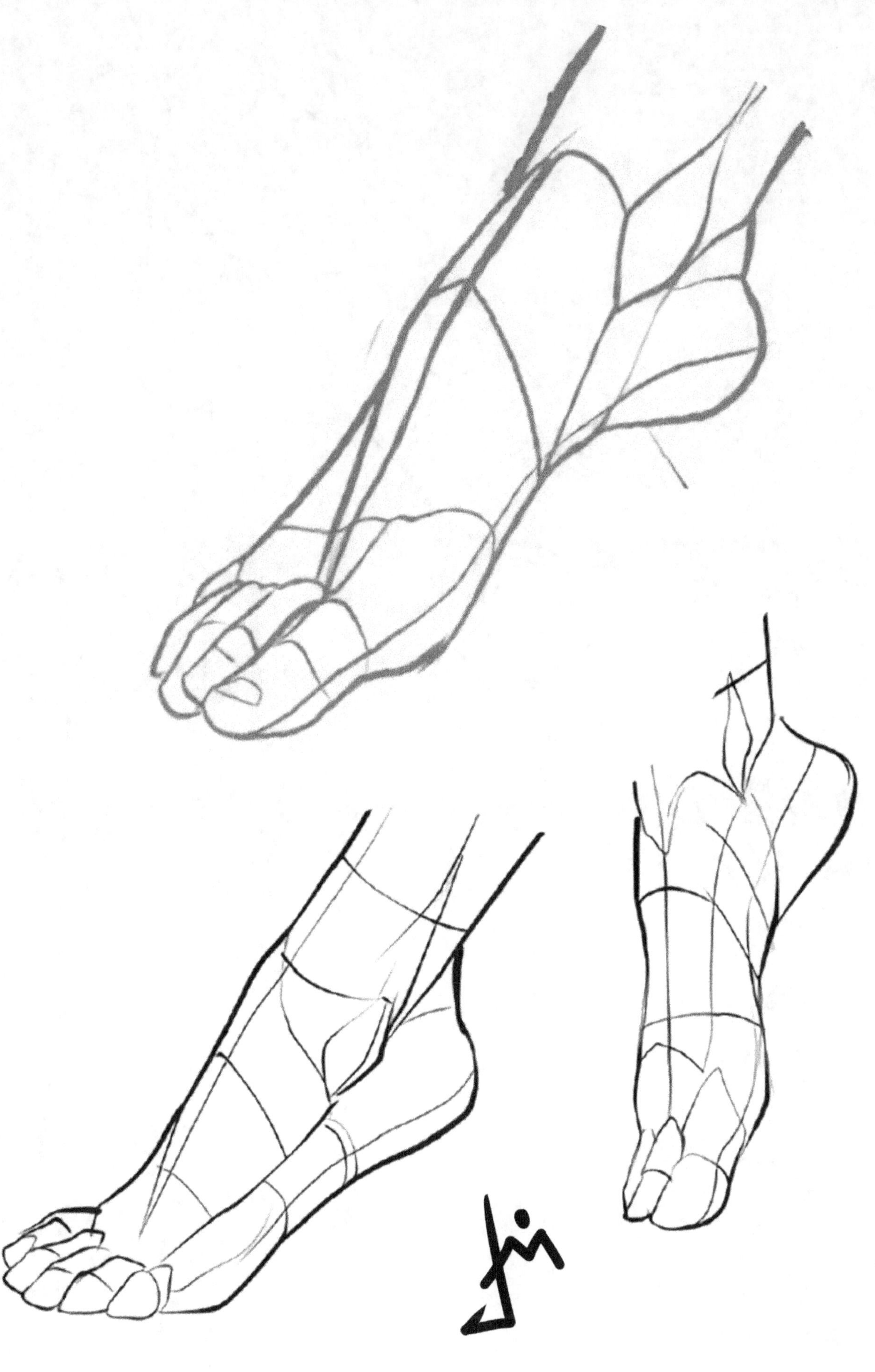

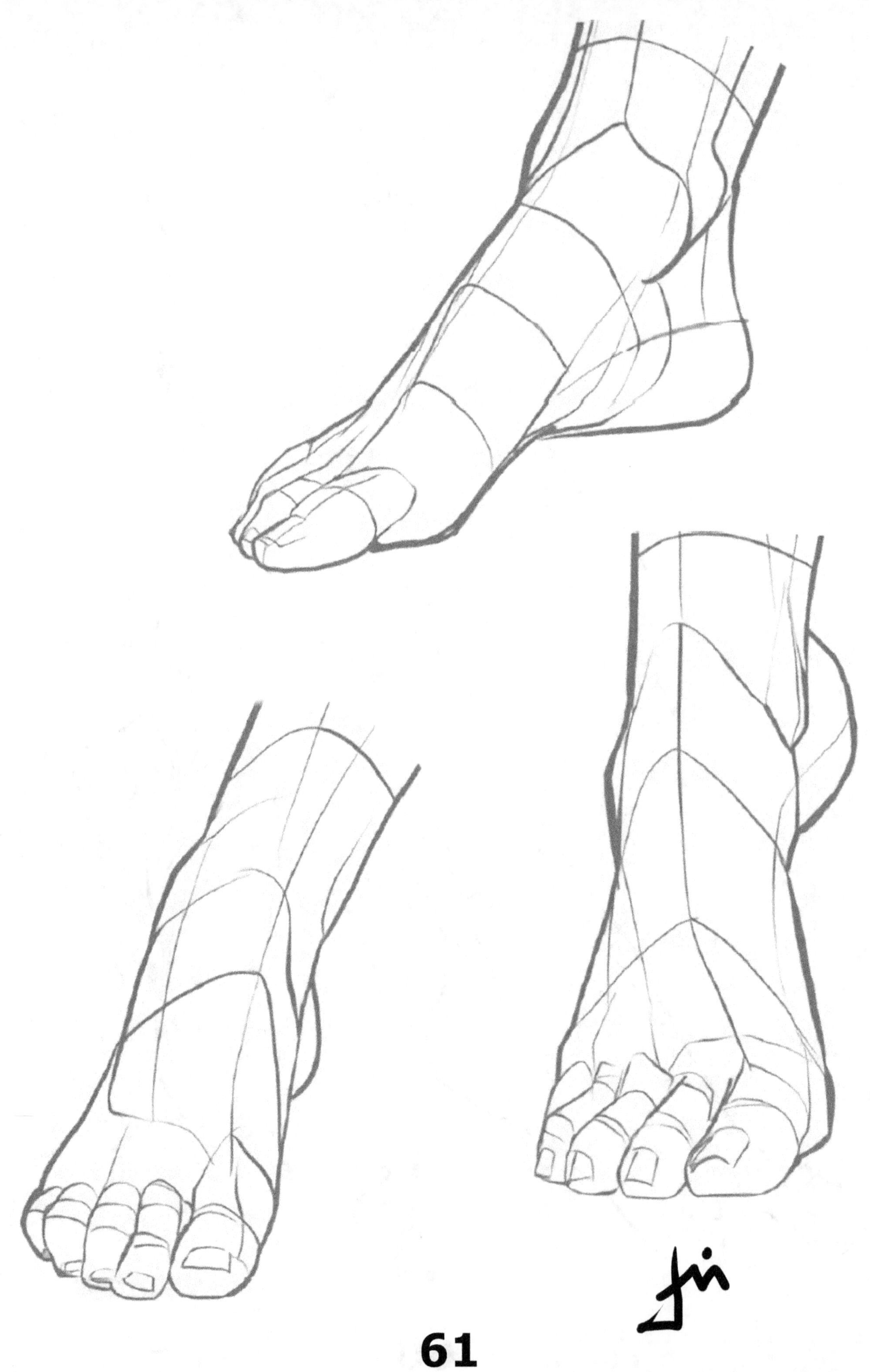

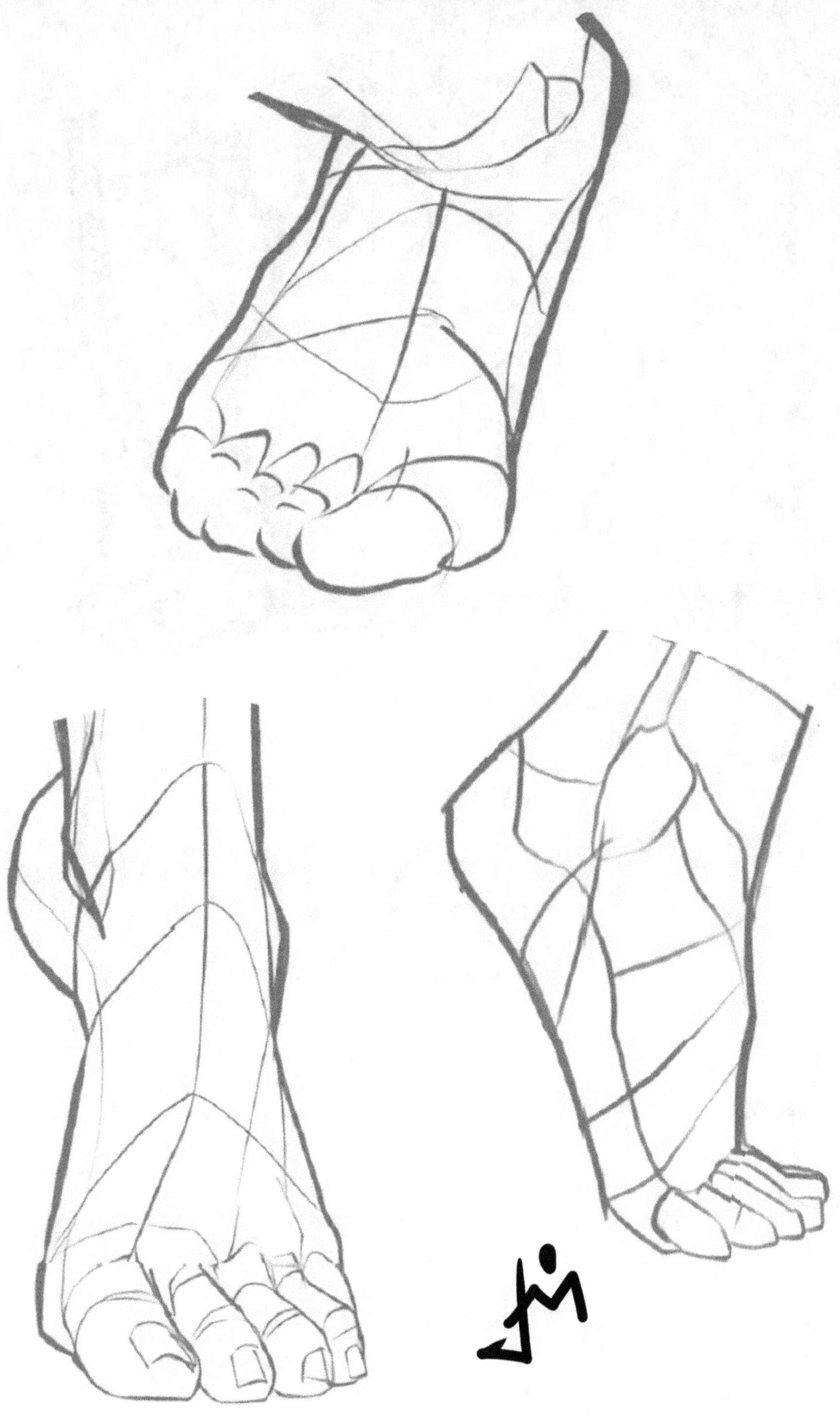

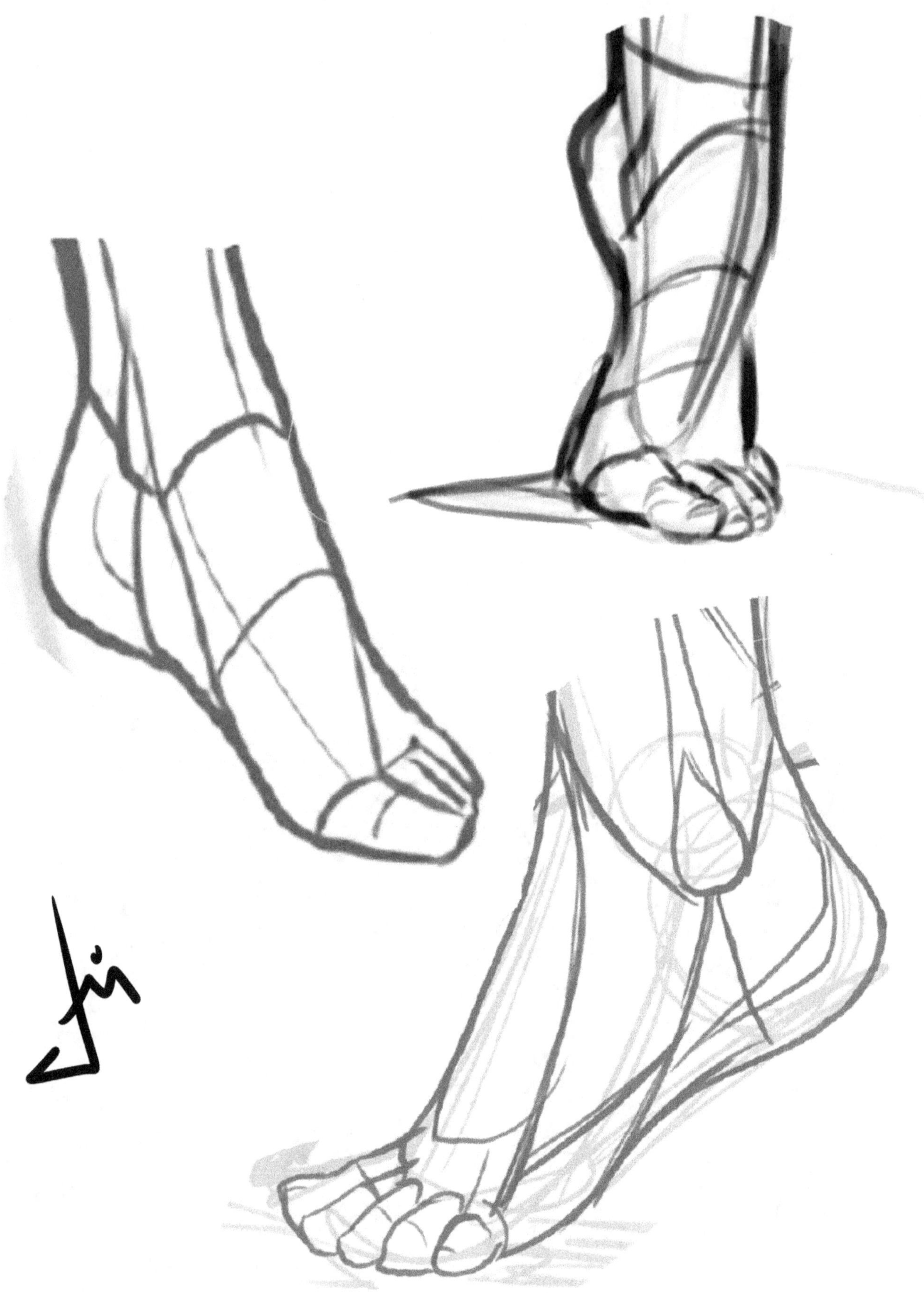

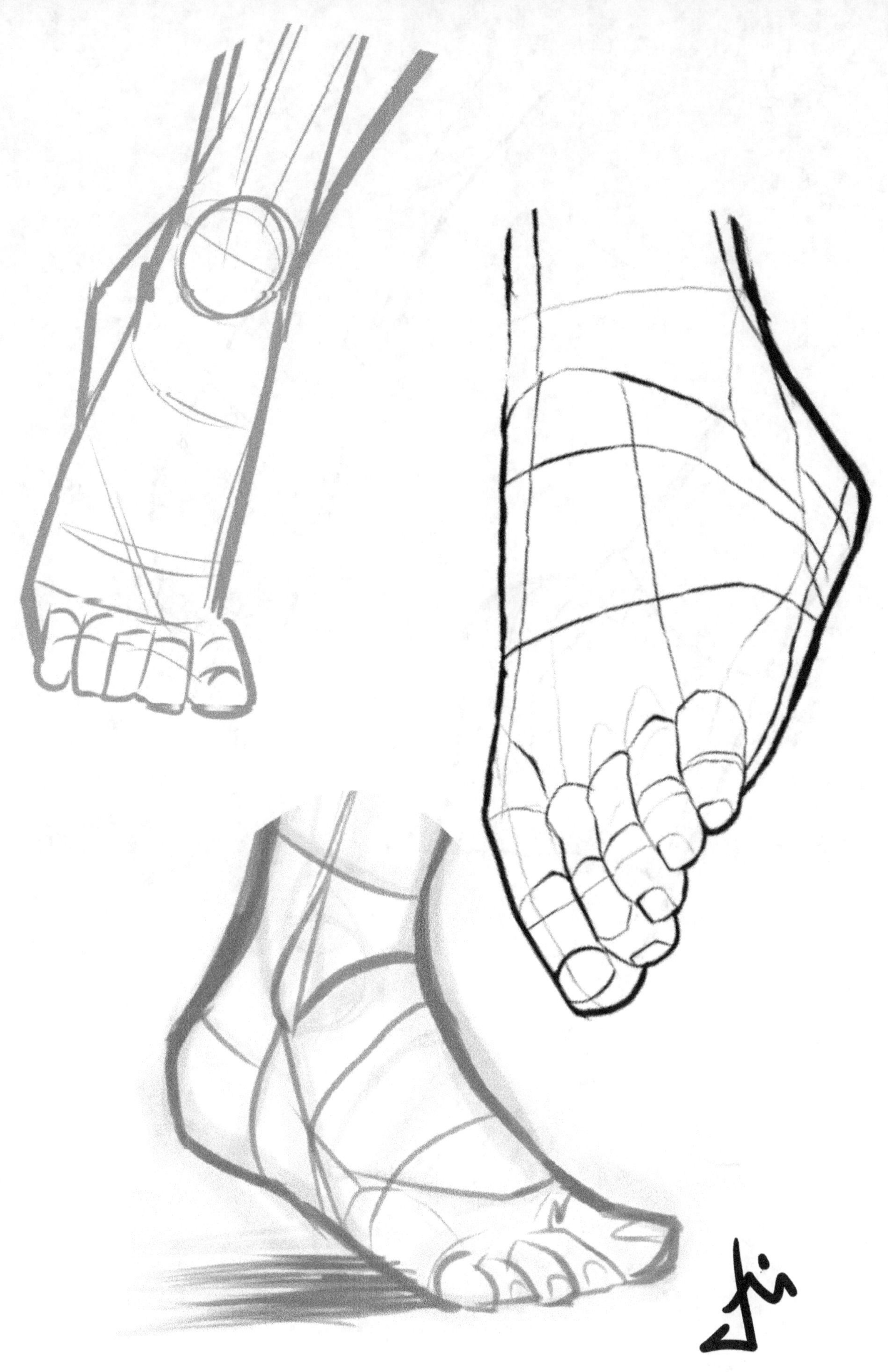

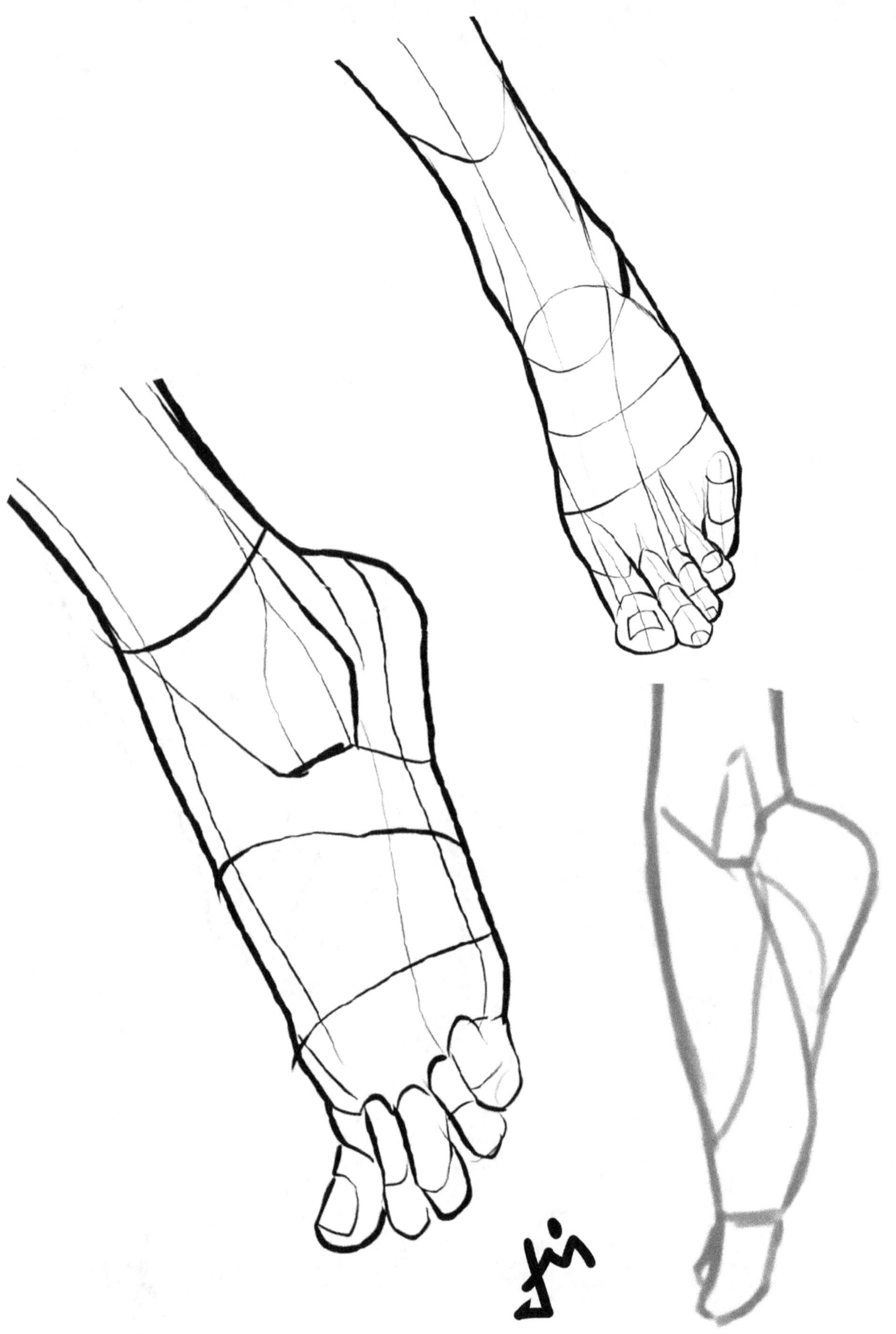

65

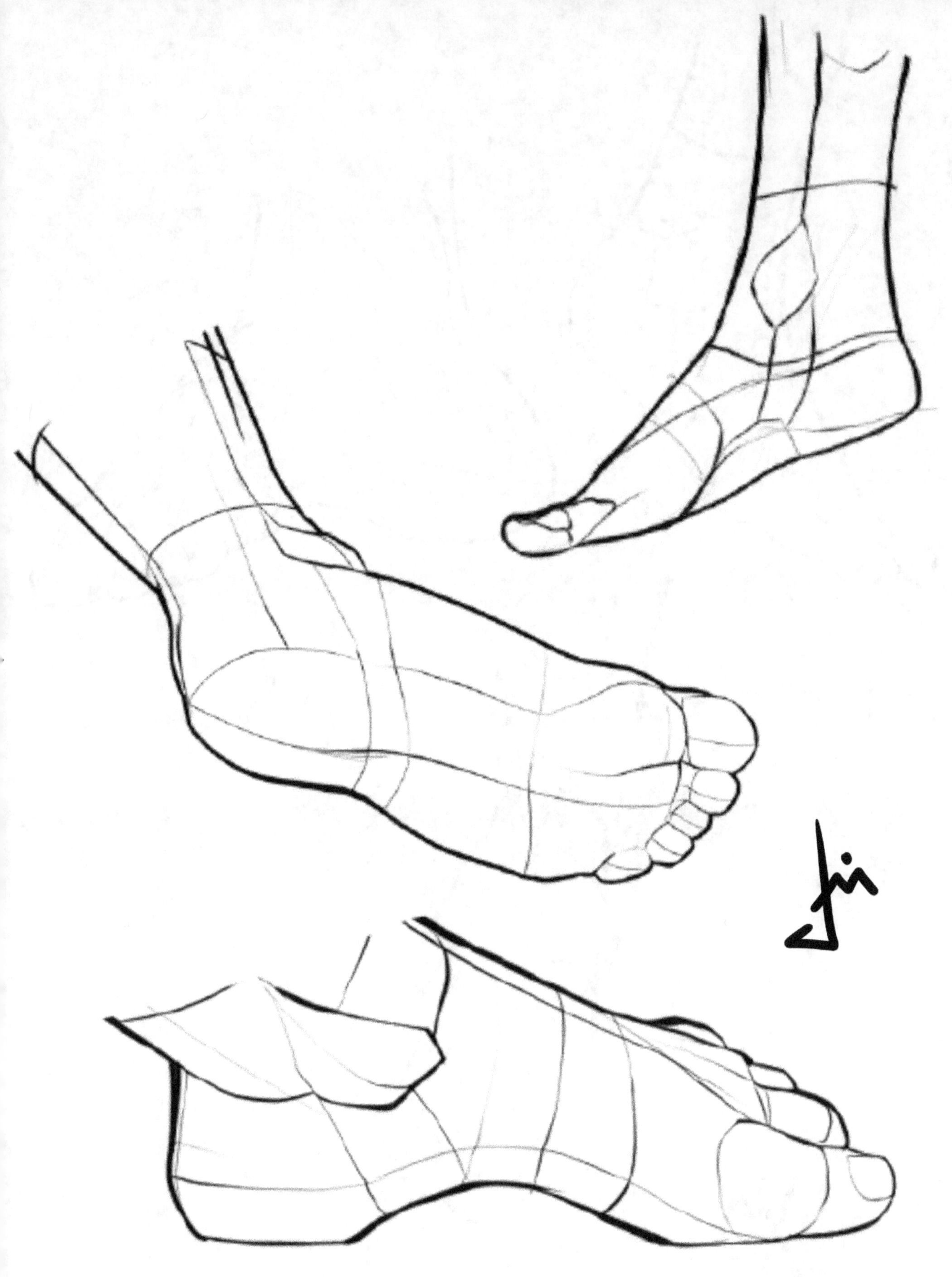

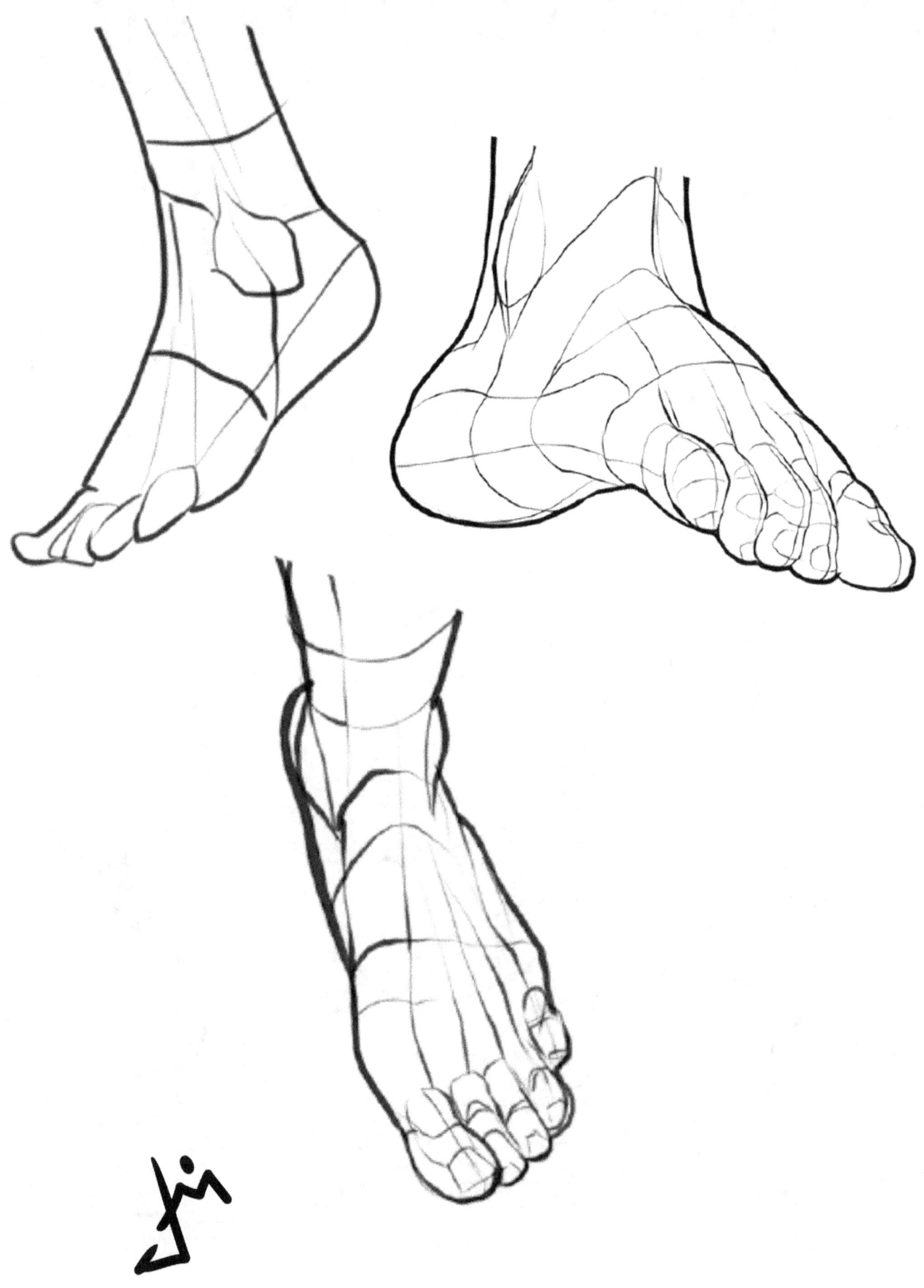

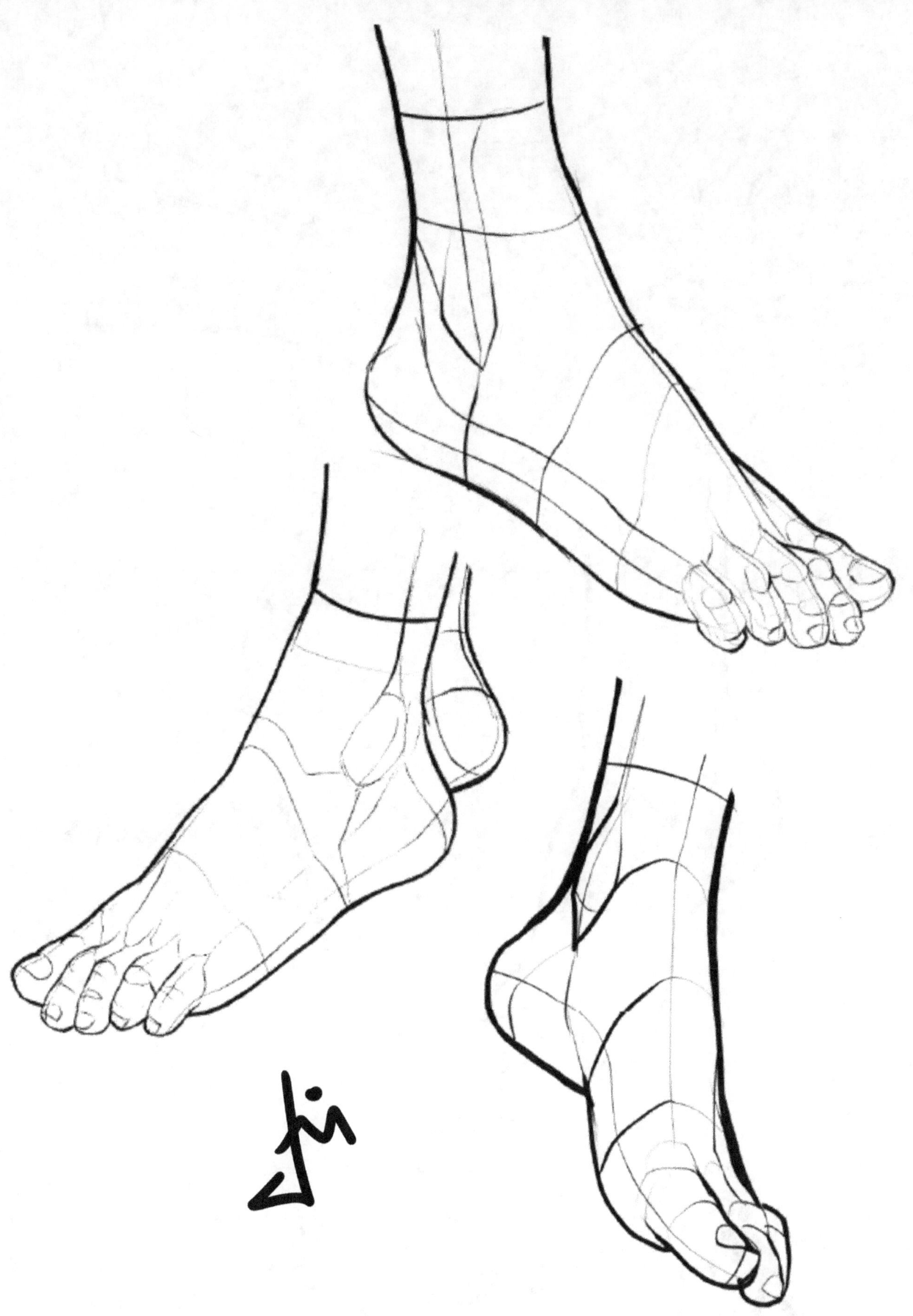

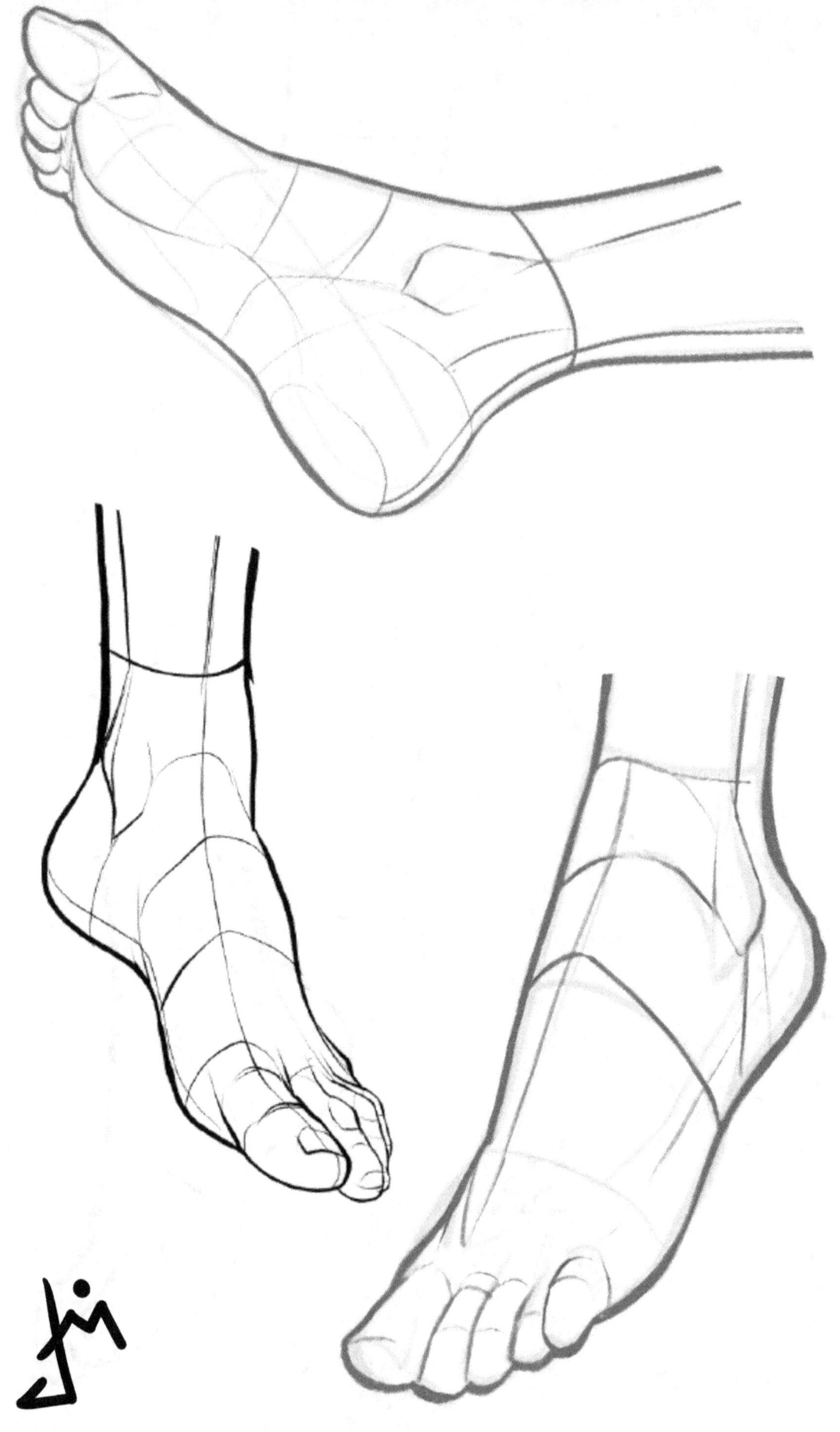

69

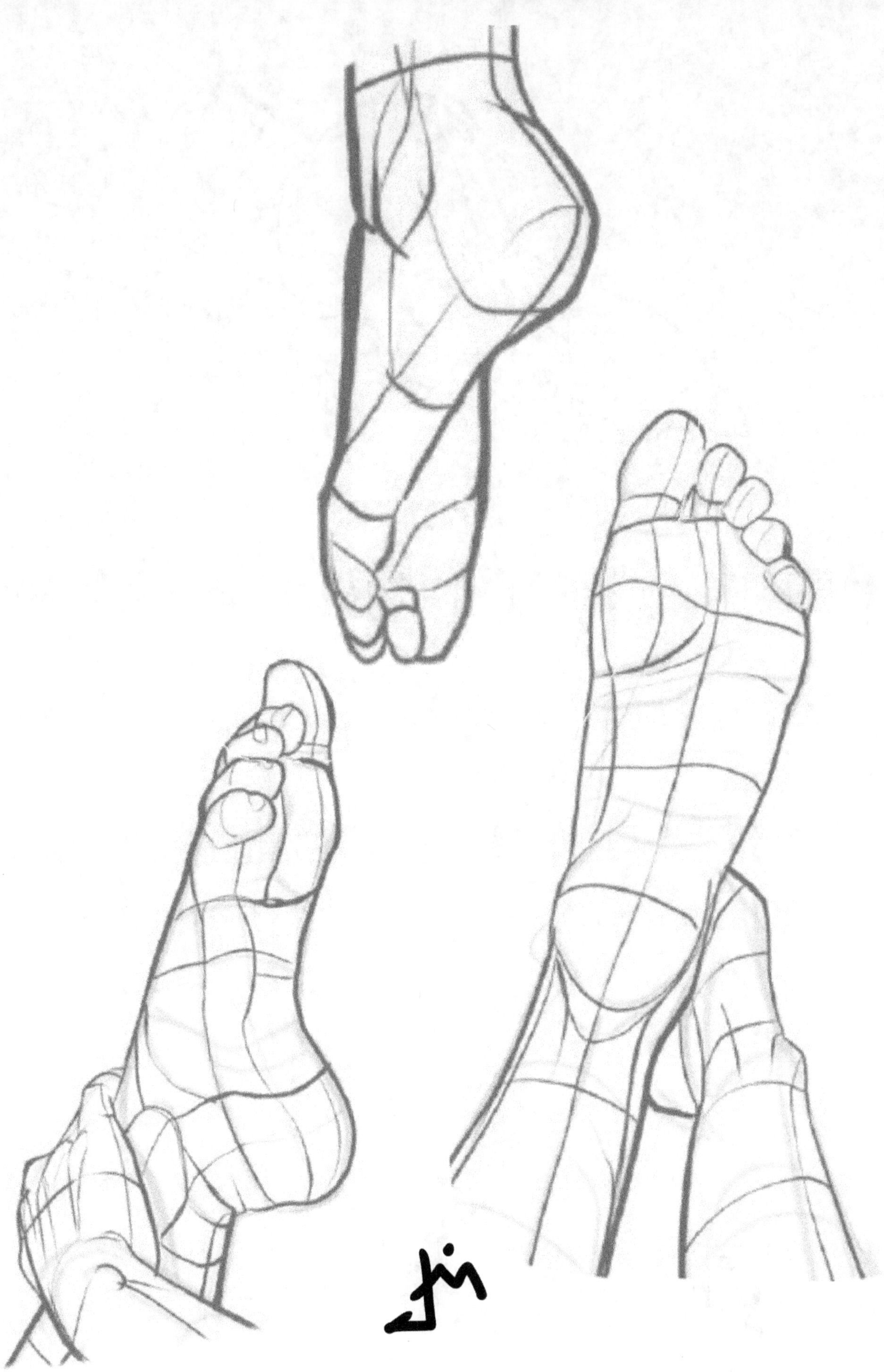

70

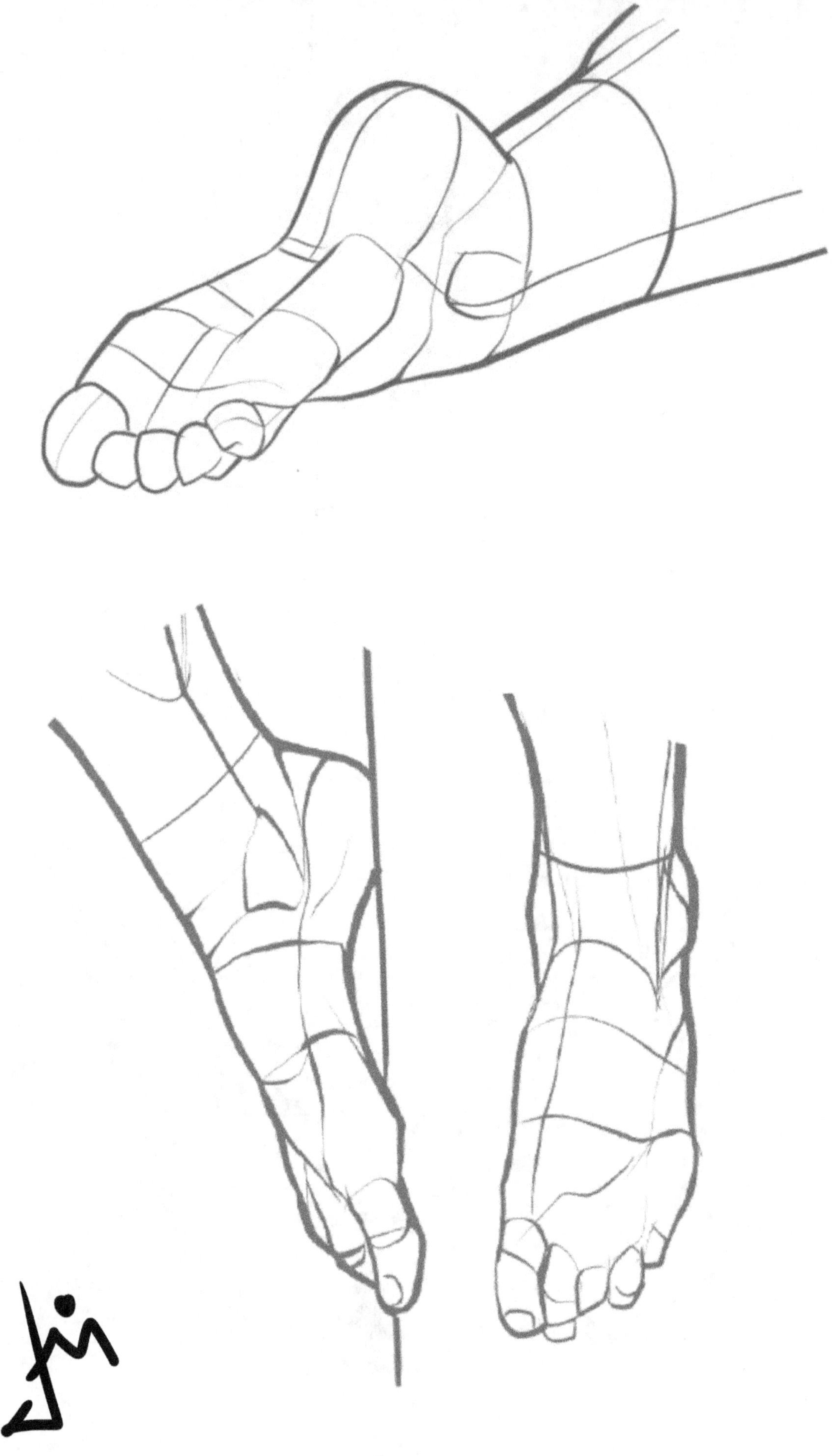

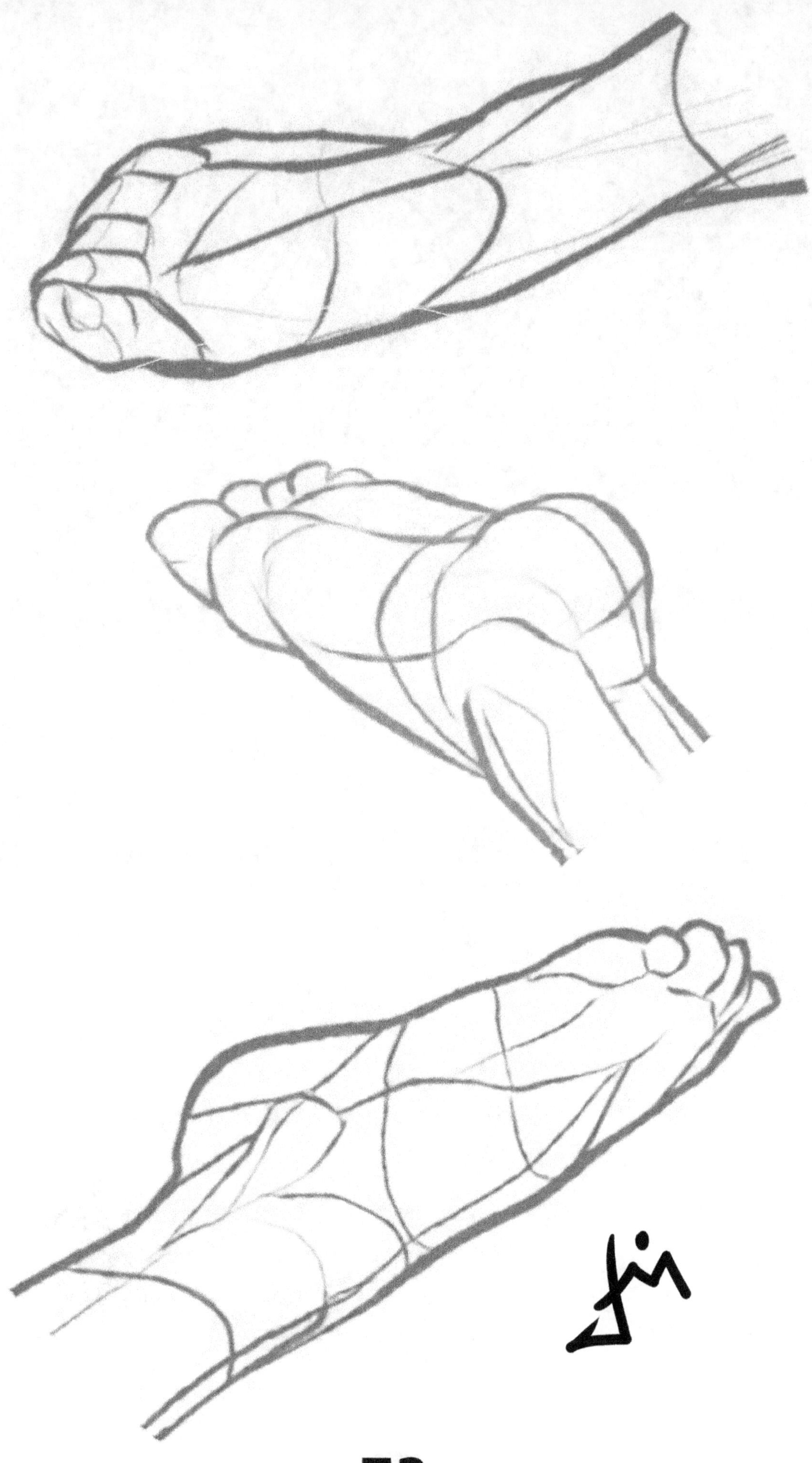

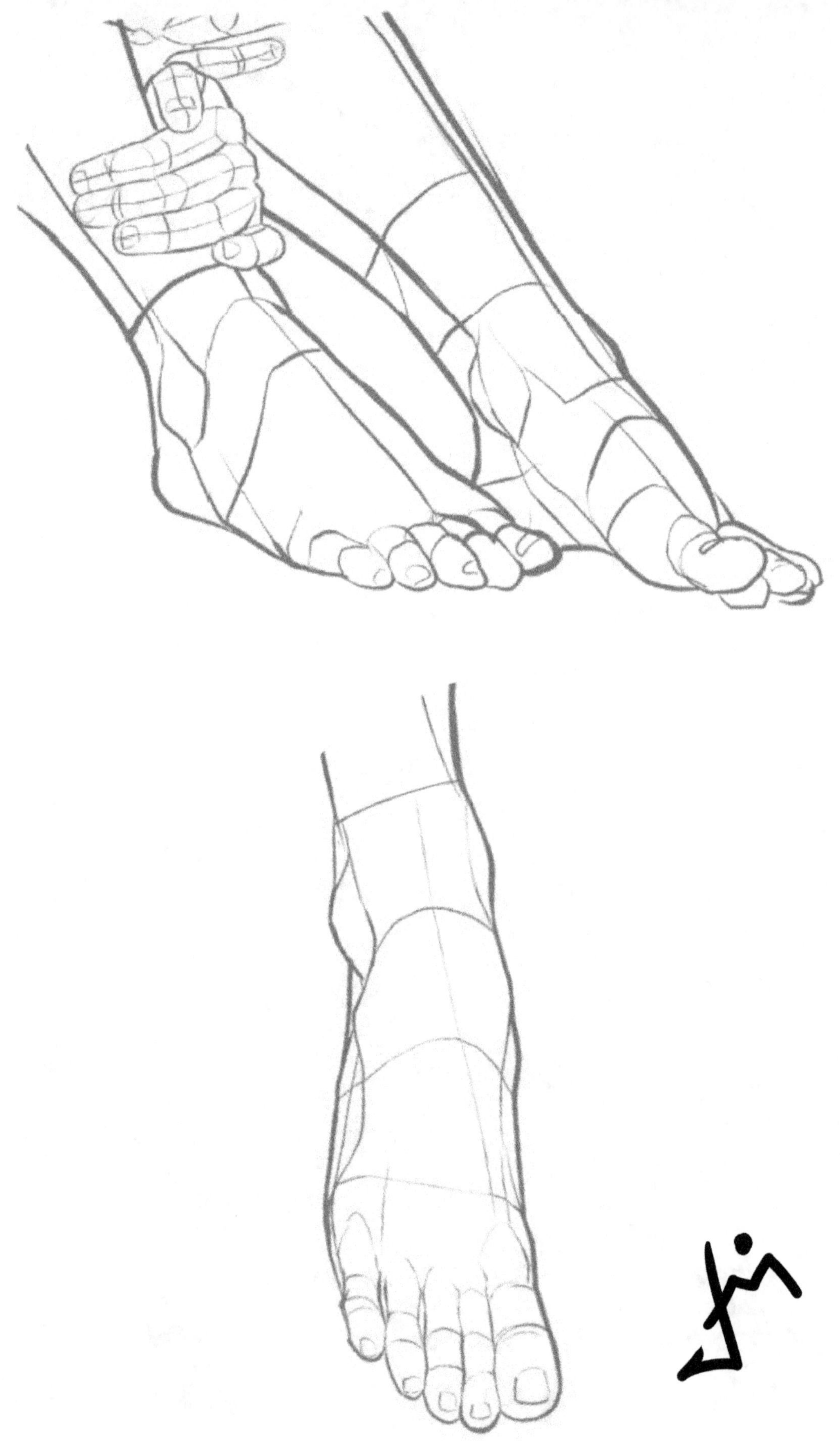

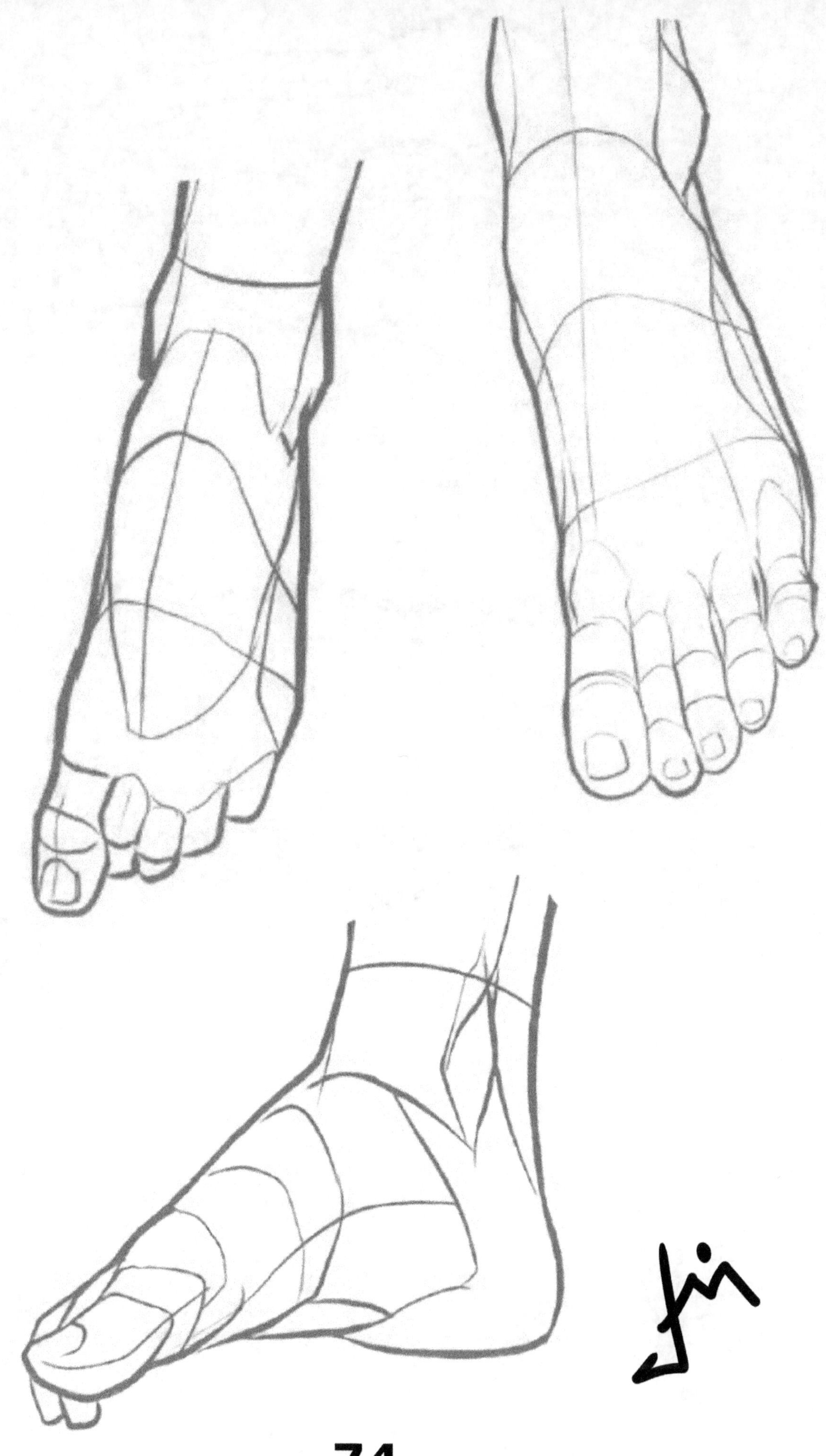

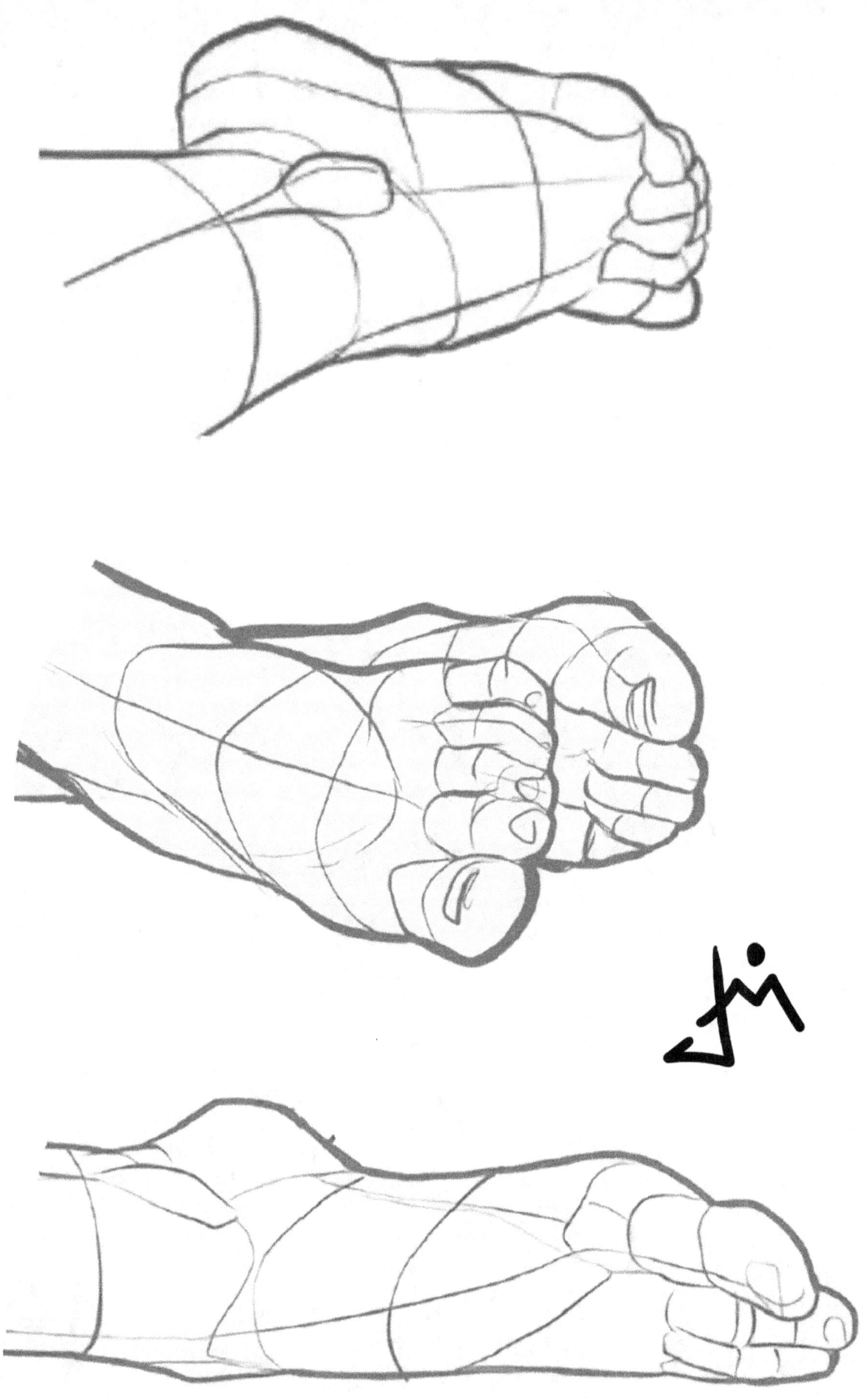

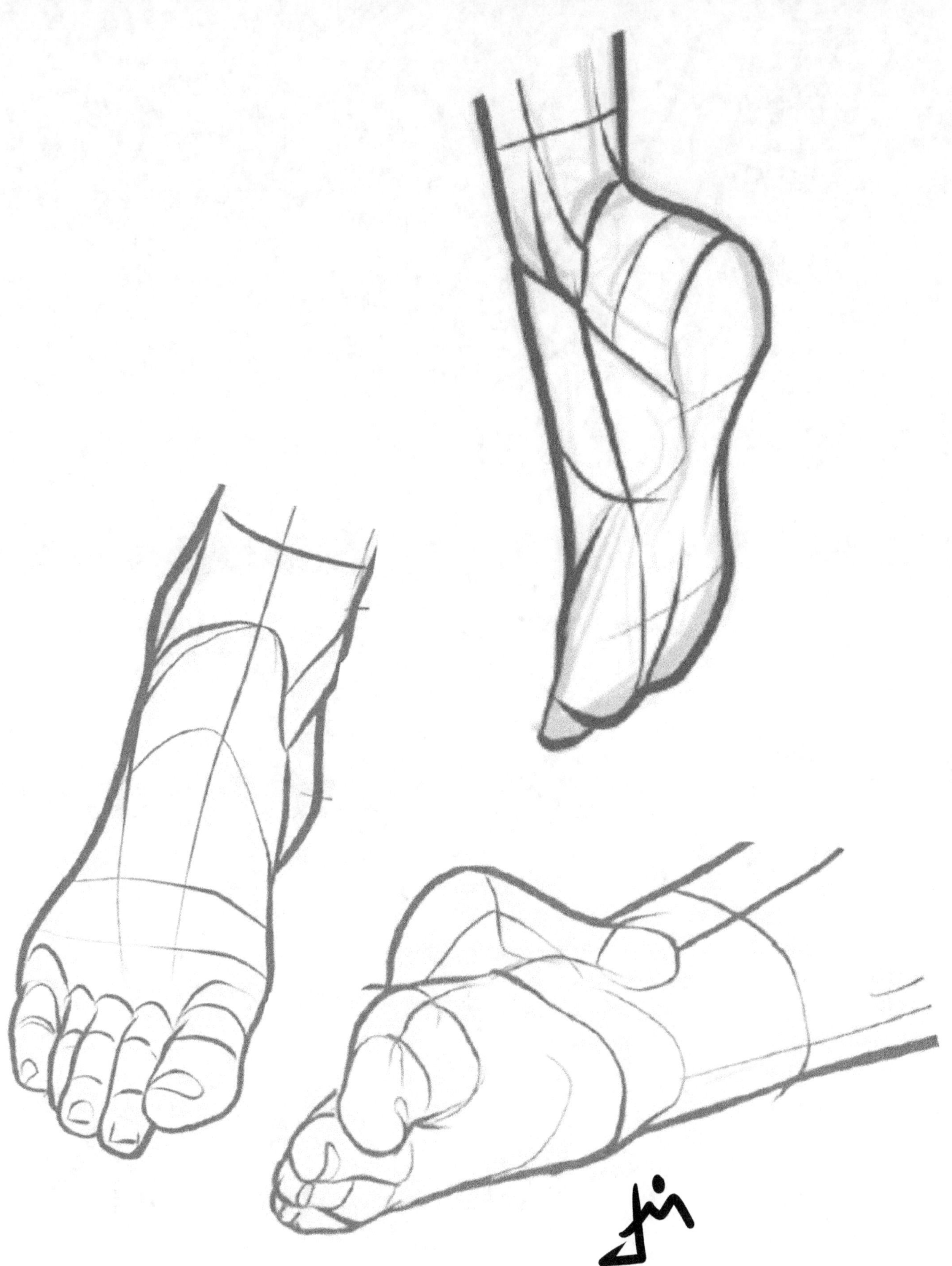

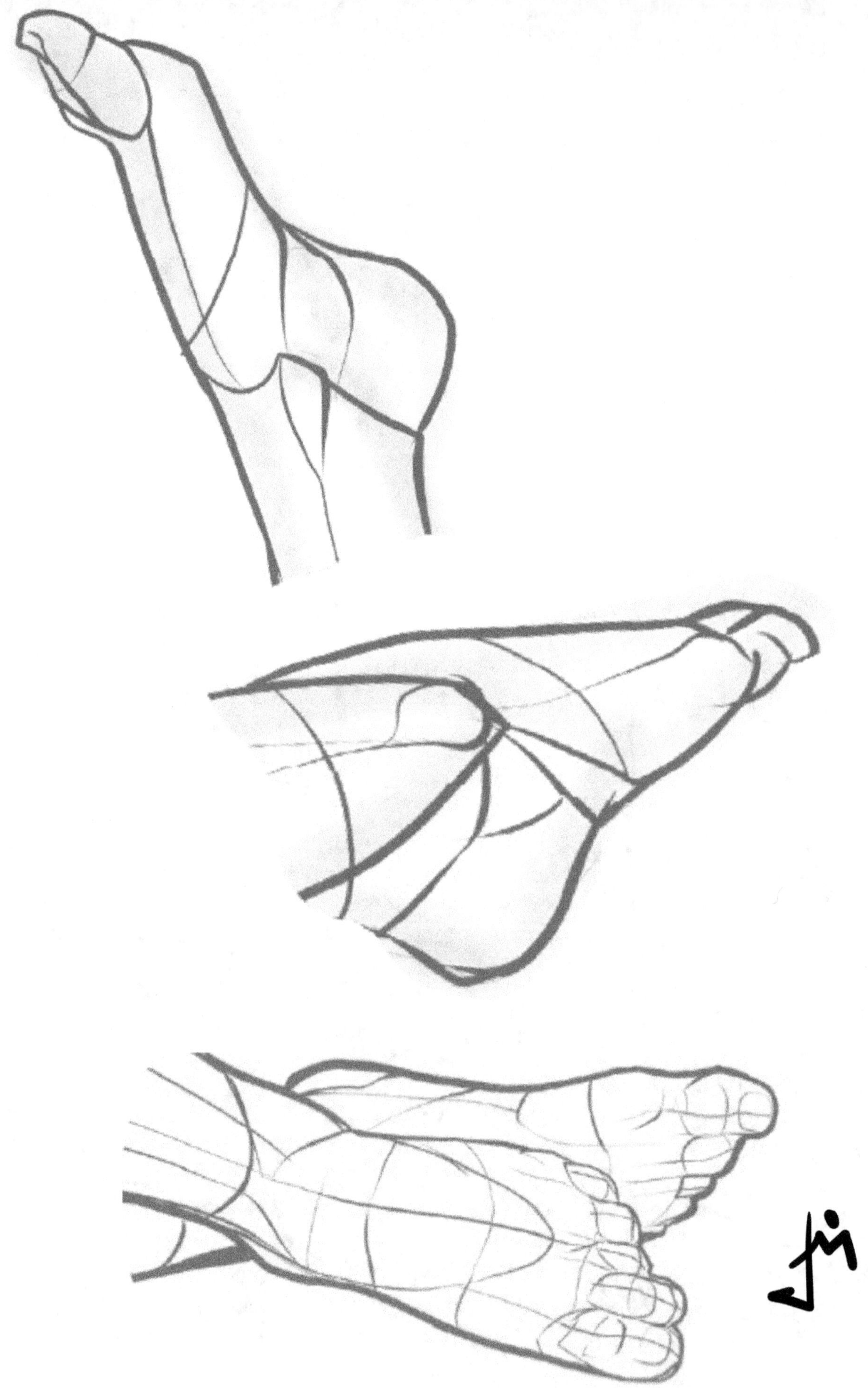

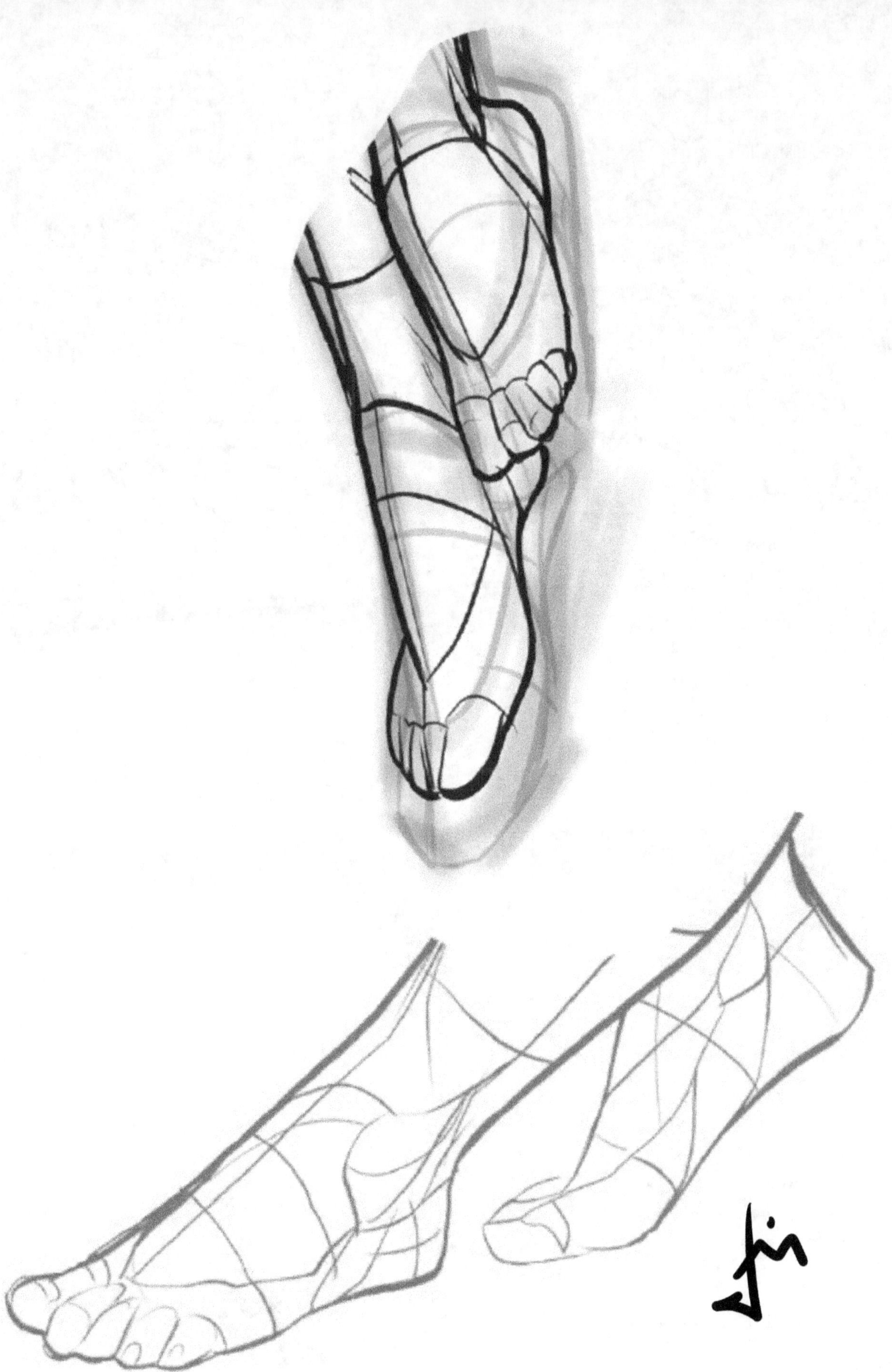

78

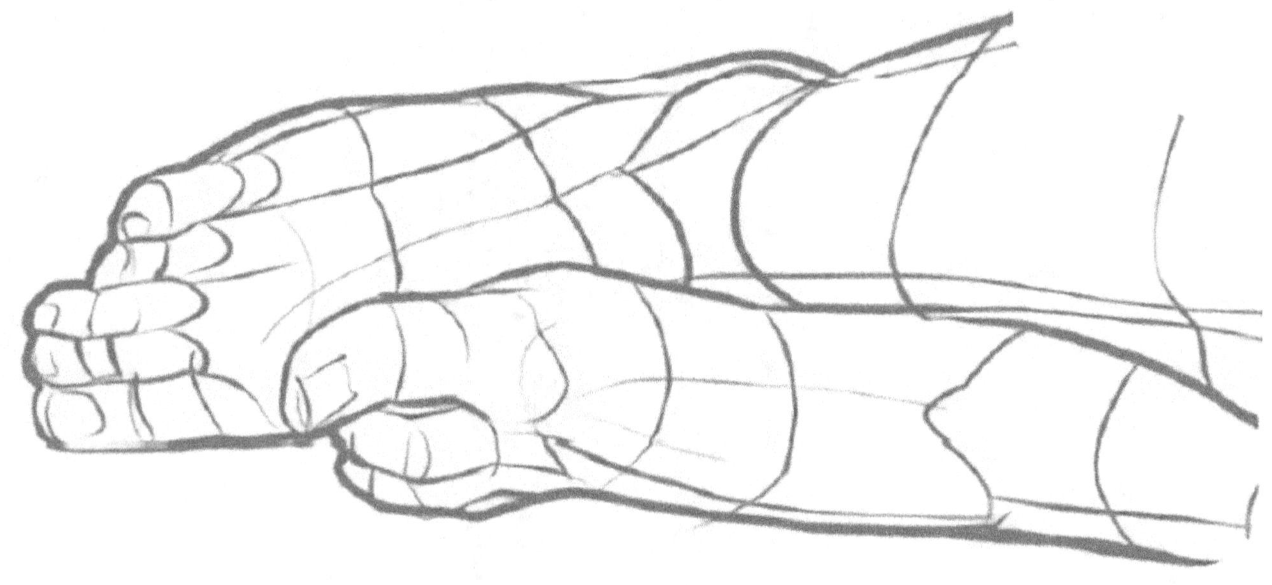

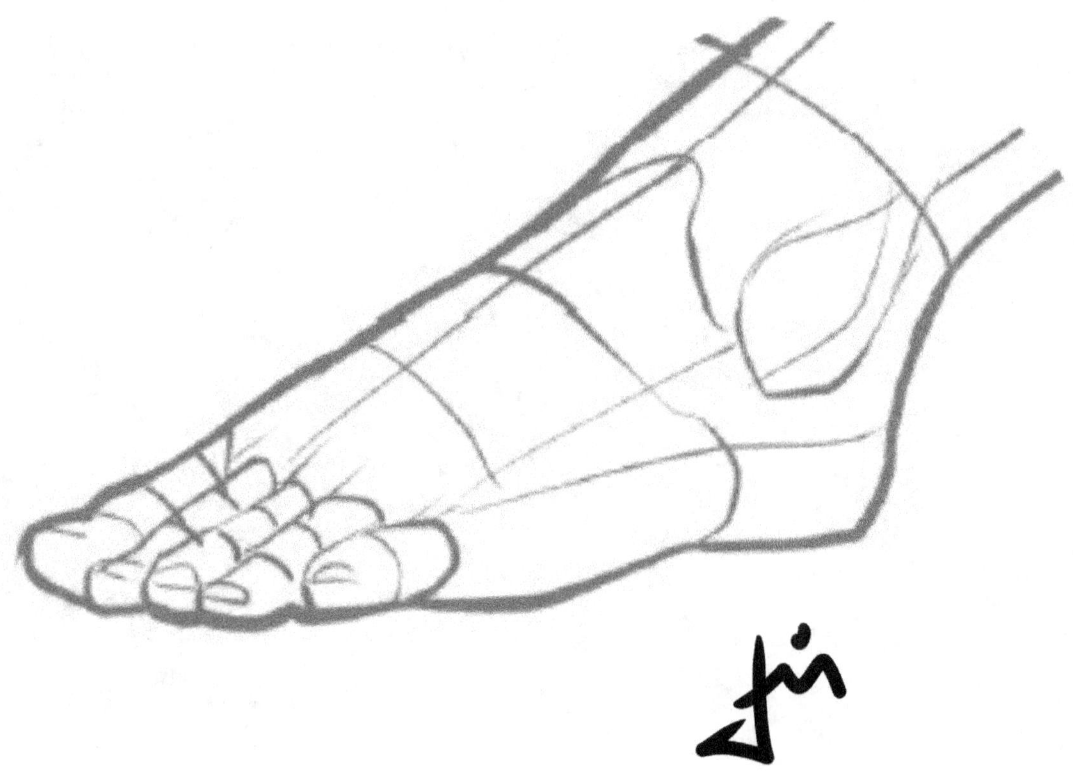

79

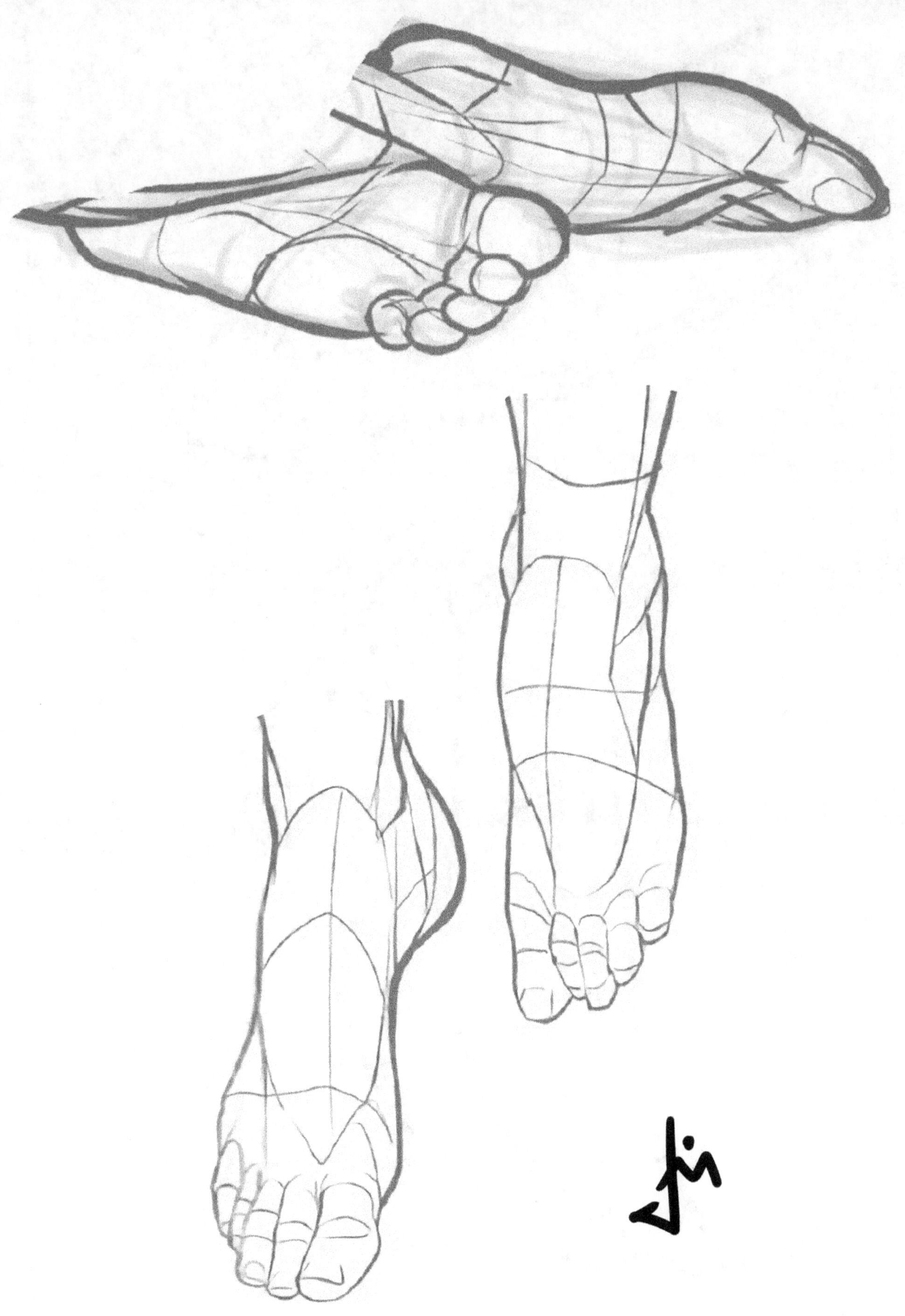

80

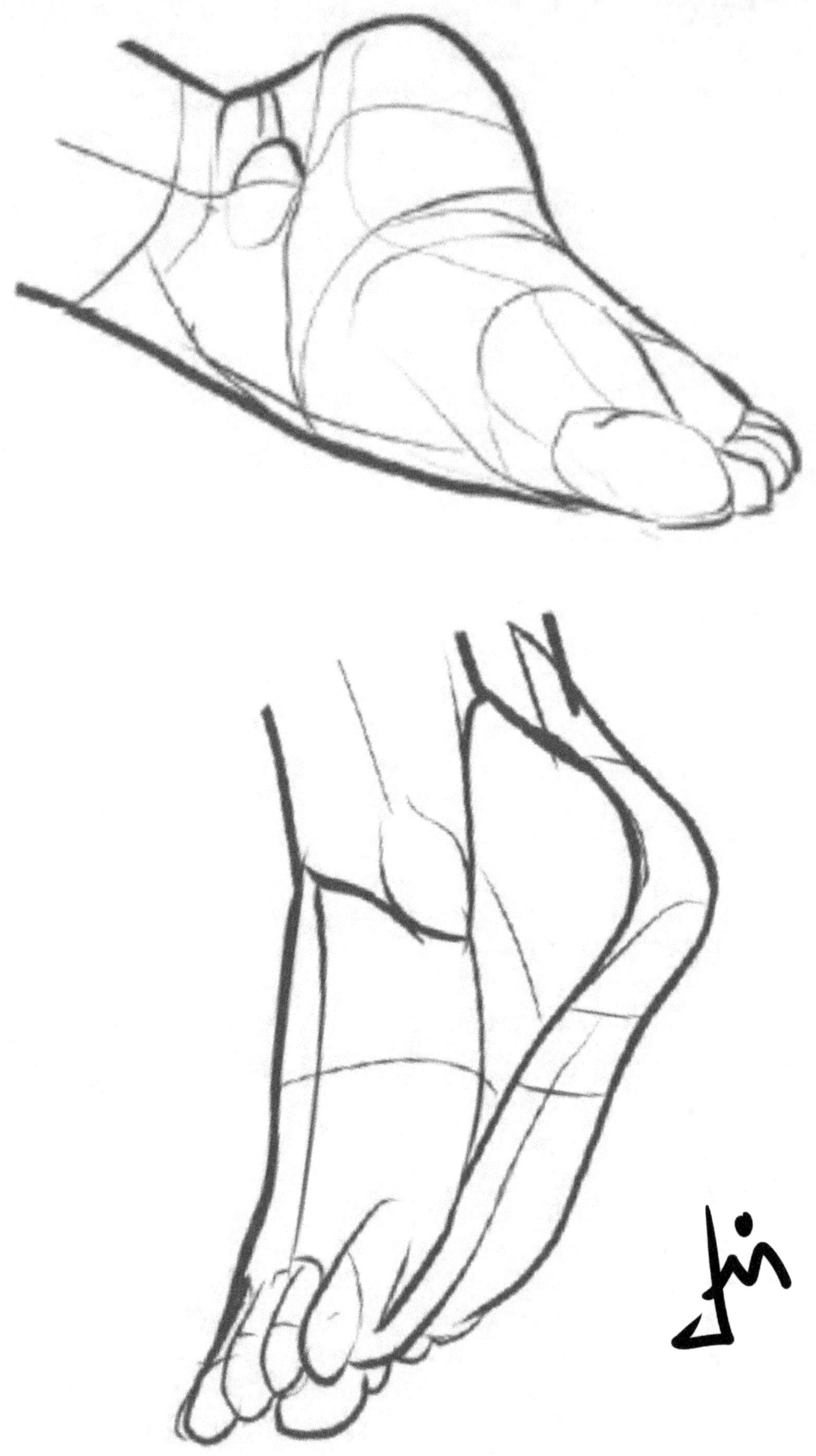

81

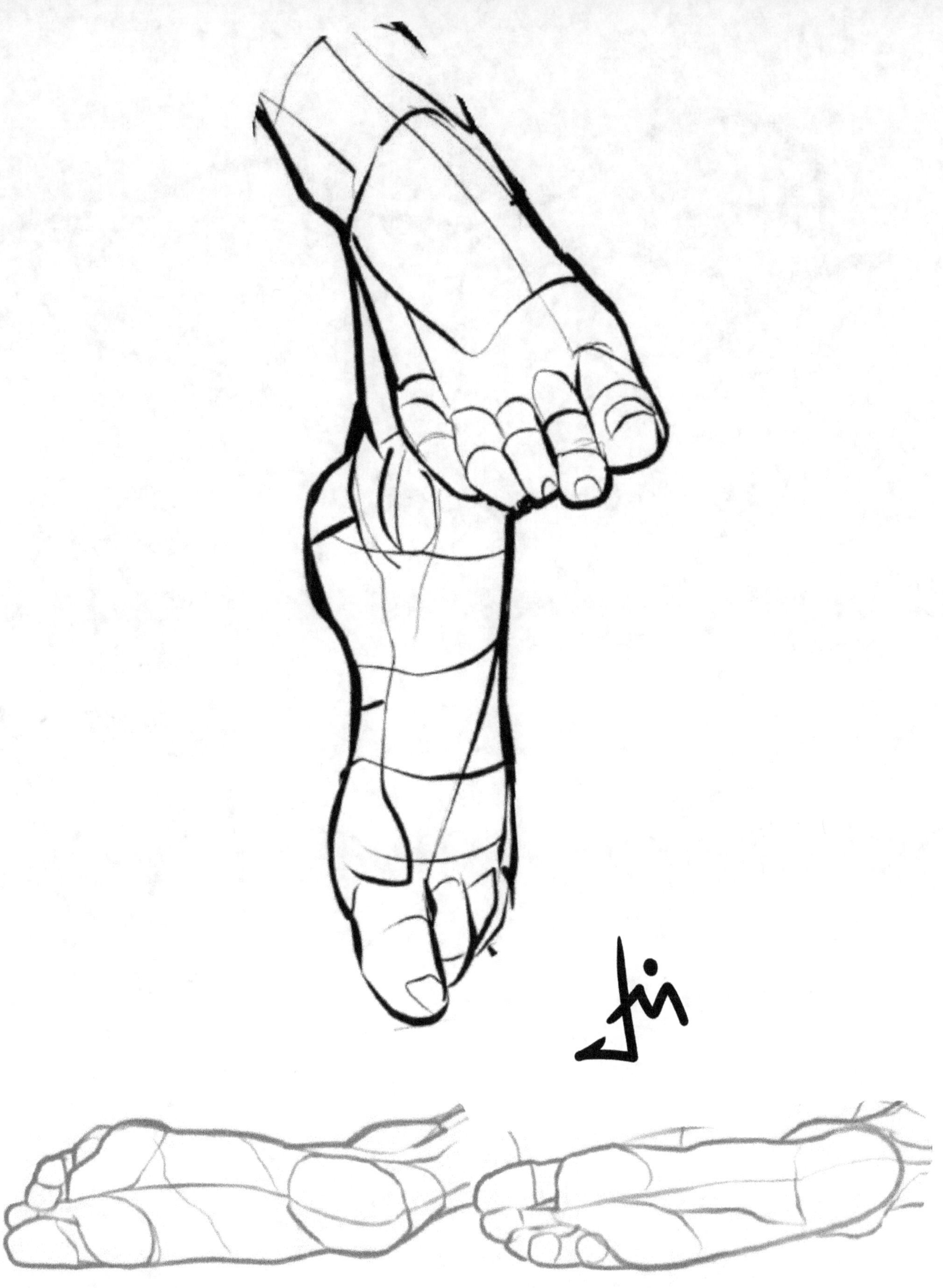

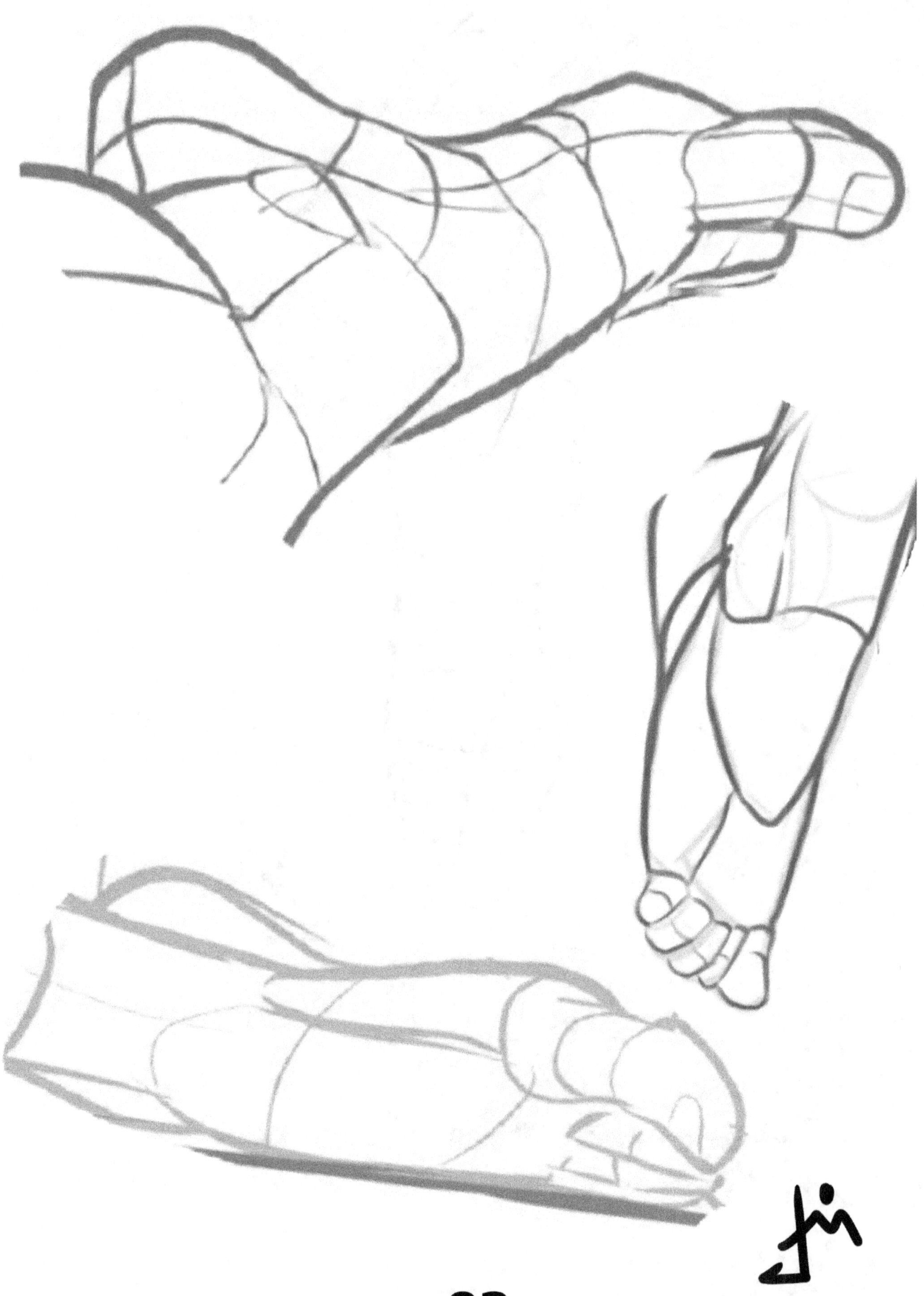

83

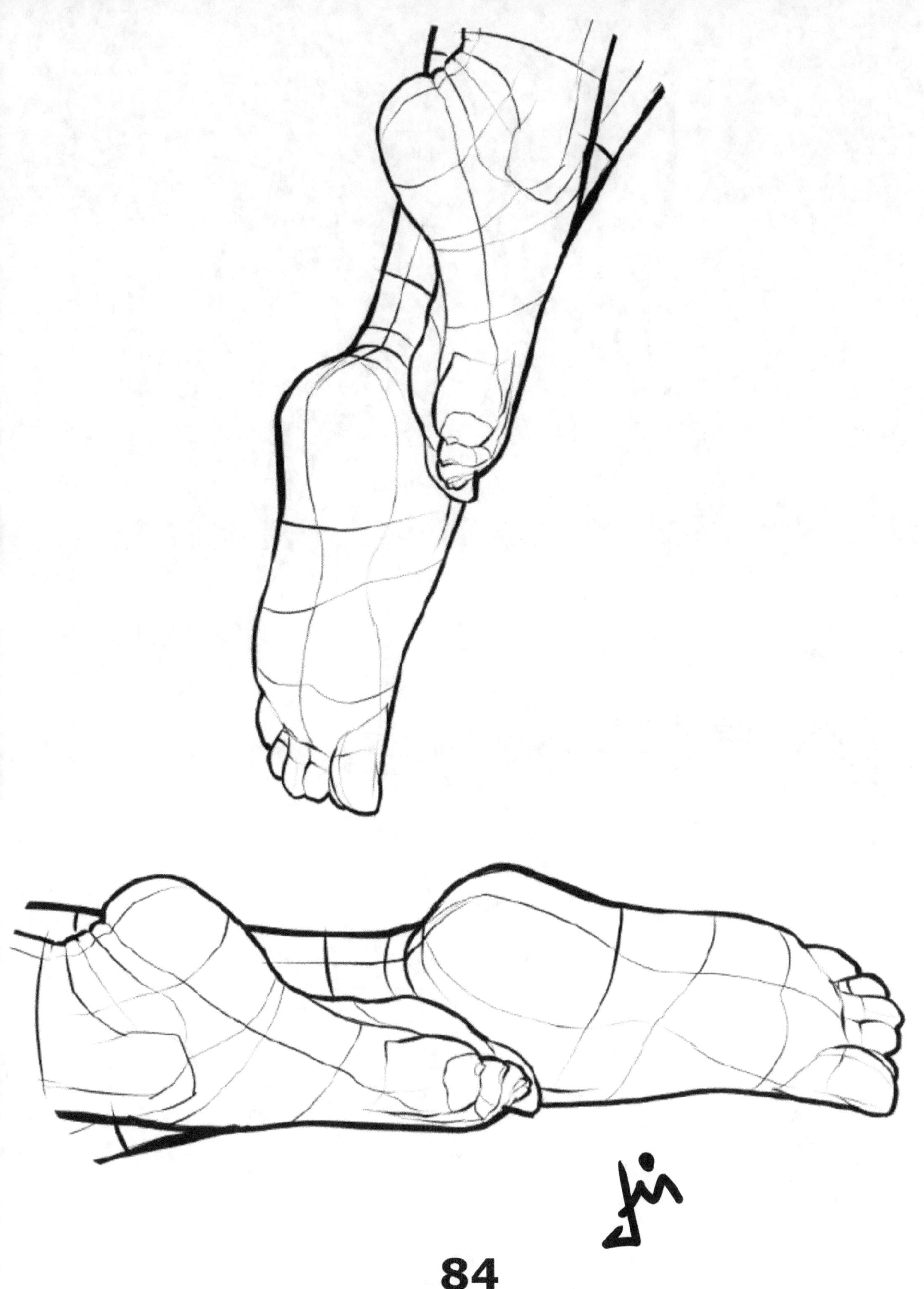

84

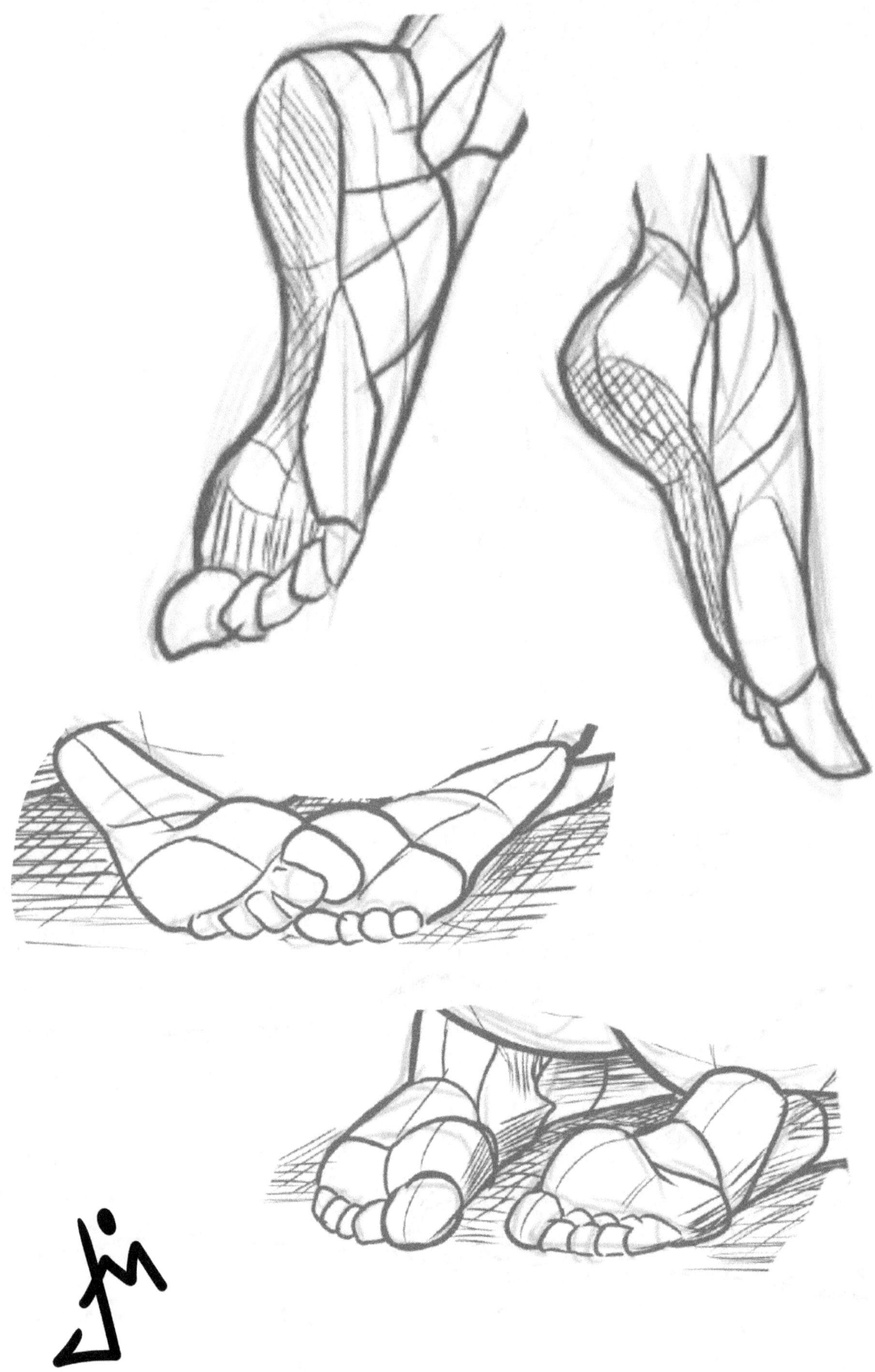

85

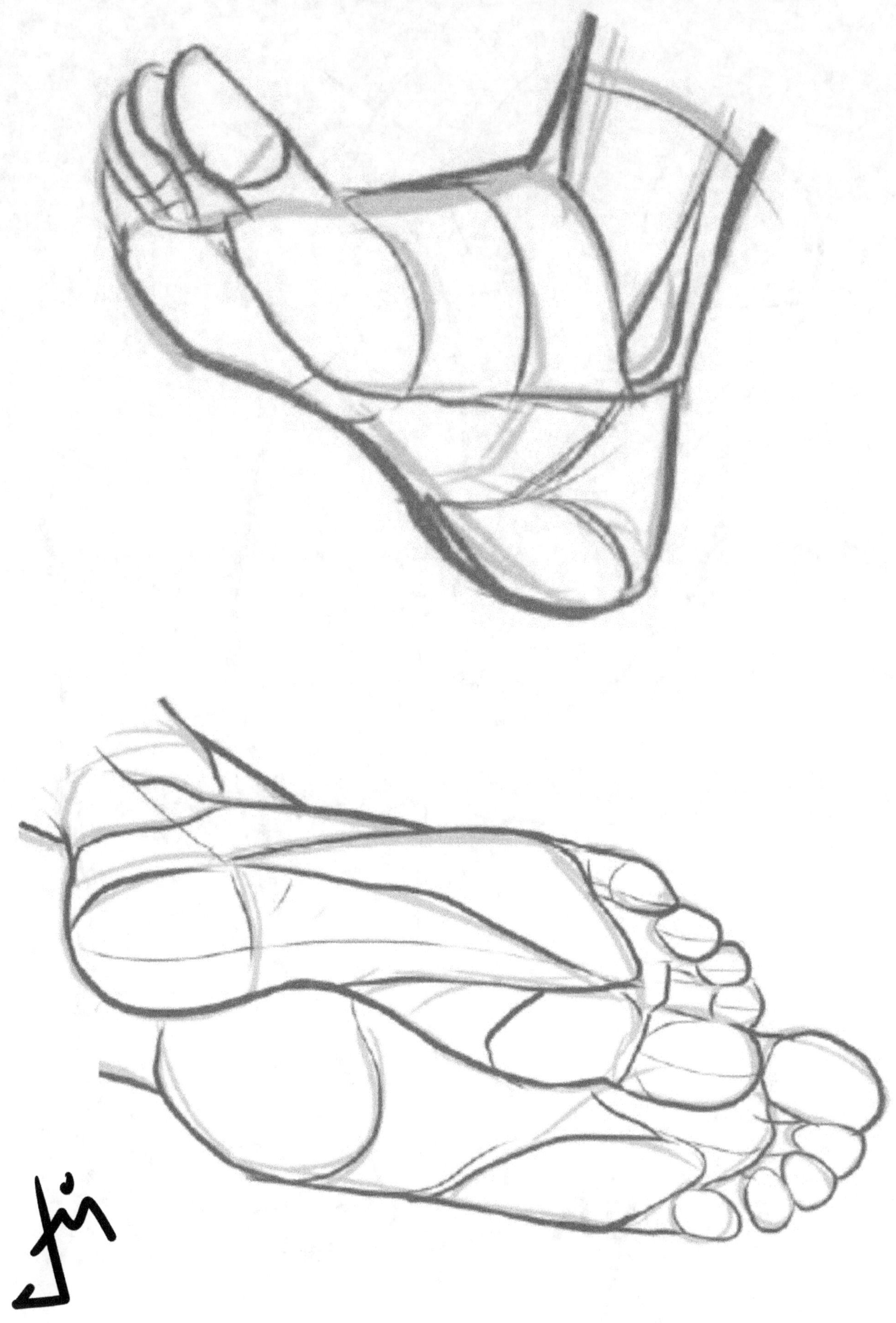

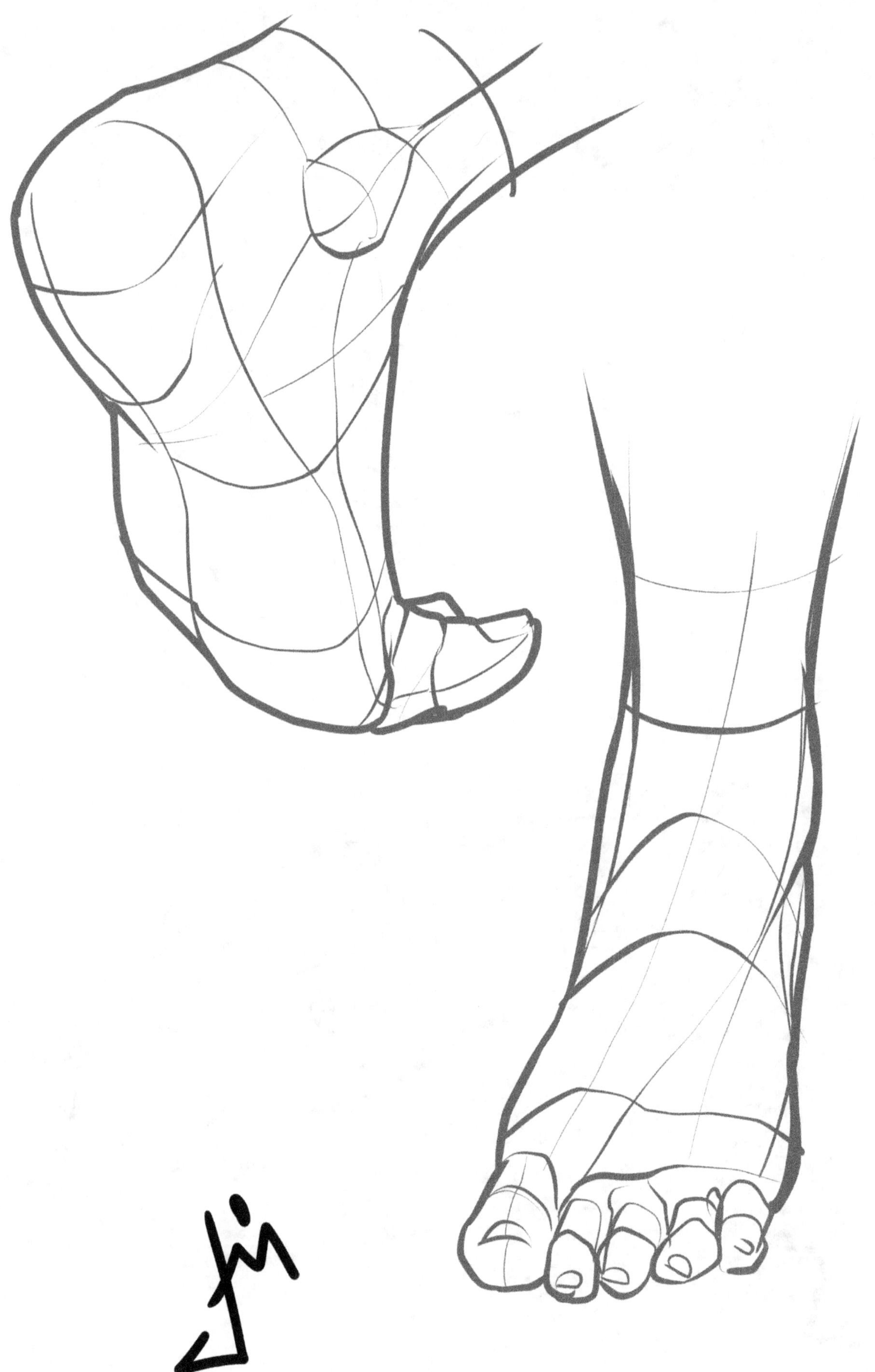

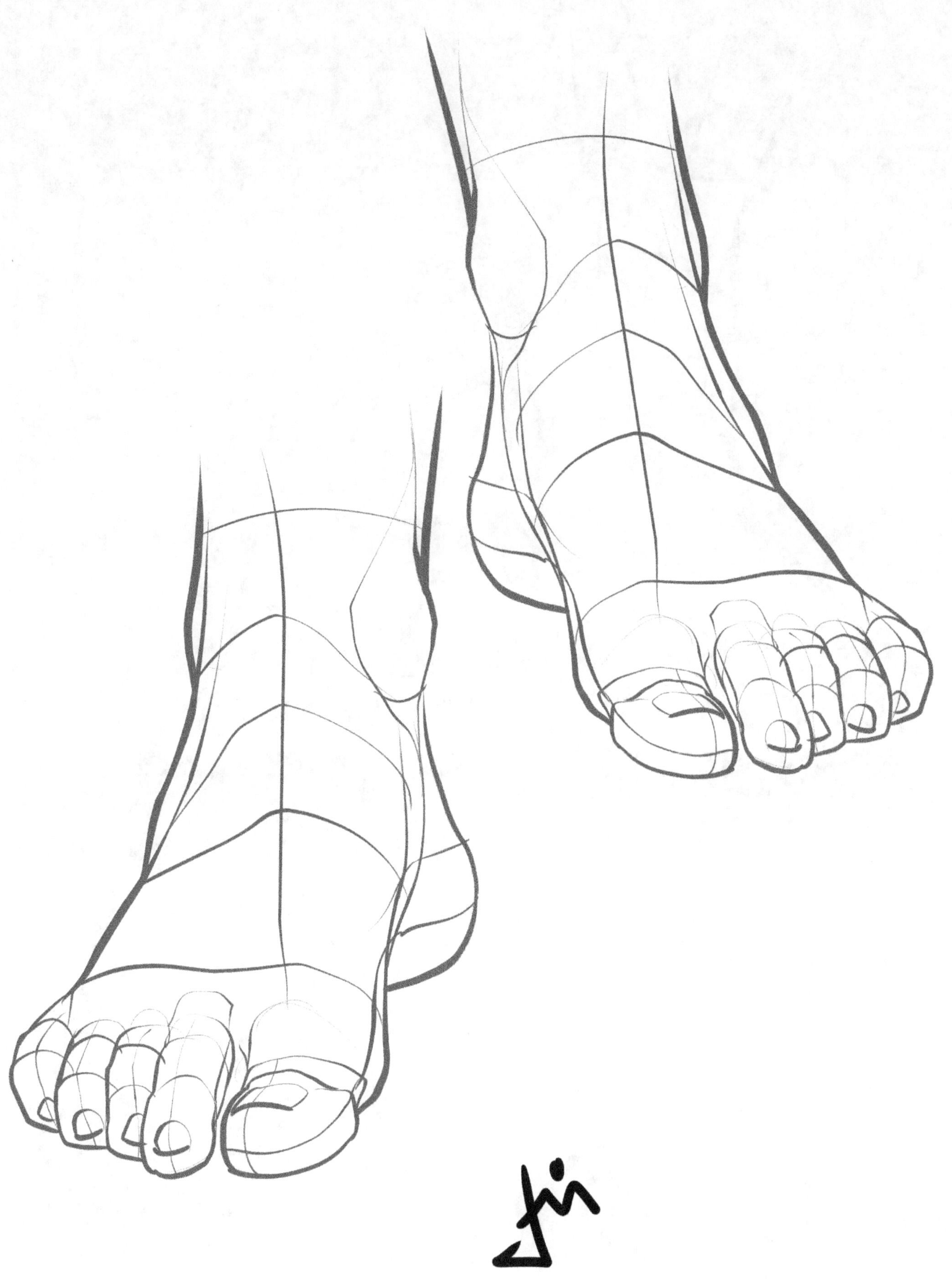

88

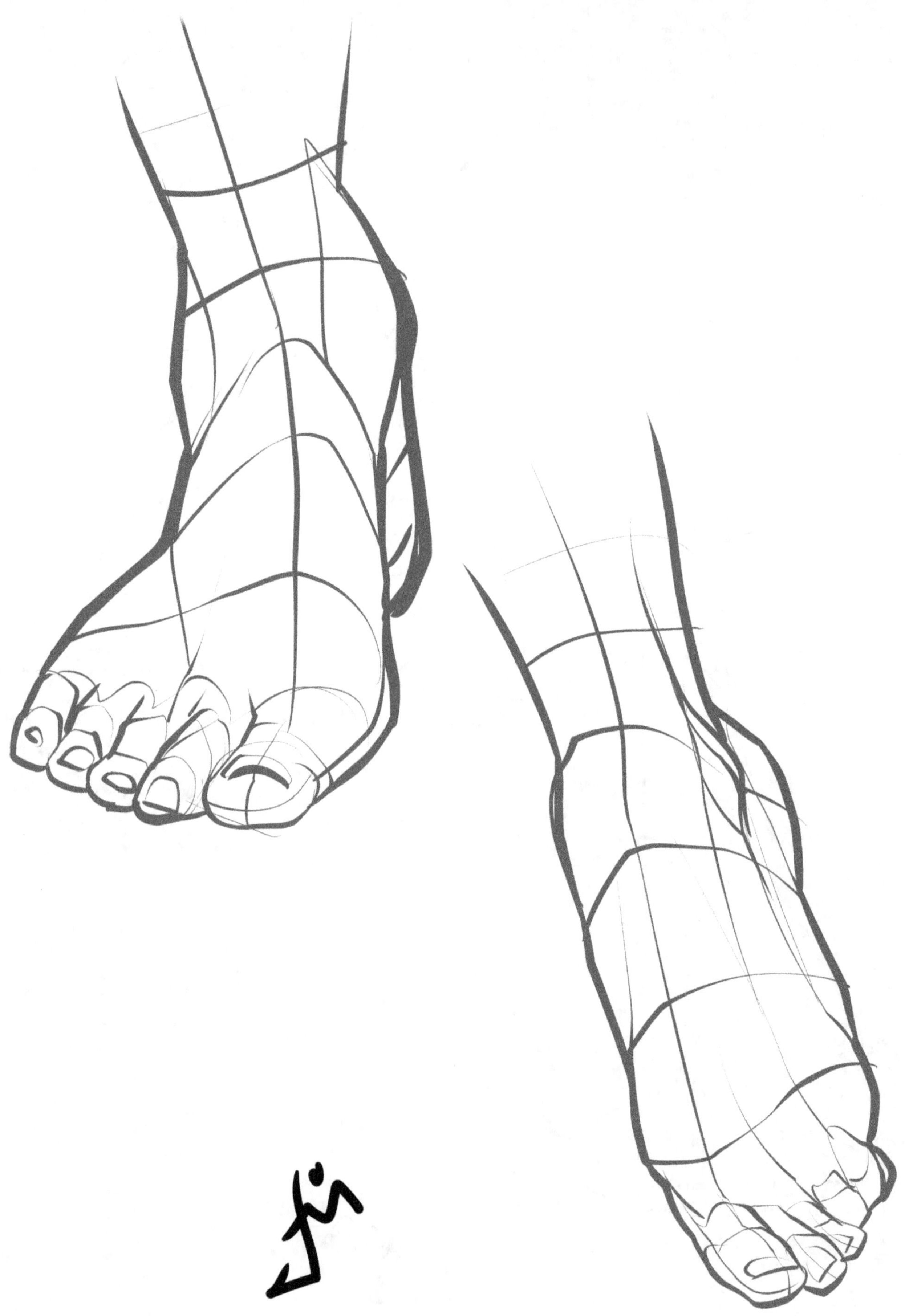

89

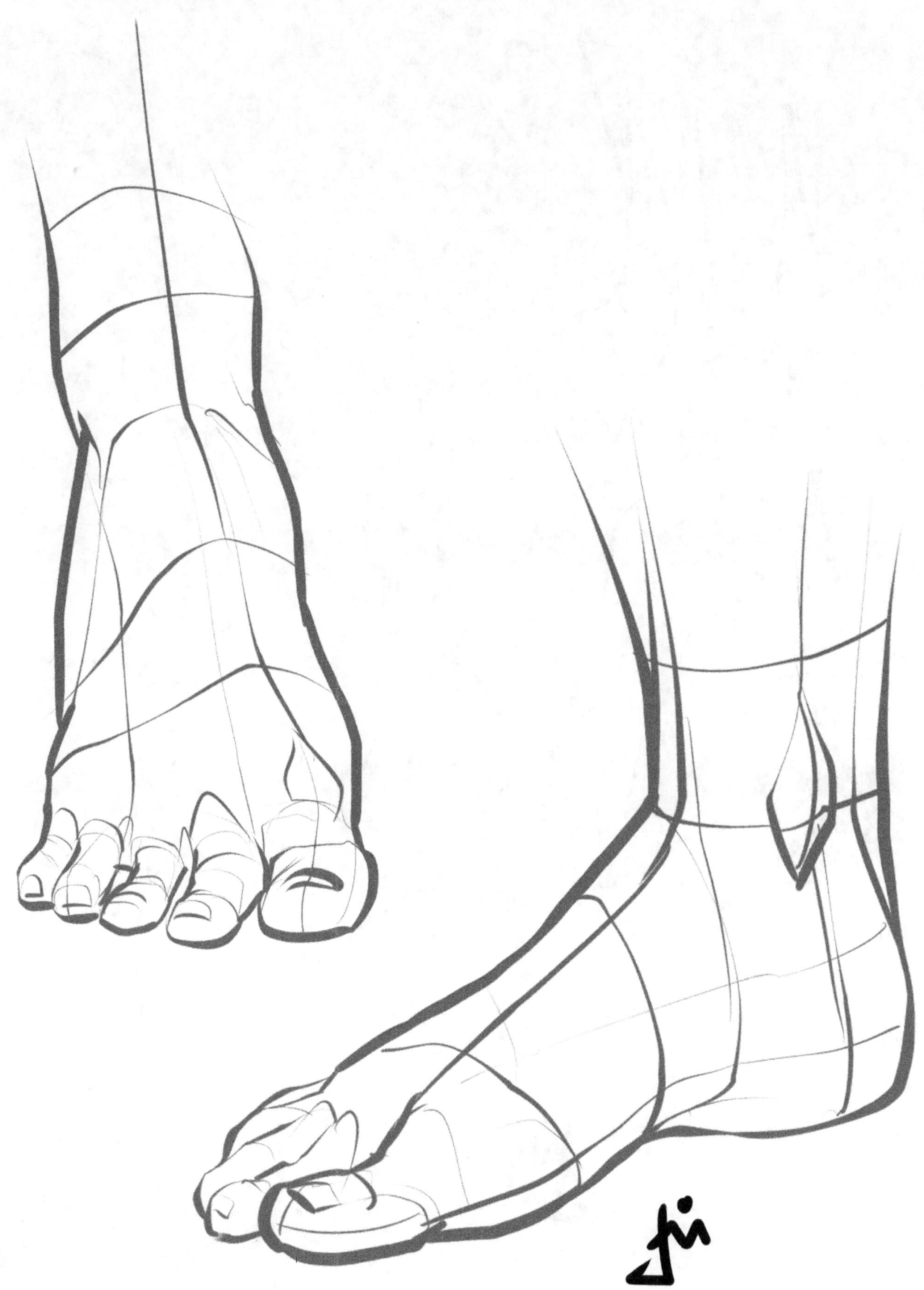

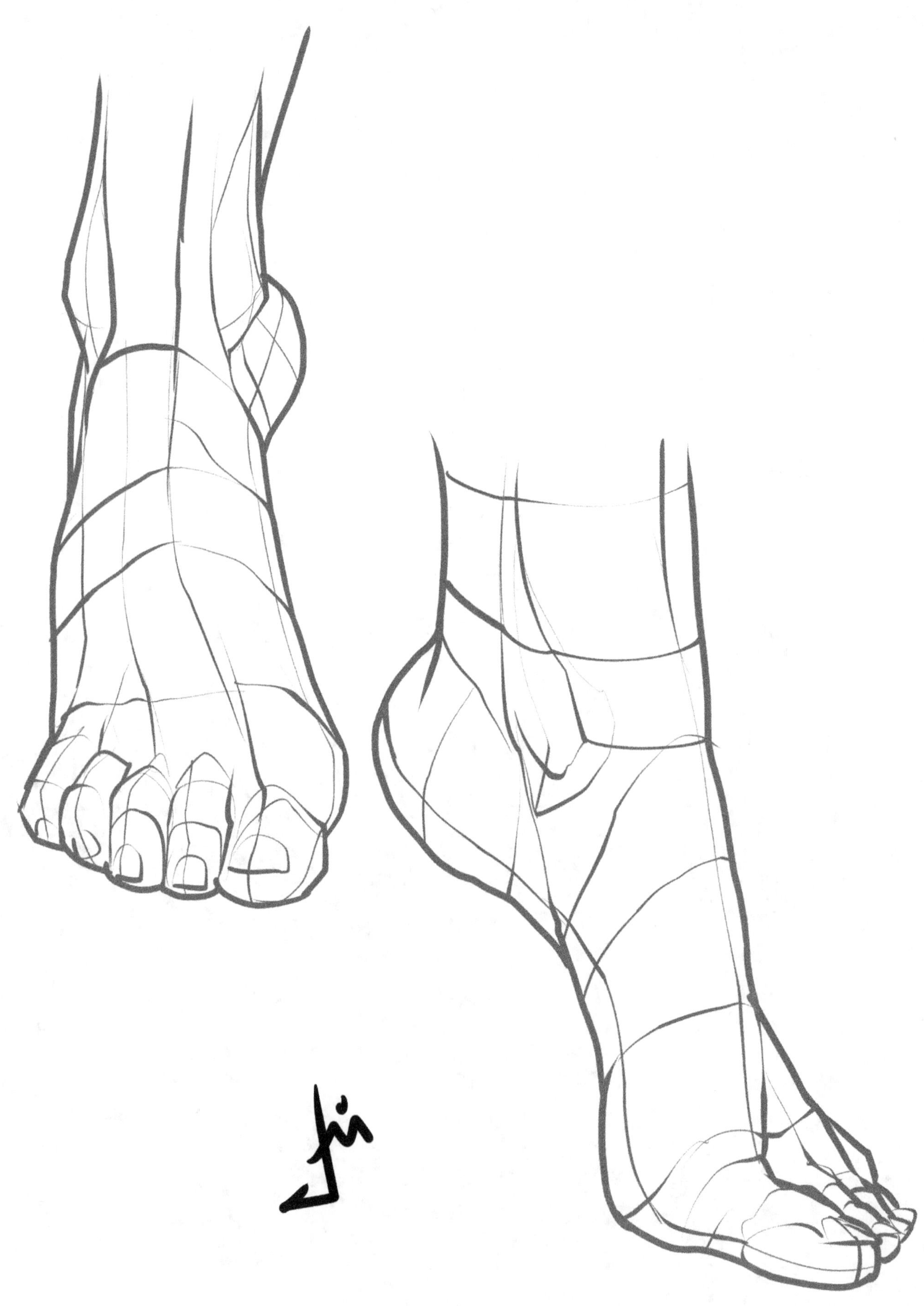

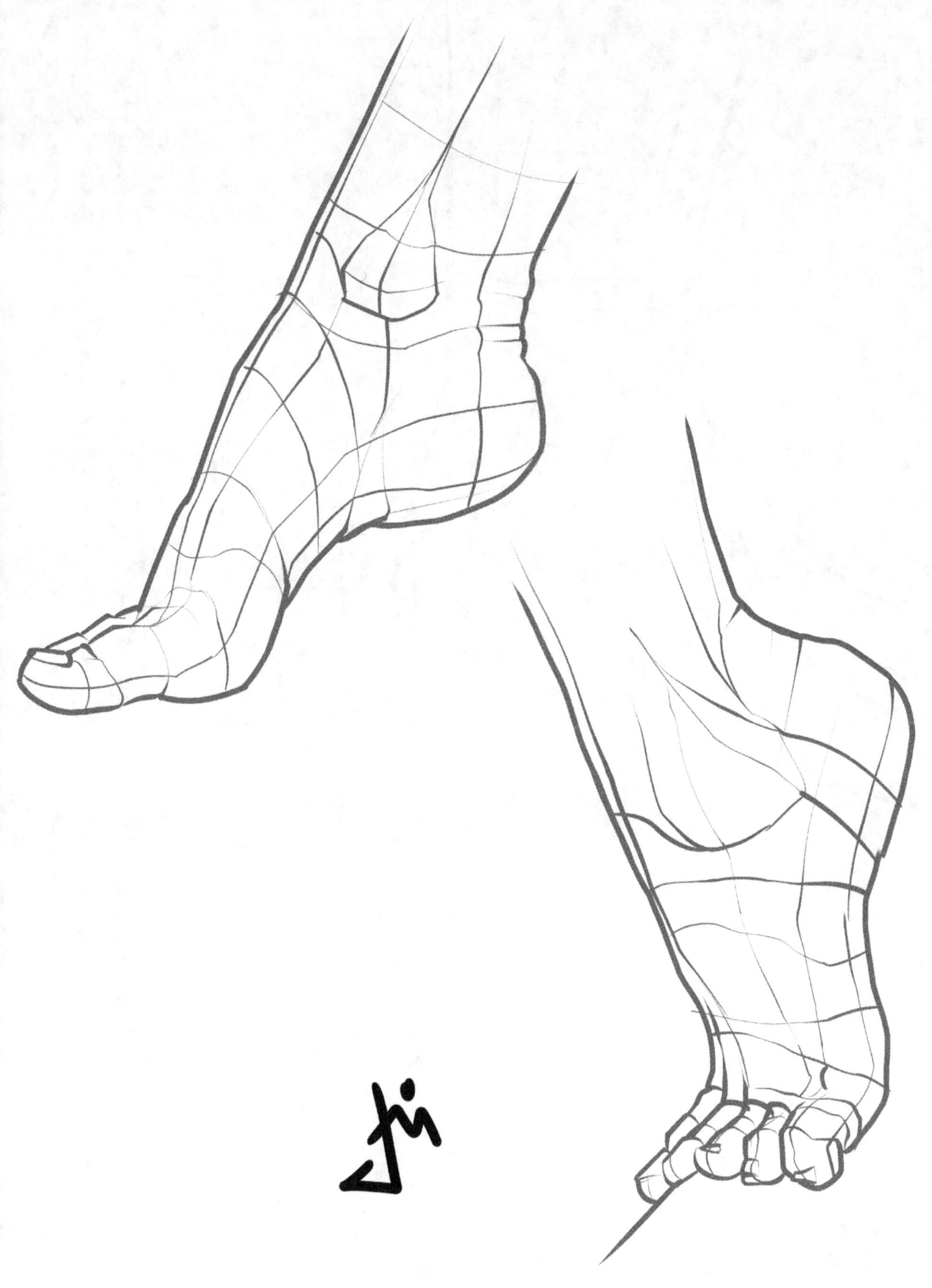

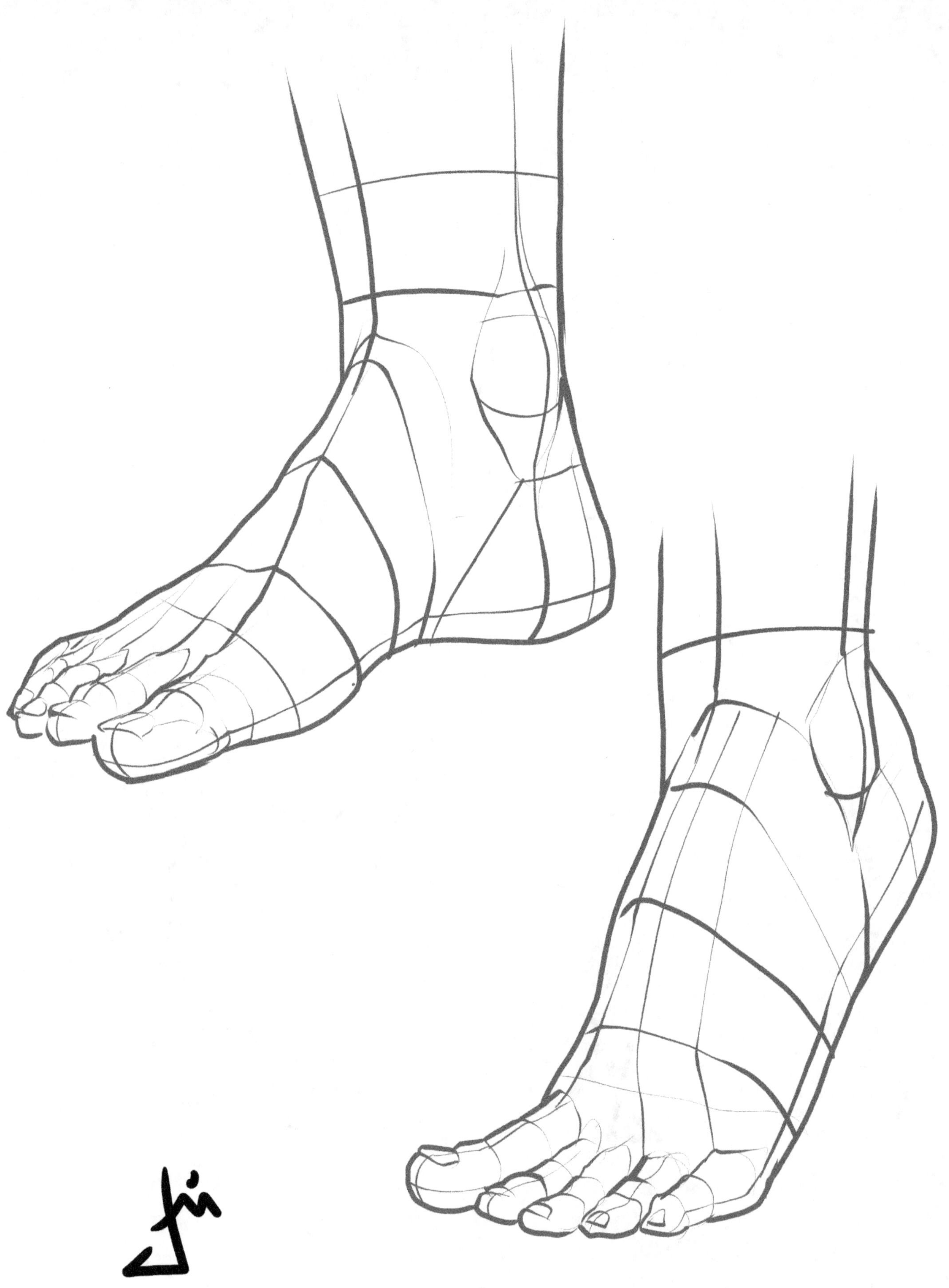

93

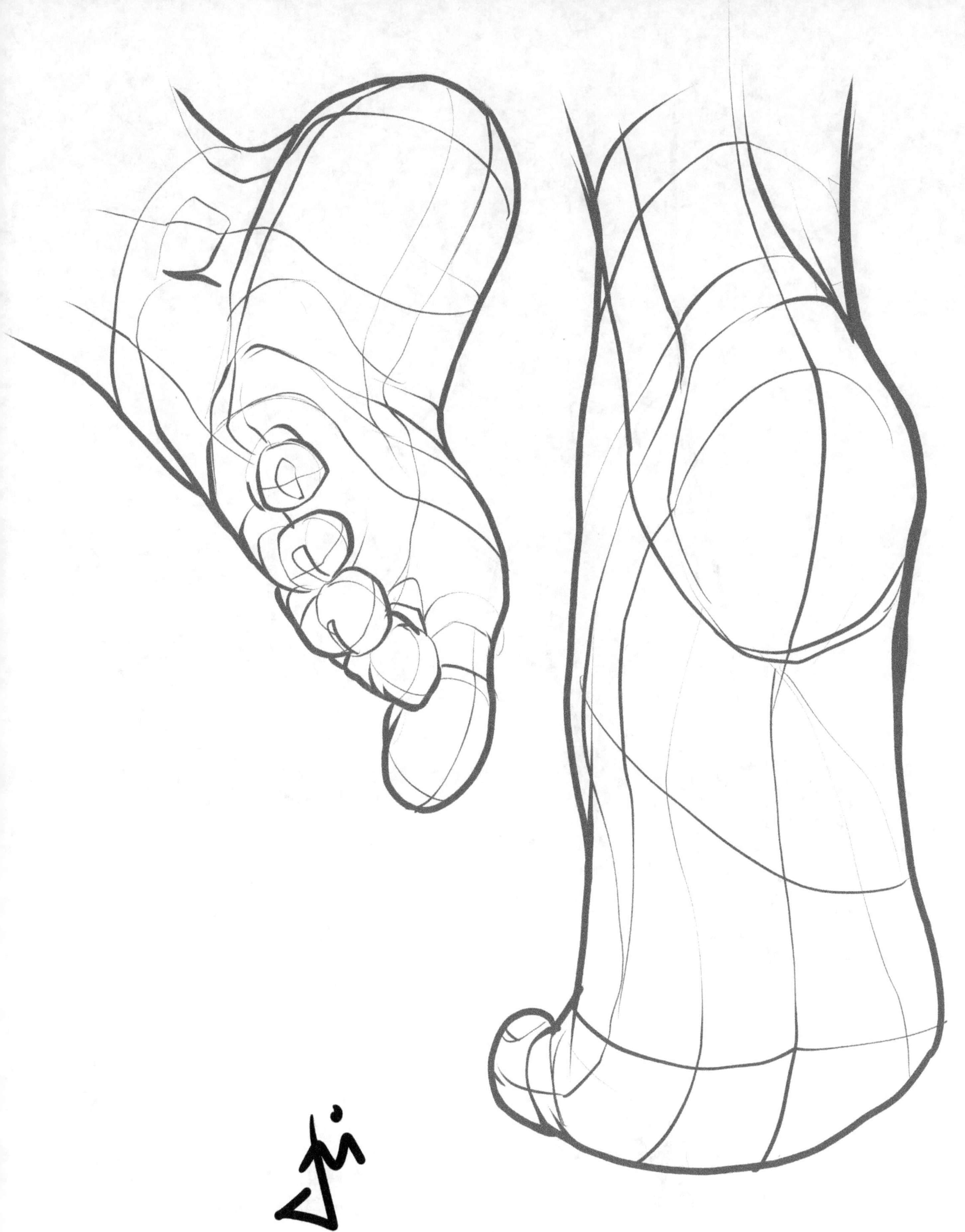

94

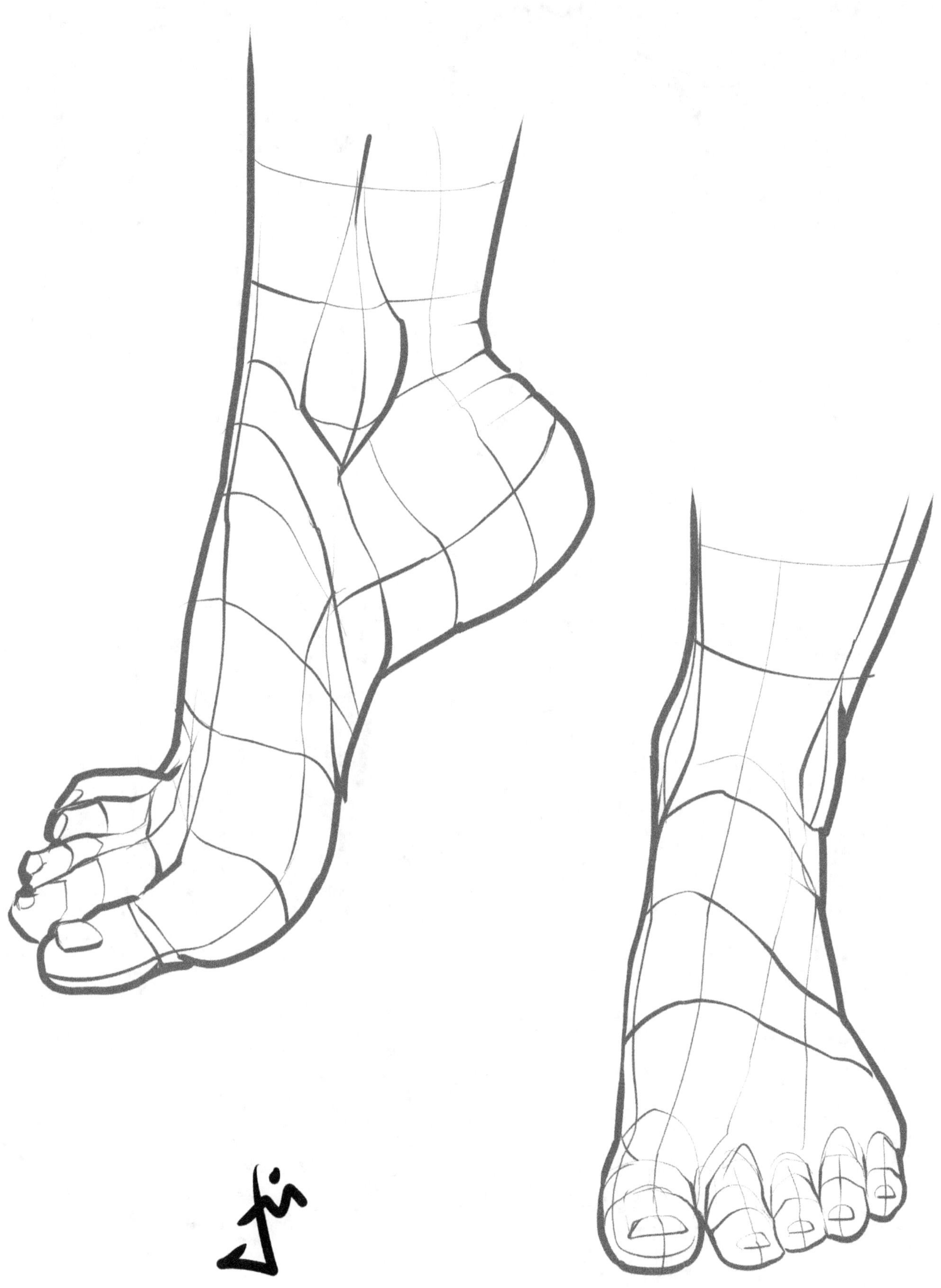

95

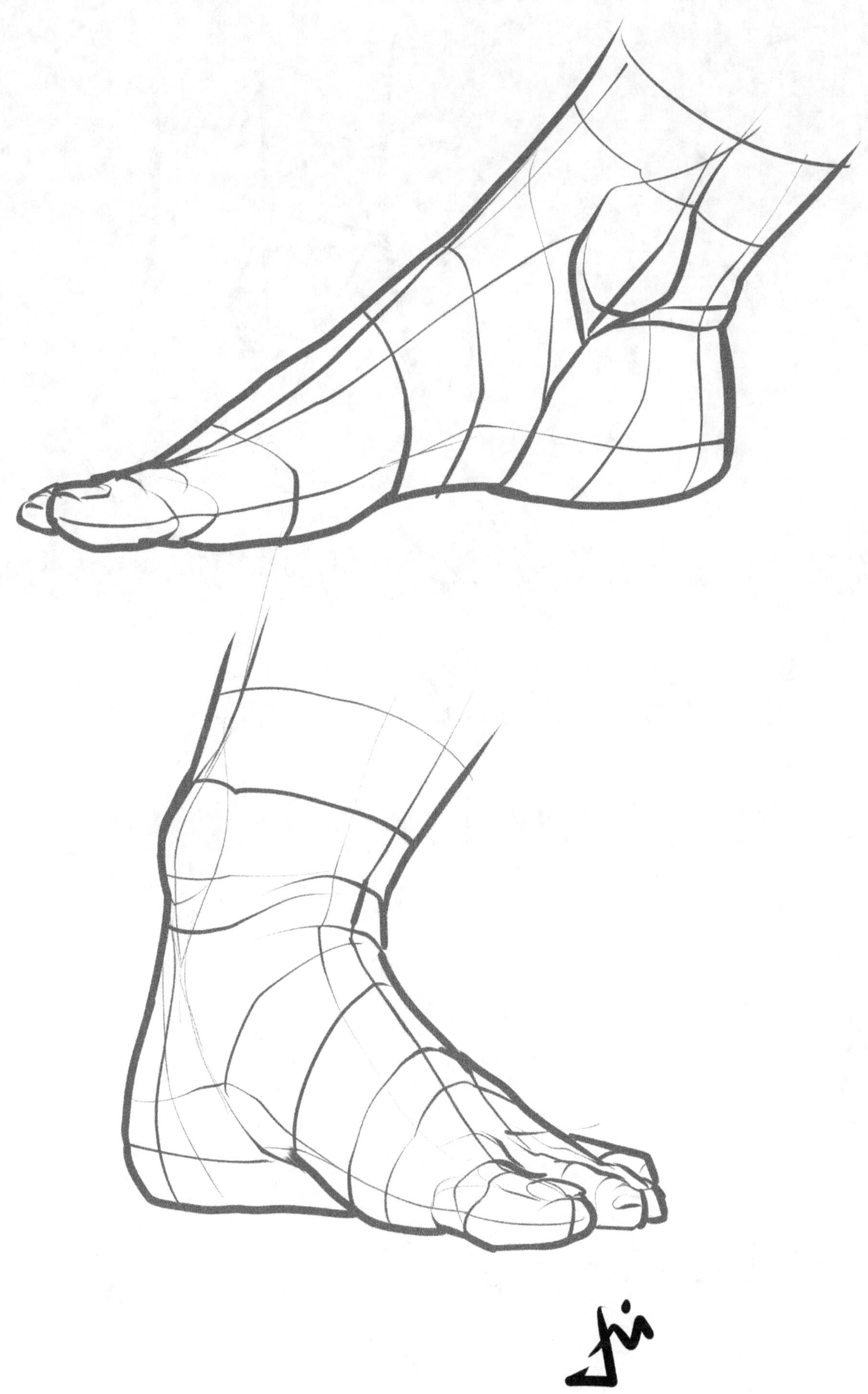

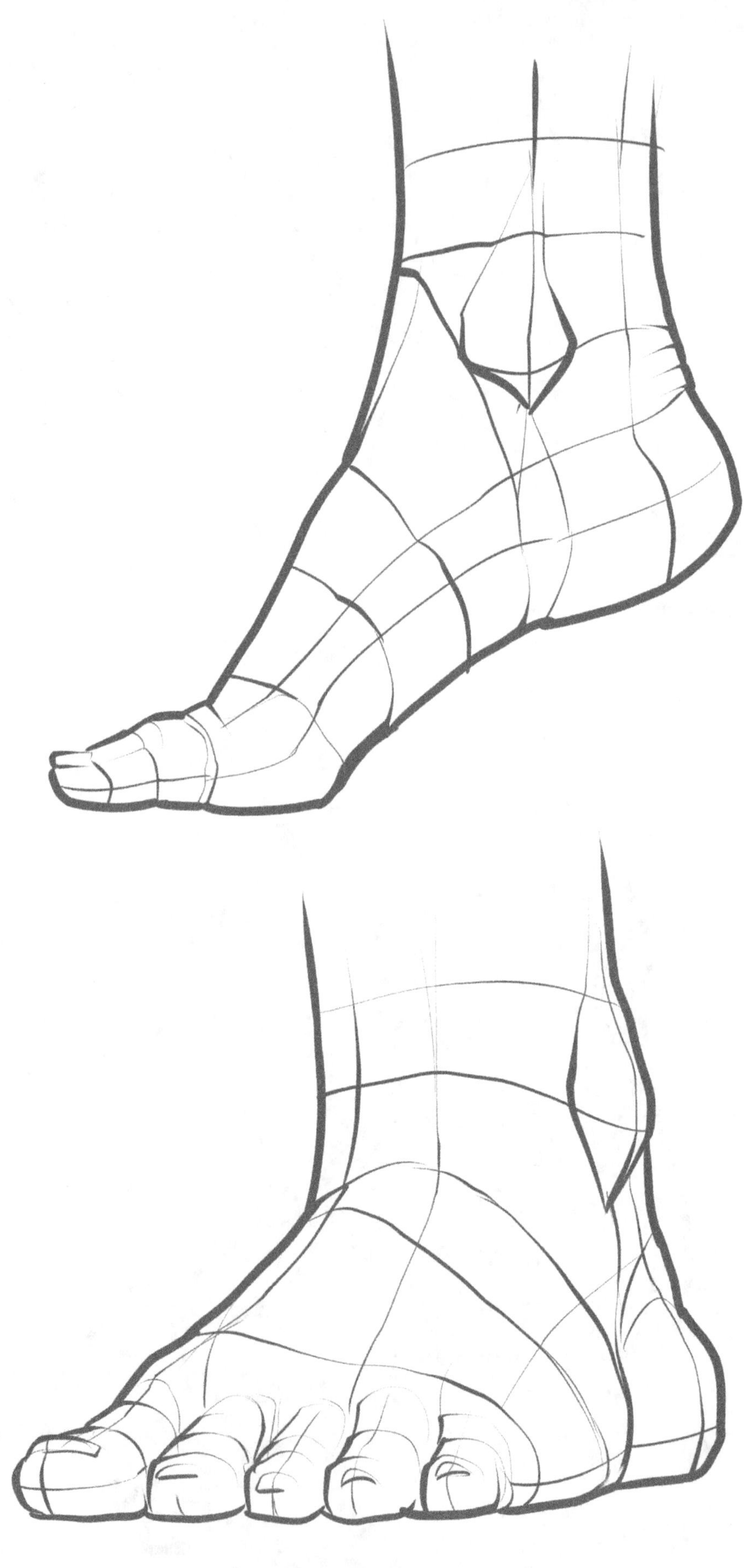

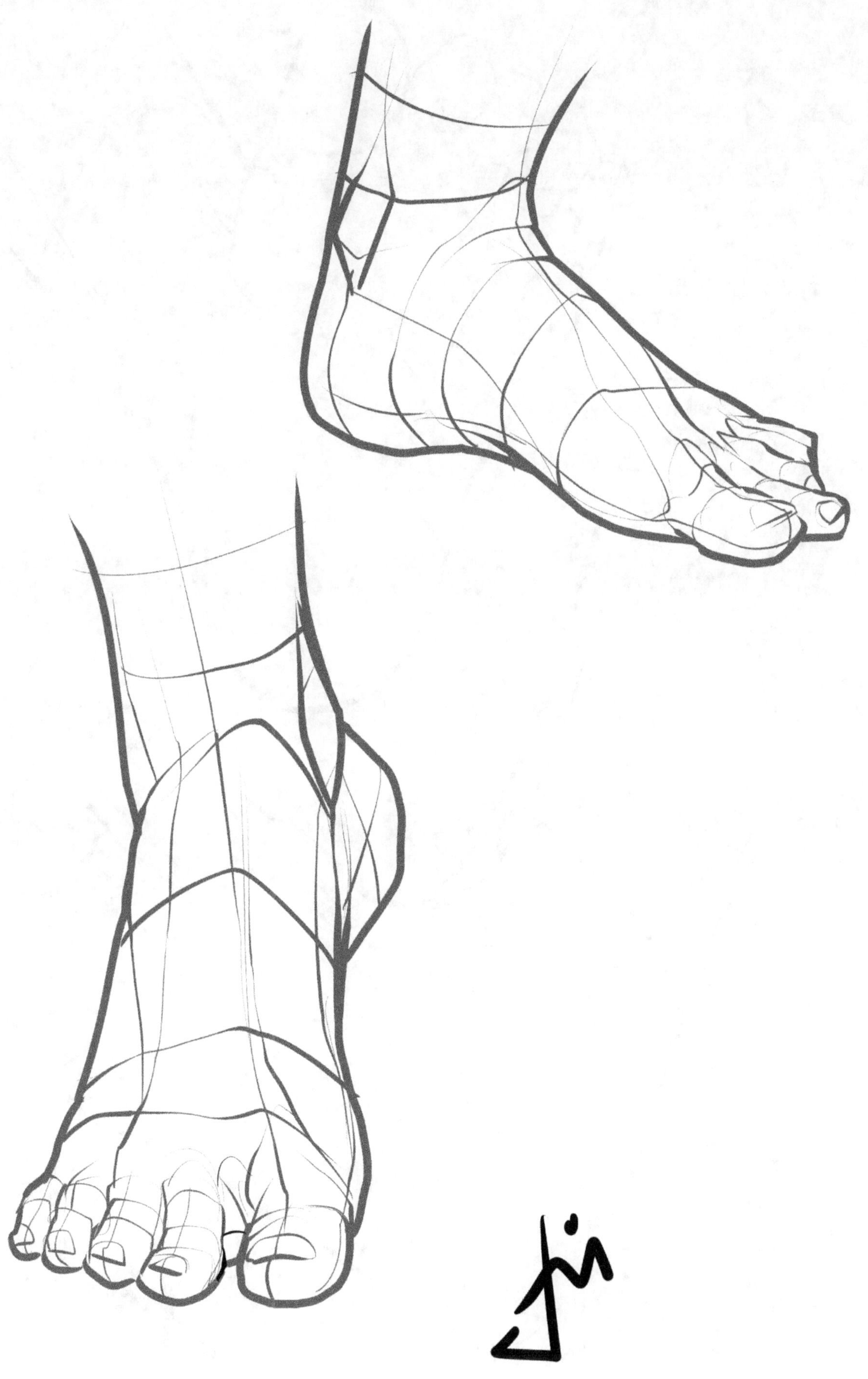

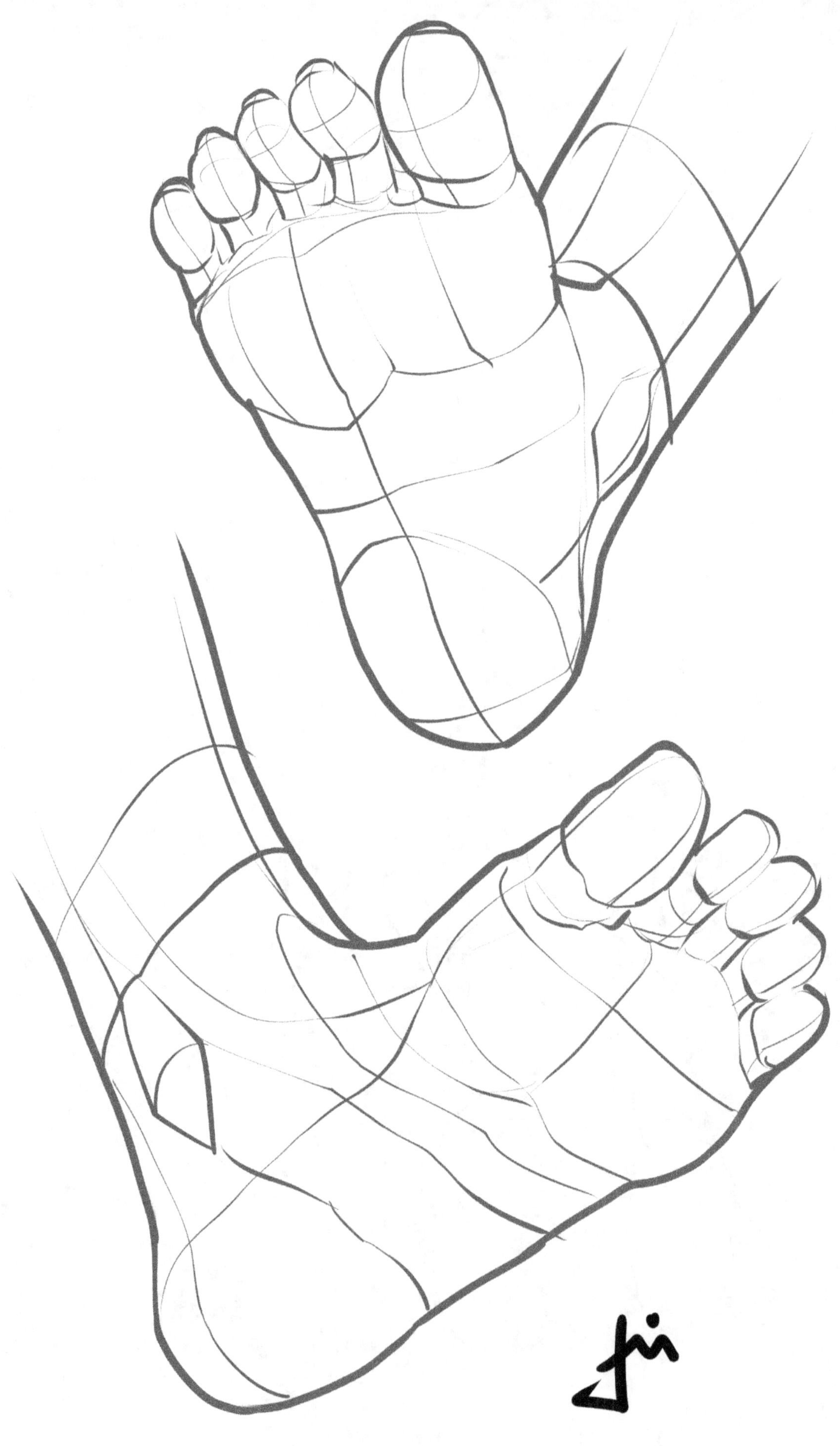

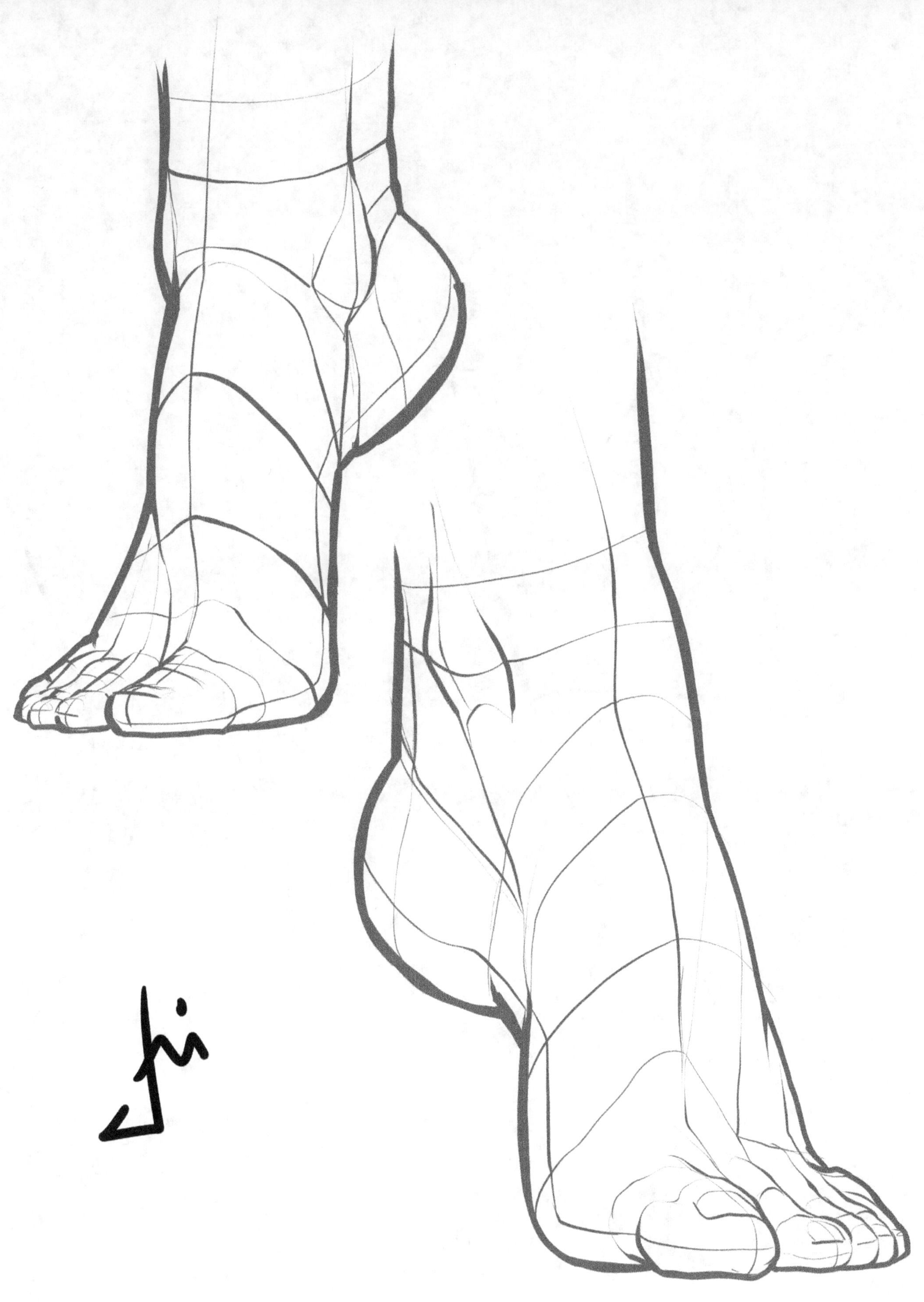

100

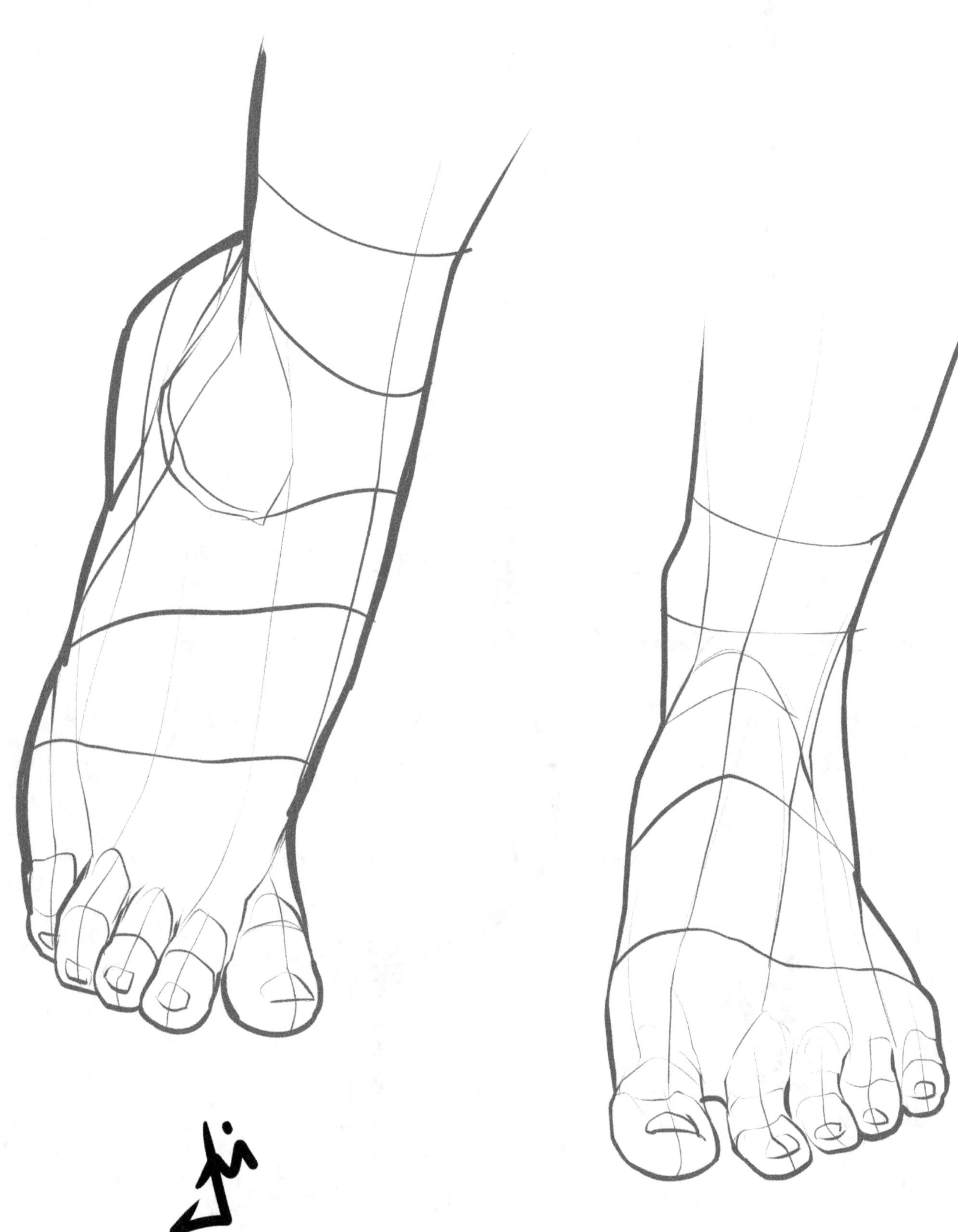

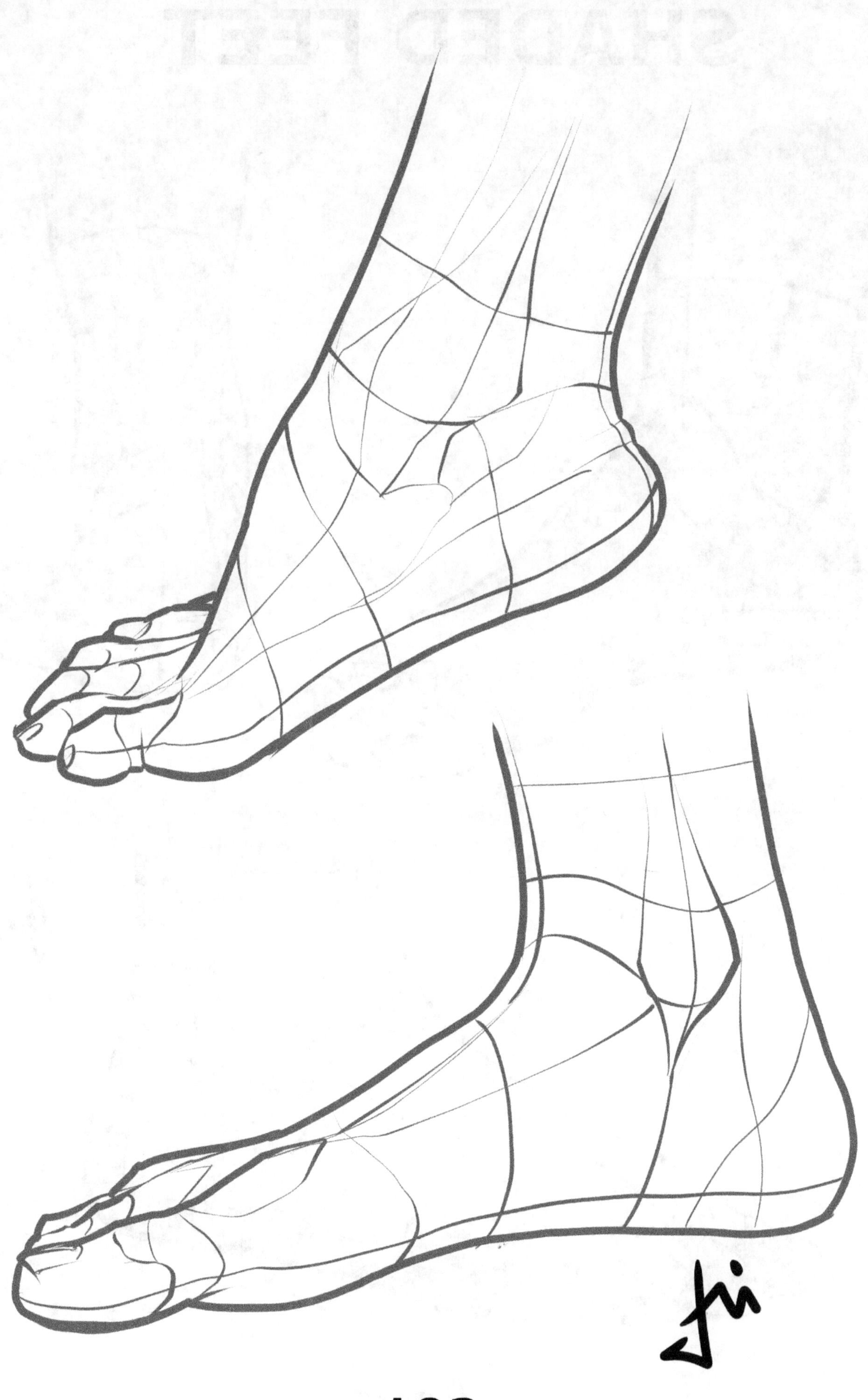

SHADED FEET

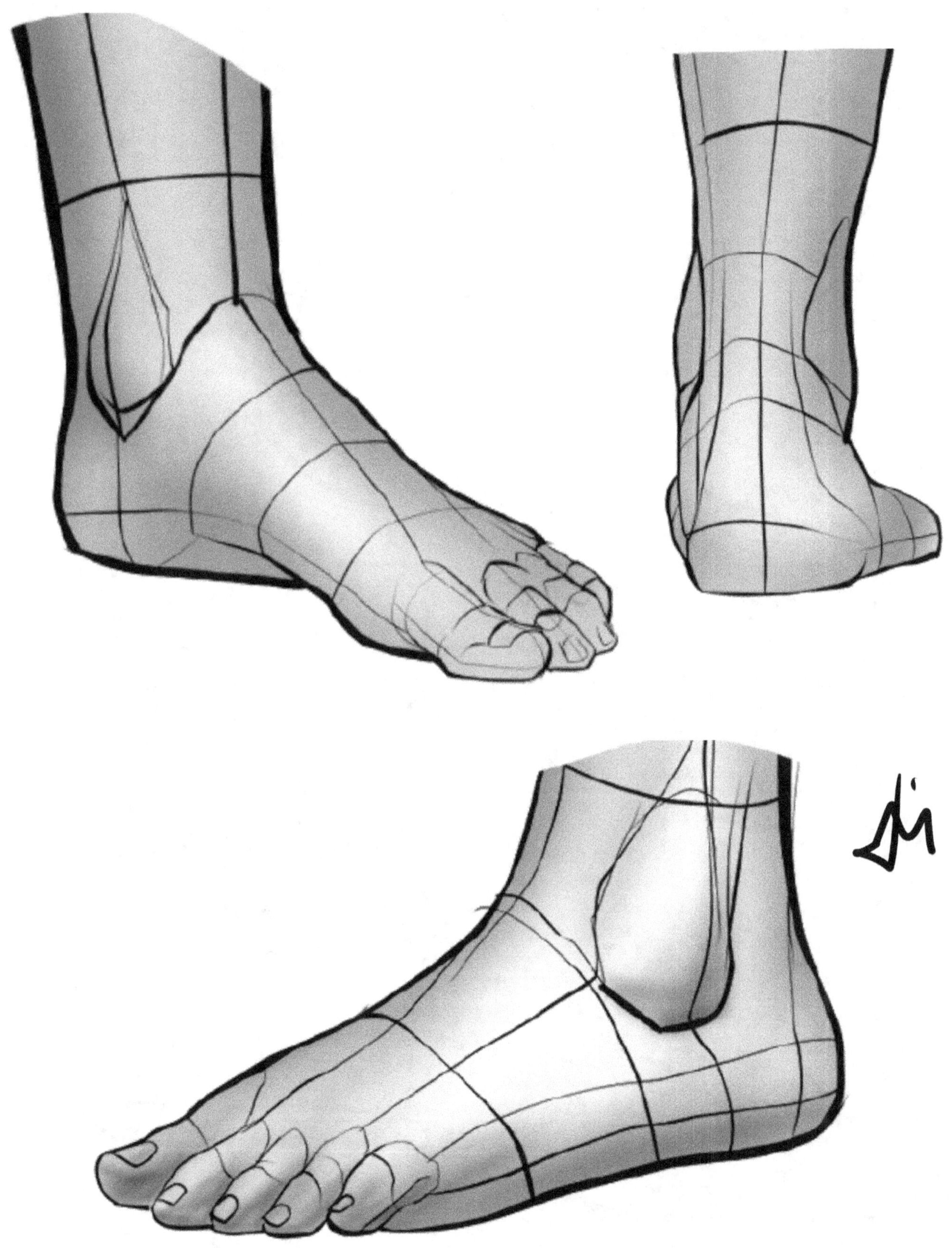

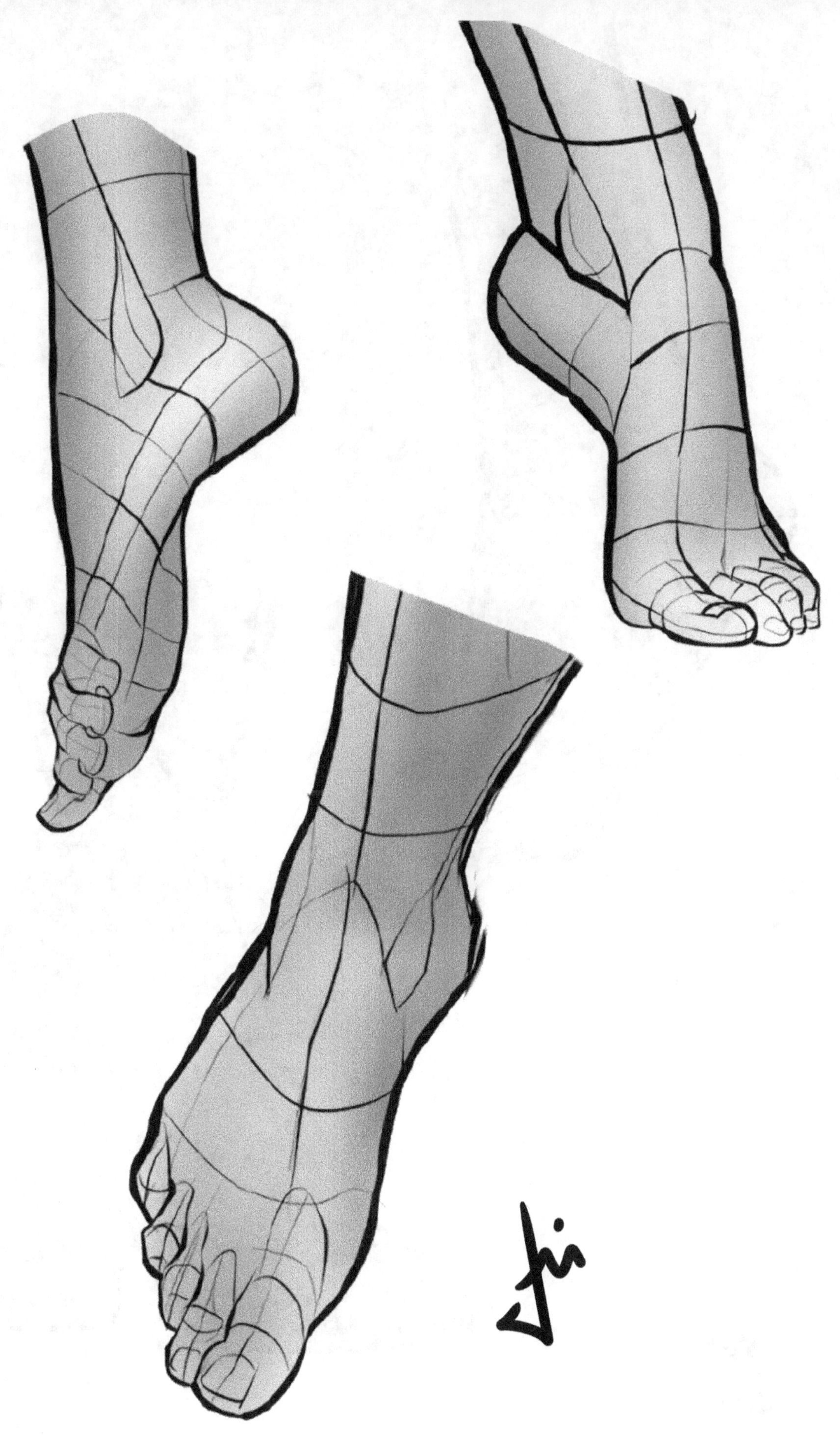

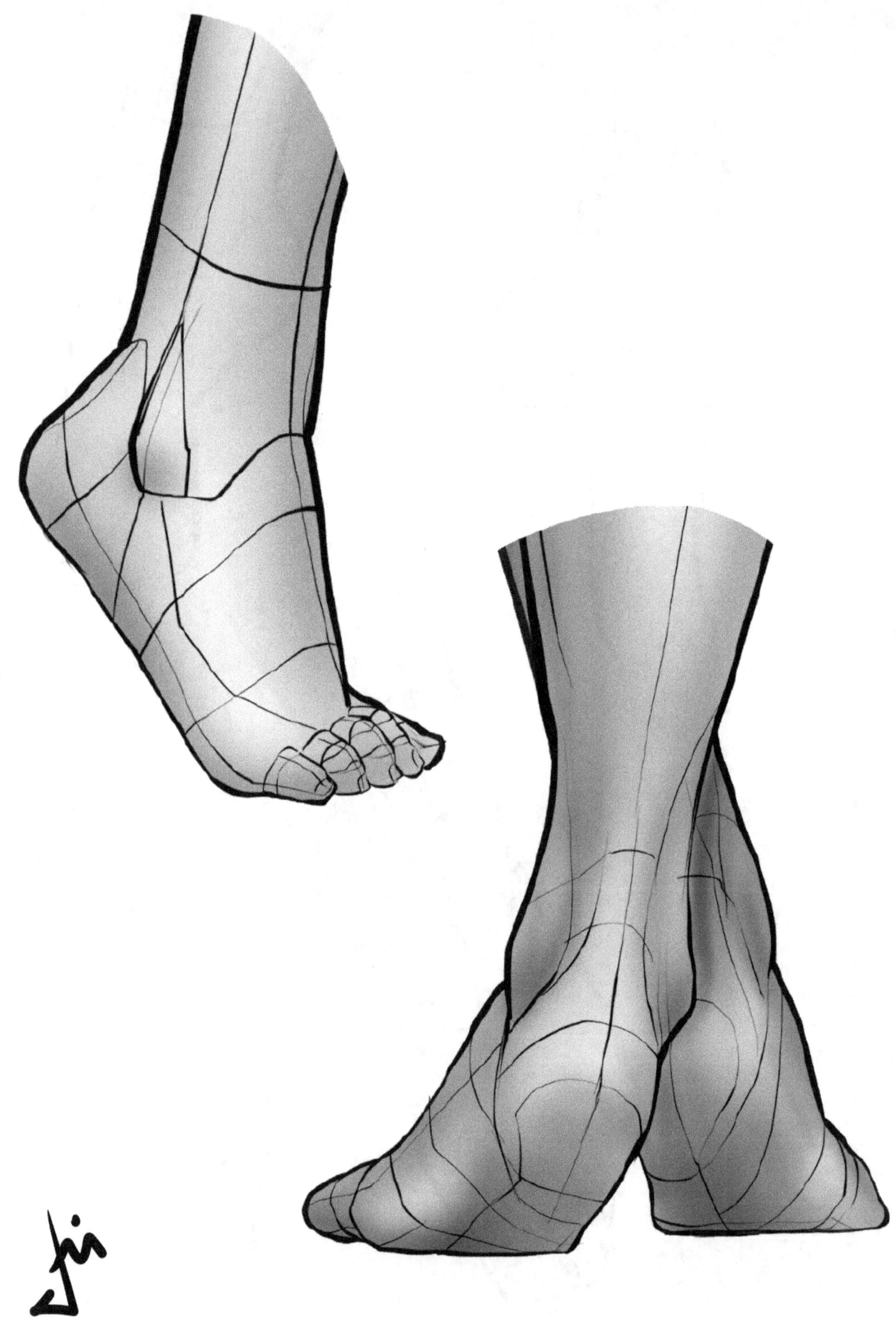

105

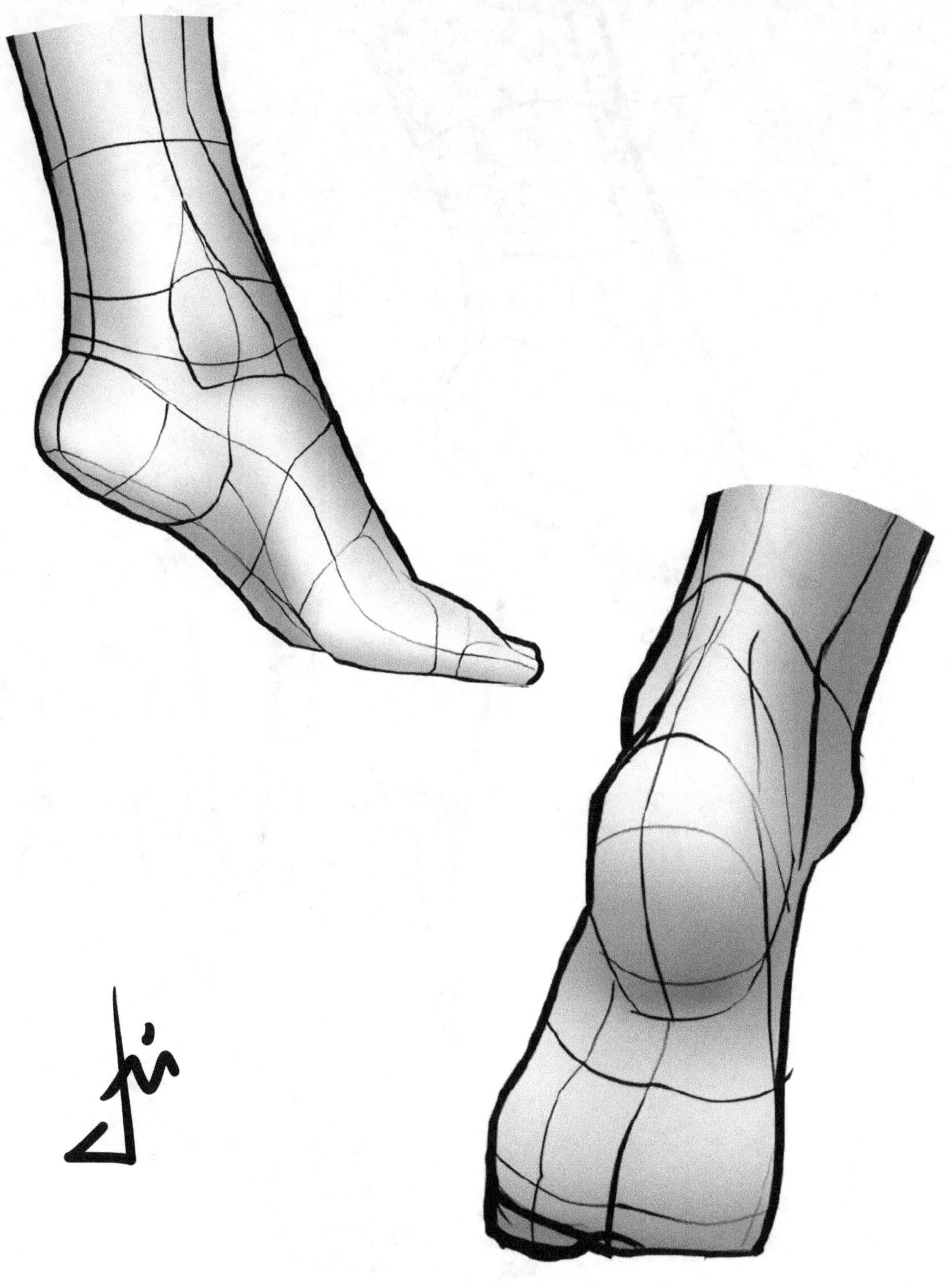

106

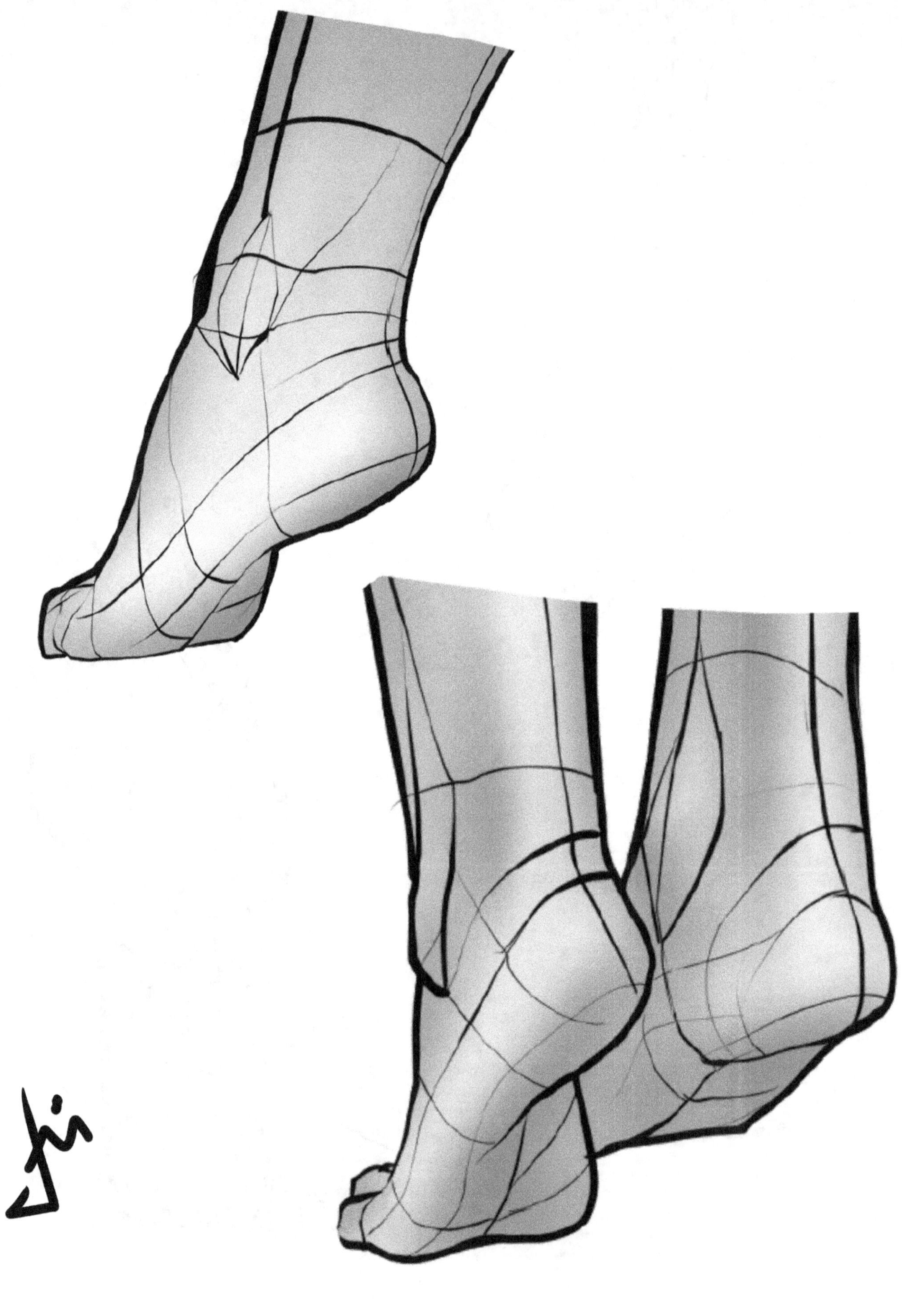

107

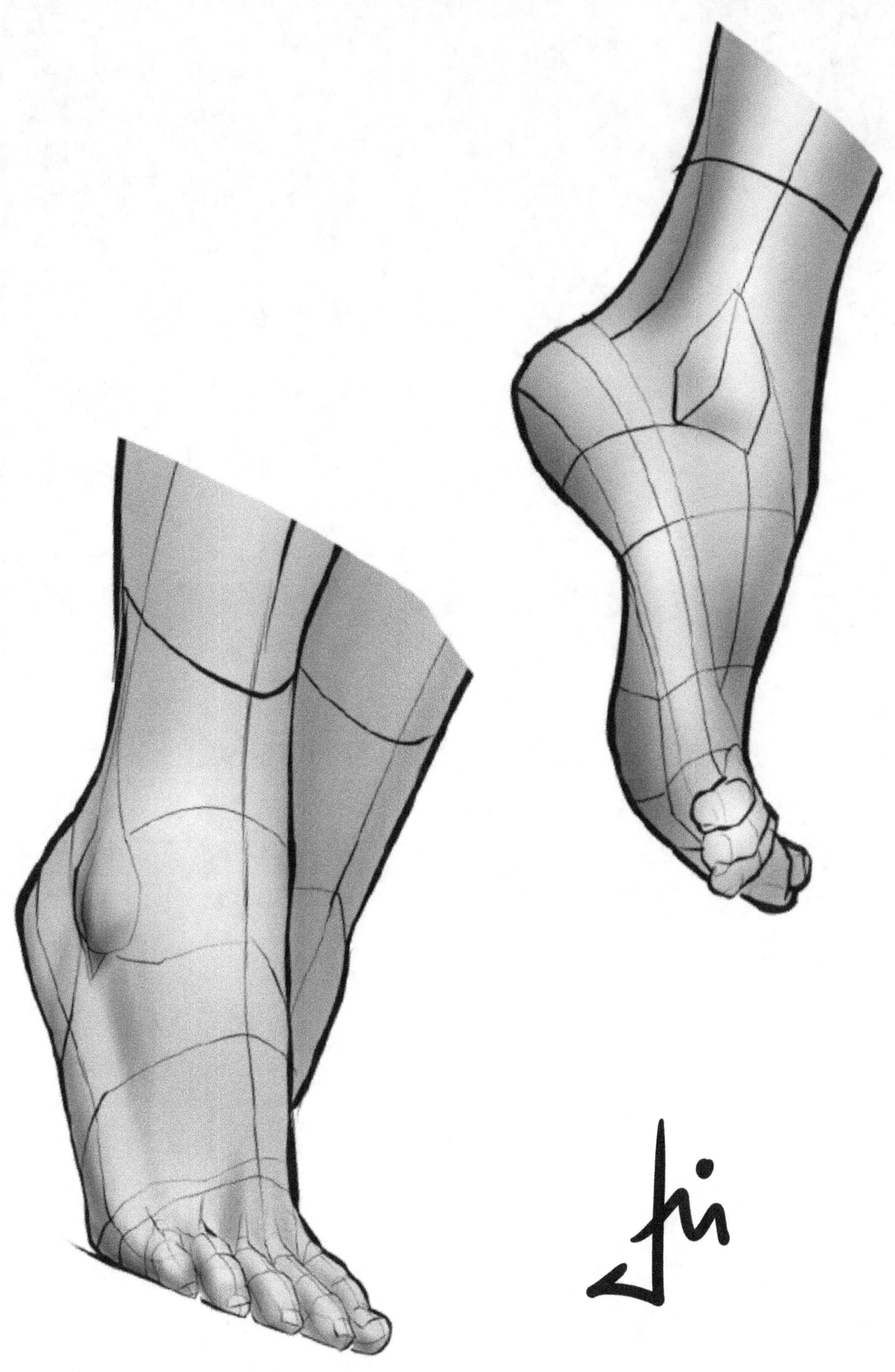

108